E98.F4 K64 2005
0/34//0/ルル7//
Koenig,

Cultures
a nativ
c20

CULTURES AND ECOLOGIES

EDWIN C. KOENIG

Cultures and Ecologies

A Native Fishing Conflict on the Saugeen-Bruce Peninsula

UNIVERSITY OF TORONTO PRESS
Toronto Buffalo London

© University of Toronto Press Incorporated 2005
Toronto Buffalo London
Printed in Canada

ISBN 0-8020-8847-3

Printed on acid-free paper

Library and Archives Canada Cataloguing in Publication

Koenig, Edwin C., 1951–
Cultures and ecologies : a native fishing conflict on the Saugeen-Bruce peninsula / Edwin C. Koenig.

Includes bibliographical references and index.
ISBN 0-8020-8847-3

1. Indians of North America – Ontario – Bruce Peninsula – Fishing.
2. Indians of North America – Fishing – Law and legislation – Ontario – Bruce Peninsula.   3. Fishery management – Ontario – Bruce Peninsula.
I. Title.

E98.F4K64 2005   333.95'6'08997071321   C2005-905128-0

This book has been published with the help of a grant from the Canadian Federation for the Humanities and Social Sciences, through the Aid to Scholarly Publications Programme, using funds provided by the Social Sciences and Humanities Research Council of Canada.

University of Toronto Press acknowledges the financial assistance to its publishing program of the Canada Council for the Arts and the Ontario Arts Council.

University of Toronto Press acknowledges the financial support for its publishing activities of the Government of Canada through the Book Publishing Industry Development Program (BPIDP).

Contents

Acknowledgments vii

Maps ix, x, xi

Introduction 3

1 Getting to Know the Peninsula and Its People 9

2 The Fairgrieve Decision and Its Impact 19

3 Fishing in the Distant Past 37

4 Change and Adaptation: Late Historical Fisheries 59

5 Mixed Economies: Twentieth-Century Fisheries 79

6 'Conservation' 105

7 Local Perspectives on Conflict Issues 122

8 Traditional Knowledge 152

9 Toward Dialogue 178

Appendices 187

Notes 197

References 207

Index 225

Acknowledgments

I would like to thank those who supported my thesis work, which is the basis of this book. I am grateful to the Social Sciences and Humanities Research Council of Canada for funding provided through award number 752-95-1686, and to the School of Graduate Studies at McMaster University for a grant that covered some of my fieldwork expenses.

I feel fortunate to have been able to participate in McMaster University's exceptional graduate program in anthropology under the supervision of Dr Wayne Warry, along with Drs Richard Preston and Trudy Nicks. I also benefited greatly from my undergraduate anthropology training at the University of Waterloo. I am grateful as well to many fellow students who shared ideas and concerns; Charles Mather, Marcia Barron, and Christopher Justice were especially supportive as friends and mentors.

Thanks also go to several university departments (and their members) where I taught while completing thesis and manuscript drafts. These include anthropology departments at Laurentian University, the University of Waterloo, Wilfrid Laurier University, and St Thomas University (Fredericton), along with the sociology department at Brock University. I also learned by working outside of universities with Janet Armstrong, Victor Lytwyn, and researchers on Manitoulin Island.

I would also like to thank the editors and staff at University of Toronto Press who worked diligently on my manuscript (especially Virgil Duff, Stephen Kotowych, Charles Stuart, Anne Laughlin, and Doug Hildebrand) and the anonymous reviewers who contributed valuable suggestions.

A special debt of gratitude is owed to the people who extended their friendship and allowed me to conduct research within their communities. I am thankful to Chief Richard Kahgee, who went out of his way to help get my thesis project going, and to Chief Ralph Akiwenzie, who oversaw community approval of my research at Nawash. I am grateful as well to Ted and Phyllis Johnston for providing accommodations and genuine hospitality. A very special thanks goes to Darlene Johnston, who is an inspiration within the peninsula's native communities and beyond.

At Nawash, Donald Keeshig took time to show me around the reserve, and Ross Waukey always made me feel welcome. Ernestine Proulx allowed me to participate in her language classes, Carlene Elliott offered advice during the early stages of my research, and Clayton Akiwenzie was a research partner for some of the early interviews. Band researchers Austin Elliott, David McLaren, and Stephen Crawford also provided assistance, as did Paul Jones. At Saugeen, Timm Rochon and Harold Thompson helped me coordinate my research, Rita Root generously helped out as language consultant, and Mindy Gill and Adrienne Kahgee were research partners for the first interview I did there.

I would like to thank Sharon George for granting permission to use the cover photo: a picture of her as a young girl, and a lake trout, taken on the Saugeen reserve in the early 1950s. And thanks to Rita Root for helping to identify and locate the person in the picture, and arranging permission.

I also acknowledge support from personal friends and relatives who have long shared some of my interests. In particular, I thank my brothers, Al Koenig and Arthur Koenig, and their families for much congeniality. In memory of my father, sister, and mother, and in the company of Sandy, Cory, and Christina, I recognize lifetimes of encouragement.

Maps ix

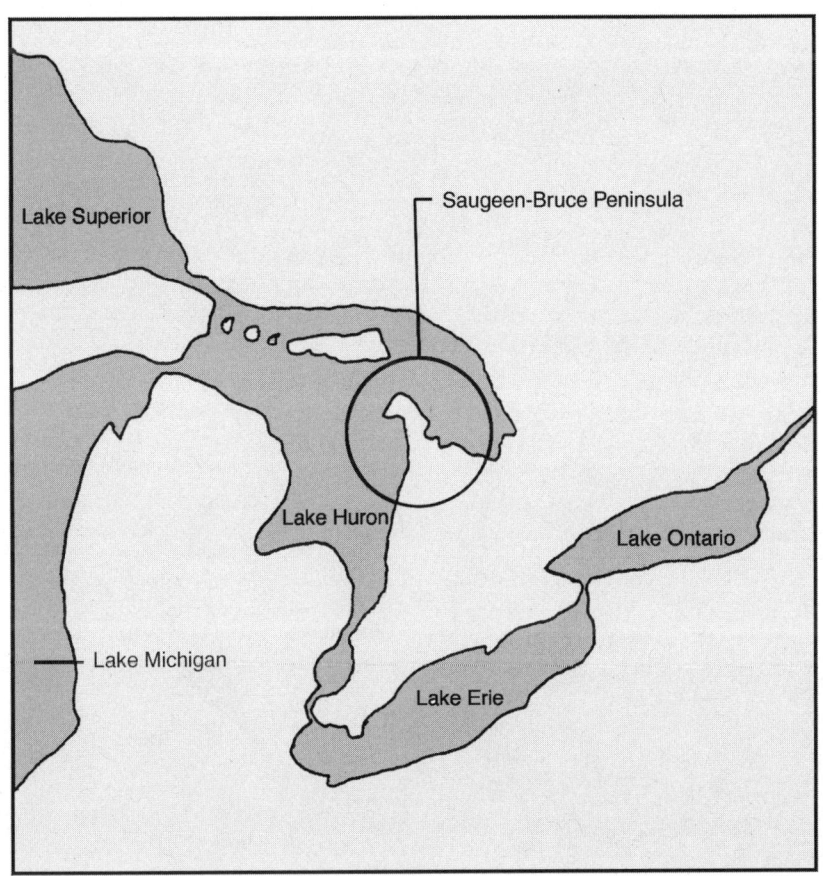

Map 1. Study Area: The Saugeen-Bruce Peninsula

x Maps

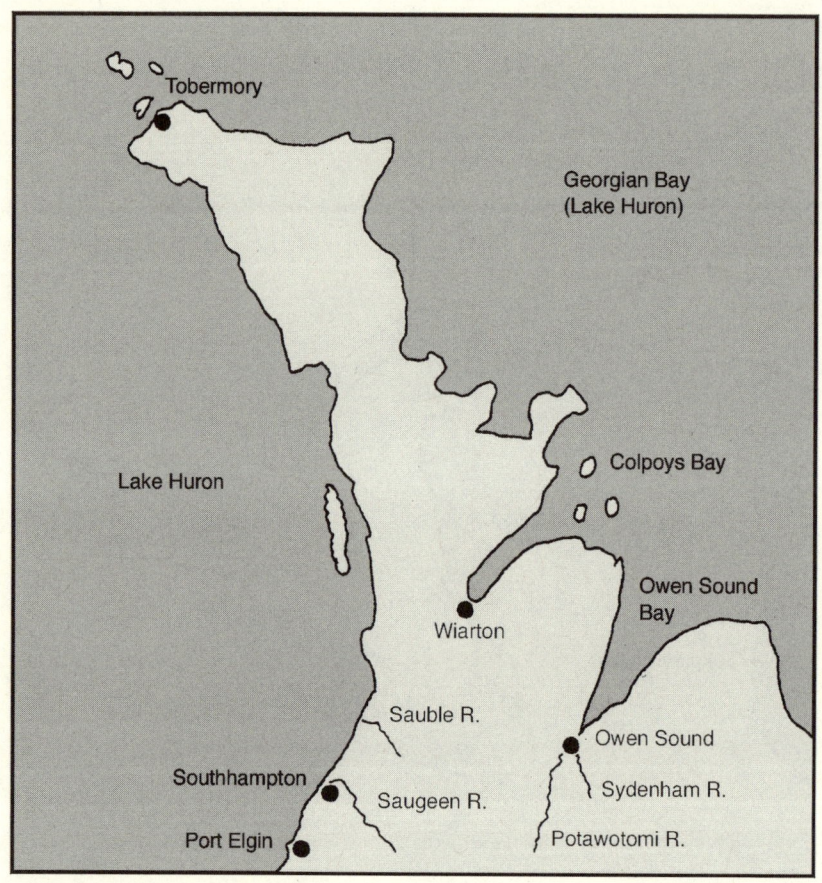

Map 2. Main Towns, Water Bodies, and Rivers

Maps xi

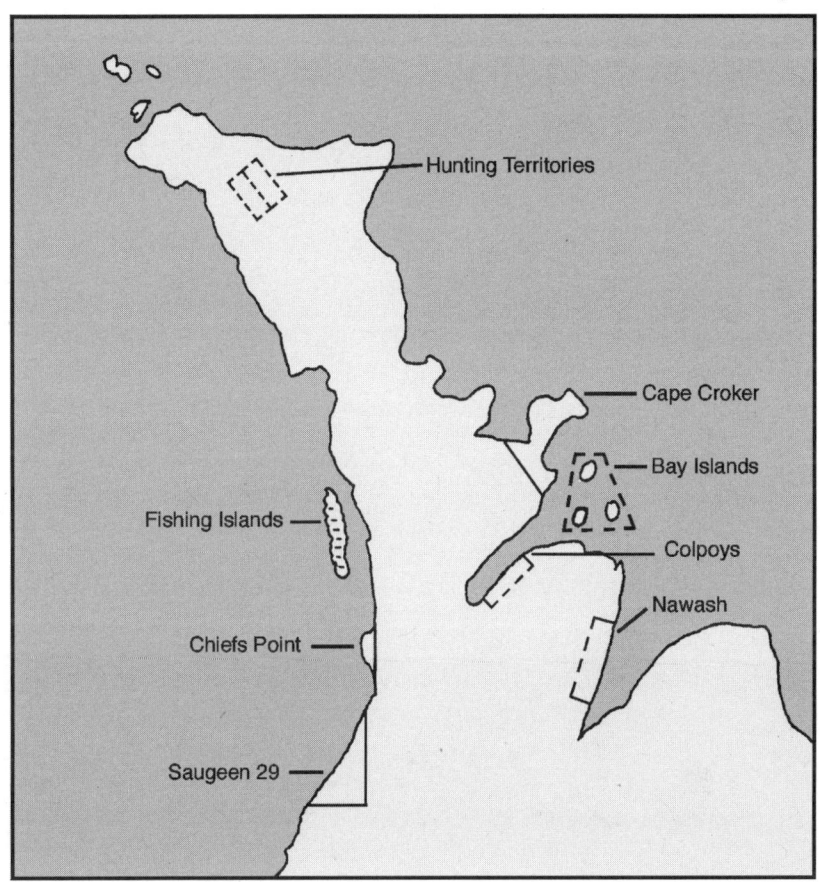

Map 3. Reserves

CULTURES AND ECOLOGIES

Cultures and Ecologies: A Native Fishing Conflict on the Saugeen-Bruce Peninsula

Introduction

During the last several decades native people in Canada have increasingly asserted their rights to natural resources. These rights are regarded as historical entitlements and as key to the rehabilitation of native communities. Increased local control of natural resources is recognized by Canadian government policymakers and native leaders alike as an important initiative toward self-government, but realizing this goal is not easy. Native representatives are asking for greater access to and control of resources for reasons that include enhanced economic opportunities and also involve broader social, political, and cultural issues. Activities related to the use of natural resources figure prominently in the histories and traditions of native peoples, and in their cultural identities. Positive change in native communities requires both economic and broad cultural solutions.

Although fishing is just one of the resource areas that are of concern to native peoples in Canada, fishing conflicts are especially conspicuous. Many of Canada's precedent-setting native-rights court cases are about fishing, a fact that illustrates the importance of this resource to many native communities and points to the widespread history of imposed restrictions by which native peoples' access to this resource has been diminished. Fishing-rights issues are also often at the centre of the table because they invoke especially challenging questions about the quality of our resource relations – about resource management and conservation.

In a more immediate sense, conflicts over native fishing rights also get attention because they are conducive to dramatic media coverage.

Many Canadians, when they hear mention of native fishing conflicts, will think about the incidents that occurred in September and October of 1999. They may recall television images of the showdown between the then federal fisheries minister, Herb Dhaliwal, and native fishers from the Burnt Church reserve who declared that they had rights to trap lobster in New Brunswick's Miramichi Bay, rights that superseded the Fisheries department's authority (*Record*, 30 Sept. 1999:A3). The urgency of this conflict subsided after a few months. Most reserve communities in New Brunswick signed agreements that gave them more rights to fishery resources, but reminders of unresolved issues in this region resurface intermittently.

Conflicts over native fishing rights have erupted recently in other parts of Canada as well, especially in British Columbia (see Newell 1993; Sharma 1998).[1] Events in adjacent regions of the United States (see Doherty 1990; Satz 1991:101–24) also have a bearing on the situation in Canada.

Access to fisheries is an issue for many indigenous groups around the world who are engaged in a global struggle for rights to resources (see Magallanes 1999; Sorrenson 1999). In a yet wider context, native fishing conflicts in Canada can be seen in relation to predicaments faced by fishing communities that are not necessarily aboriginal, in Canada's various regions and beyond (e.g., Derman and Ferguson 1995; Newell and Ommer 1999). Insights into cases where fishing rights are disputed can contribute to a better general understanding of the effects that outside forces can have on local communities, and how local communities can deal with them.

The level of media exposure that native fishing conflicts receive in Canada increases their potential for invoking social change. Their conspicuous nature makes inaction a problematic political option for government policymakers. However, there are no easy solutions to native fishing conflicts. It is not clear how far most Canadians are willing to go in recognizing native rights that can be seen as limiting non-natives. Special rights for a particular ethnically or culturally defined group are seen by many as inconsistent with fundamental principles of Canadian nationhood and citizenship. Native rights can be viewed as a challenge to the very legal and political processes through which we are trying to resolve fishing conflicts.

This book is an attempt to sort through some of the complex issues associated with one particular native fishing conflict on the Saugeen-Bruce Peninsula, which is located in Southern Ontario, on Lake Huron, one of Central Canada's Great Lakes. I examine many of the perspectives and assumptions on which various opposing positions within the conflict are based, in the hope that this effort may contribute to a productive rethinking of the issues and encourage a more open dialogue concerning this and other native resource conflicts.

In order for us to gain useful insights into this situation, a wide range of social and ecological issues needs to be taken into account. My approach to this task reflects my training in cultural anthropology and ecological anthropology. I borrow from three recent ecological anthropology approaches that place less emphasis on the 'ecological' qualities of our relationships with resources, and more on human dimensions – on social and cultural factors and conditions. Historical ecology, ethnoecology, and political ecology are interconnected through a shared concern for complex human aspects of resource relations. I emphasize each in various parts of this book, where they serve best as frameworks for examining particular aspects of the fishing conflict, such as its historical background, the meanings of central concepts associated with various positions on conflict issues, and its political contexts.[2]

Cultural anthropology also provides a general orientation around this topic. Anthropology can play a role in encouraging awareness of cultural diversity in our ever-changing and more globally interactive world. It is increasingly important in such an interrelated world to understand 'other' people better, and thereby see ourselves and our relations with others more clearly. Since many of the factors that contribute to the native fishing conflict have strong cultural dimensions, cultural anthropology is especially relevant.

This book is based on ethnohistorical research and ethnographic fieldwork that I conducted as part of my PhD work during 1995 and 1996. This included regular visits to the peninsula, and frequent stays in the peninsula's two First Nations communities. Where I discuss the perspectives of individuals and groups, I give most attention to ideas and concerns articulated by the native community members I interviewed. I have taken the liberty of placing their words in particular contexts, having considered the potential ethical and political issues before doing so. I see increased exposure of local perspectives as an important corrective to past conditions. Native peoples' voices have too often been ignored. The inclusion of local views in this book might contribute to a better-informed dialogue on fishing conflict issues. Direct quotes are used where possible as they may increase the chances of accurately expressing peoples' intended meanings. I am grateful to have been permitted to gather and present these ideas and opinions.

The fisheries around the Saugeen-Bruce Peninsula have long played a significant role in the life-ways of the region's human inhabitants, both in terms of subsistence and social relations. A dramatic change occurred in the early 1800s when a Great Lakes commercial fishery was created and settler governments started regulating resources that native peoples had long been harvesting. Another major shift was witnessed around the middle of the twentieth century when the lake trout that had long been a dominant species in the area's open waters all but disappeared. Recent years have also brought about a significant change in the peninsula's fisheries. A 1993 Provincial Court ruling known locally as 'the Fairgrieve decision' gave legal recognition to native fishing rights. This ruling presents new opportunities for native community members, but it poses difficult challenges for them as well, along with broader resource-management challenges. Natives and non-natives alike are apprehensive about how the Fairgrieve decision will be translated into new resource relations.

Apprehensions and uncertainties have increased tensions between those who support native fishing rights and those who oppose them. The atmosphere of conflict over native fishing rights is most evident on the peninsula itself, but angler associations and various other groups that are more broadly located have also entered the conflict. I aim to clarify fishing conflict issues by examining both historical contexts and current perspectives and conditions.

Interviewing native community members yielded rich insights, both directly, through the access to local perspectives that it allowed, and indirectly, by altering my general approach to studying the conflict. Fred Jones was one of the last native community members I interviewed during my fieldwork. Born in 1914, he was among the peninsula's most experienced fisherfolk. On an earlier occasion I had approached him about an interview concerning the history of the peninsula's fisheries, and he was straightforward about not wanting to discuss such an important community issue with a stranger. However, he did eventually take me into his confidence.

Fred Jones welcomed me into his small but cosy home and offered me a chair near the wood stove, opposite the couch where he sat with his cane at his side. Through the large window behind him I could see MacGregor Harbour, where a fishing boat was tied up at one of the small docks on Jones's Point. I began explaining my interest in the history of the peninsula's fisheries, but before I could utter more than a few words he pointed to a news article laying on the TV tray in front of him: 'It all started here,' he explained, 'when Howard Jones and the Nadjiwon boys were arrested for fishing without a licence.'

My original interest in studying the peninsula's fisheries conflicts developed from my suspicion that this was a place where anthropological approaches might be usefully applied. I assumed that I could simply provide an ethnohistorical or historical ecological study of past native fisheries involvement, and that this in itself would serve to inform people involved in the conflict in a practical way. However, through advice given by interviewees, including Fred Jones, I have come to better appreciate the need to explore the links between historical contexts and current social-political conditions more directly. I gradually shifted my research focus to current conditions, and began to focus more explicitly on how history is brought into present situations.

Chapter 1 elaborates on the background information presented in this introduction, with attention to the peninsula's people and its geography. It also includes an explanation of my information-gathering processes. In chapter 2 I describe the recent fishing trial as a pivotal event in the conflict. Chapters 3, 4, and 5 offer a glimpse into the historical and cultural depth of native fishing in the region. To clarify the time frames I use, a chronological list is appended (see appendix 1). While depicting the past importance of fishing activities in these historical ecological chapters, I note the difficulties encountered when interpreting the past and defining the cultural groups engaged in early fishing activities. I also question the simplified cultural distinctions often assumed when considering past fishing activities, and suggest that cross-cultural fishery involvements should not be ignored. These chapters also illustrate adaptations that native people have made in the past, which are relevant for assessing current conflict issues.

In chapter 6 the main focus shifts to ethnoecological areas – how environments are viewed as part of the cultural constructions of particular groups, and how these views are symbolically expressed. I give special attention to notions linked to 'conservation,' since these are deeply intertwined with conflict issues.

Chapter 7 extends these ethnoecological insights into more explicit political ecological domains. I discuss native community members' views on various political issues. All three ecological-anthropology approaches are incorporated in chapter 8, where I examine the idea of 'tradition,' its role in the conflict, and its possible contributions to resource-management solutions. In the conclusion, chapter 9, I reiterate the need to more openly examine the issues involved in this conflict, and point toward challenges and opportunities.

Increasingly, anthropologists consider questions about biases in their own writing as well as in the information that they gather or borrow. Knowledge of any sort is inherently shaped by particular purposes, and I do not deny that this book is subject to my own perspectives. I cannot hope to account for all such factors, but I have made every effort to include information in a way that matches the importance of the issues I discuss.

The overall purpose of this book has undoubtedly had an impact on my choices about how to present information, my main intention being to explain the conflict issues and encourage critical and productive discussion of them. One of my basic assumptions is that open discourse is an important step toward resolving conflict issues. Trying to contribute to this end demands careful reflection, but the goal itself supports my effort to present a conscientious balance of perspectives on fishing conflict issues.

1 Getting to Know the Peninsula and Its People

Among various peoples of the world, geographic place names may be highly expressive and convey much information. Such names are frequently descriptive, indicating notable qualities of landscape features. Mythical individuals are sometimes connected with particular places through stories that explain how geographic markings were formed. Such stories can contribute to social and ecological knowledge; by referencing ancestral ties, this knowledge can serve to define and regulate social relations and territorial privileges (see Cruikshank 1990; Tonkinson 1991; Davidson-Hunt and Berkes 2003). This function of place naming has been recognized through ethnographic research among 'unfamiliar' groups, but it might apply in more familiar contexts as well.

On the frontiers of colonial expansion in Canada, newly designated places were commonly named in honour of European aristocrats, government officials, and military officers. These place names also served to evoke allegiance to a particular social order. Colonial naming practices, like the more obviously mythical ones engaged by less familiar groups, can have implicit functions of social and territorial control. On the peninsula, territory has been controlled in more explicit ways as well.

The stretch of land commonly known as the Bruce Peninsula (see map 1) is the northern extension of Bruce County. The county was named in 1849, when the land below the peninsula was first surveyed, in honour of James Bruce, Earl of Elgin and Kincardine, and Governor General of British North America (Robertson 1971:38–9). In 1836, under a treaty negotiated at Manitoulin Island by Lieutenant Governor Sir Francis Bond Head, about 1.5 million acres below the peninsula

10   Cultures and Ecologies

were surrendered, and the peninsula was reserved as territory of the 'Saugeen Indians.' Until around 1854, when most of the peninsula was also surrendered (see Surtees 1984:101–5), it was commonly referred to as the 'Saugeen Peninsula.' During the 1800s, it was also called the 'Indian Peninsula.'

Some First Nations members prefer the name 'Saugeen Peninsula' because it speaks to their historical connection with the region, which is relevant to land claims that are being pursued (Darlene Johnston 1995, pers. comm.). A few contemporary writers, for example Spangler and Peters (1995:105), do refer to the peninsula as the Saugeen. This may reflect its proximity to the Saugeen River (see map 2), which empties into Lake Huron at the peninsula's southwest corner, but it also suggests recognition of a historic native presence on the peninsula, and perhaps support of current native concerns.

I use the name 'Saugeen-Bruce Peninsula' to mark both a historical sequence and a cultural relationship. This two-part name acknowledges the peninsula's multicultural history, and underlines the difficult task of finding a workable balance of perspectives when considering the peninsula's current fisheries problem and its underlying issues.[1]

The Peninsula Past and Present

The peninsula extends along the raised edge of an arched bedrock plate that is visible south of the Great Lakes, up through Southern Ontario, and across Manitoulin Island and beyond. A gradual slope between the peninsula's jutting eastern limestone cliffs and its western lowland shores causes its watersheds to drain primarily westward into Lake Huron (see Chapman and Putnam 1966).

By about twelve thousand years ago the ice sheets had begun to recede from most of the central Great Lakes region. Since then, the peninsula has been shaped and reshaped by major changes in water level (see Karrow and Warner 1990:28–33). Closed spruce forests that were established in areas of Southern Ontario by 12,500 BP began to spread onto the peninsula. Fossil pollen from peninsula lakes suggests that as early as 10,000 BP pine forests had replaced spruce growth. However, forest makeup fluctuated with lake levels: spruce dominated again when the water was high.[2]

Not long after the glacial recession first exposed the peninsula, it was almost completely submerged under water. During a period of low water that followed, Manitoulin Island and the peninsula were connected by land. Episodes of high water occurred later, around 5000 BP and then again around 3000 BP (Daechsel 1994). At these times the peninsula's lowlands were under water, making the top section into an island. Fox (1990a) speculates that an aboriginal (Iroquoian) name for the peninsula, 'Onenditiagui,' indicates knowledge of a time when the upper peninsula was separated from the mainland by water.[3]

There are several estimates of when Southern Ontario's biological environments first approximated today's conditions. Fitting suggests that the end of a period of environmental fluctuation around 5000 BP coincided with the beginning of new cultural forms in the development of 'essentially modern environmental associations' (1978:14). With reference to ecological environments apart from cultural adaptations, Trigger (1985:76) places the beginnings of modern environments a bit earlier, at 6000 BP, and Ellis et al. (1990:68) see 8000 BP as a workable estimate. Given the numerous criteria we might use to define and compare 'environments,' this variation in estimates might be expected.

Today, the peninsula is about one hundred kilometres long and thirty kilometres across at its widest points. It roughly follows a north-south axis, leaning slightly to the west. The southern boundary, recognized in the 1836 treaty that partitioned the peninsula as territory of the Saugeen Indians, runs from the bay at Owen Sound across to Southampton.

Colpoys Bay, about a quarter of the way up the peninsula, cuts more than halfway through its width. A network of rivers and lakes made this an ideal crossing point for early native peoples and later for the first non-natives in the region. Today a paved highway follows part of the old portage trail, joining Wiarton to cottage communities on the Huron shore. The peninsula's eastern, northern, and especially its western shores are dotted with islands.

In 1990 the Niagara Escarpment, which includes the Georgian Bay coastline of the peninsula, was declared a UNESCO World Biosphere Reserve. The peninsula's geological features and unique plant ecology are well known to naturalists and vacationers alike (see Fox 1952; Larson 1996). Bruce Peninsula National Park and Fathom Five National Marine Park are located at its northern end.

The peninsula can be characterized as an out-of-the-way place in a cultural as well as an ecological sense. Other parts of Southern Ontario have been more obviously affected by industry and urban expansion. Settlers came to the peninsula later than they did to most other parts of

12   Cultures and Ecologies

Southern Ontario: it was the last large area of Southern Ontario to be ceded in treaties.

The People

Unlike most of Southern Ontario, the number of non-native residents has not increased substantially since shortly after the peninsula was opened for settlement in the last decades of the 1800s, though many vacationers visit or pass through, especially during the summer. Apart from the larger centres of Owen Sound, Southampton, and Wiarton, most current non-native residents live in smaller communities along the shore and on the main highway that runs the interior length of the peninsula and serves as a corridor for north-south traffic. A large ferry, the *Chi-Cheemaun*, carries more than eighty thousand vehicles and two hundred thousand passengers between the peninsula's northern tip and Manitoulin Island most years, from May to October.[4]

Visitors may notice the occasional road sign that suggests the presence of native people on the peninsula – a hand-made sign advertising native crafts, or a professional one marking the boundary of a reserve. But who these people are is not readily apparent to most. The Saugeen 29 reserve, known locally as Saugeen, is located on the main highway that crosses the peninsula's base (see map 3). Heading east, at the edge of Southampton one crosses the Saugeen River bridge, from which the end of Southern Ontario's largest watershed can be seen flowing deep and wide into Lake Huron. The road winds along the top of the bluffs that follow the river, passes the golf course, and takes you onto the Saugeen reserve.[5]

Saugeen is a typical reserve in many respects, with its conspicuous band office, marked by a brightly coloured traditional band logo, and its widely spaced rows of small frame houses, interspersed with the occasional larger more modern building. The Sauble Beach road runs up the Lake Huron shoreline along the western side of the reserve. Along the inland side of the road, picturesque wooded sections stretch for more than ten kilometres, defining the reserve as a place undisturbed by modern development. On the lake side of the road, the stretch from Southampton to Sauble Beach is lined with cottages built on lots leased from the band. This section is indistinguishable from non-reserve lands, except perhaps for the high number of signs advertising 'cottages for sale.'

More intimate impressions of the Saugeen 29 reserve can be found on the few back roads that dissect its wooded interior. Several houses are clustered here and there, at a crossroad where one of the old schools stood, or where a small church has recently been built.

In the summer, the reserve's flat landscape is typically covered by still layers of dry heat that are occasionally shifted by breezes from Lake Huron. In the winter, the snow blends all but the cliff shorelines of the river and the edge of the lake into a monotone. From the outside Saugeen appears homogeneous and unchanging. But such impressions fade quickly when one enters the homes of the people who live there to find out what the peninsula's fishery means to members of this community.

Nawash, on the Georgian Bay side of the peninsula, contrasts in several ways with the reserve at Saugeen. While Saugeen is a flat section of western lakeshore, Nawash is itself a sort of peninsula extending out from the rugged eastern side of the broader Saugeen-Bruce Peninsula. Nawash is also farther away from a main town or highway. When coming onto the reserve from either of the two entrance roads, one cannot help but be struck by its dramatic landscapes. Beyond the limestone escarpment lies a narrow lowland, known on the reserve as 'the Prairie.' Further on, the road winds along the northern side of the cape toward the lighthouse.

There was once a community called Nawash (or Newash) about fifty kilometres to the south of the present reserve location, at the northern edge of Owen Sound. People from this community were relocated by the government of Canada West a few years after the 1854 Oliphant Treaty was signed, and the group that came to the present reserve brought the name with them (see Schmalz 1977:107–21).

While the reserve officially belongs to the 'Chippewas of Nawash,' it is more commonly referred to on maps and in the community as Cape Croker. Less formally, it is called Cape. Another name, Neyaashiingaming, is currently being revived. Neyaashiingaming roughly translates from Ojibway as 'a body of land mostly surrounded by water' (Ernestine Proulx 1995, pers. comm.).

Houses are more widely dispersed at Nawash than at Saugeen, though here too some are concentrated around places where the first churches and schools stood. There are also some newly developed areas where a few modest cottage-like houses are grouped together. The band leases a small number of cottage lots to non-reserve members, and runs the 'Indian Park' for campers, some of whom hike reserve sections of the Bruce Trail. Except for during the annual powwow weekend, this park is not as busy as other peninsula parks.

The visually idyllic settings of the reserve at Nawash are, like the first impressions noted in my descriptions of the Saugeen reserve, only surface pictures. At Nawash, too, people bring a variety of individual perspectives to community issues.

Another reserve section, known as the Hunting Territories, is located farther up the peninsula on the main highway. It belongs to both Nawash and Saugeen. Wilmer Nadjiwon, who was chief at Nawash for several terms and is a past president of the Union of Ontario Indians, runs a tourist shop here. He sells various items including his 'Indian carvings.' Behind the modern but rustic shop is a small interpretive area where tourists can learn about the native heritage and participate in traditional native activities. Visitors can explore the inside of a tipi and join in story circles.

Proximity to outside centres may account for some differences between Saugeen and Nawash. Many Saugeen community members have worked in Southampton, which is close enough to reach on foot or bicycle. People from Nawash, on the other hand, are more isolated from the main towns. Fewer local economic opportunities may account in part for the fact that there is a larger off-reserve membership at Nawash. There are roughly six hundred Saugeen First Nation members living on reserve and about eight hundred off reserve. Nawash has approximately the same number on reserve, but around twelve hundred (about one-third more than Saugeen) off-reserve.[6]

When looking at the various group names associated with the peninsula's native peoples, one begins to appreciate the region's historical cultural complexity. Ojibway is typically regarded as the main tribal affiliation of both communities. Chippewa is generally synonymous with Ojibway here, as it is elsewhere, though the former term is used mainly with reference to the official band names: 'Chippewas of Saugeen' and 'Chippewas of Nawash.' Many native community members note some Potawatomi lineage, though they see Potawatomi and Ojibway (both Algonquian-speaking groups) as closely linked. As among probably all reserve populations in the Great Lakes area, there is non-native ancestry as well, including French and British.

Many native community members use the Ojibway name 'Anishinabe,' or an abbreviation, to distinguish themselves from non-natives. Basil Johnston (1992, pers. comm.) has translated this roughly as 'the original person,' or 'a person spontaneously coming up from the ground.' This name is found in historical literature; for example, William Warren referred to the 'Anishnabay' in the late 1800s (Warren [1885] 1984:46).

Another designation used to distinguish native peoples is 'First Nation,' a term that came out of political discussions in the late 1970s and early 1980s concerning constitutional recognition. The peninsula's two native communities have used collective names, including 'Saugeen Ojibway Nation,' and 'Saugeen Ojibway Nations Territories,' since the 1980s (Darlene Johnston 2000, pers. comm.) to indicate their shared involvement in political causes, especially the fisheries trial.[7]

Gathering Information

Gathering information for this study posed special problems. While I relied substantially on literature research, my focus was on gathering local information through fieldwork. In light of the politically volatile nature of my topic, literature research required careful treatment and fieldwork demanded special considerations.

I examined a wide range of written materials, including historical works, government documents and records, newspapers, archaeological articles, and various reports and studies related to resource-management issues. I conducted my literature research at the National Archives of Canada, the Department of Indian Affairs library, the Archives of Ontario, at several university libraries, and at local libraries and in museum archives on the peninsula. I was also fortunate to have been given access to a substantial collection of documents compiled by Saugeen Ojibway First Nation researchers. Many of the literature sources I build on are discussed where relevant to specific issues examined throughout this book, and I provide a brief review of the main historical fisheries sources in appendix 2.

Many of the community members with whom I discussed written accounts of past fisheries involvements on the peninsula were suspicious of histories written by non-native peoples. There is a view that native perspectives have been overlooked, and that history has been written to support the political agendas of non-native authorities. I recognize this as a valid concern and attempt to address it in part through my focus on interviews that allowed people to tell their own histories. I also gathered and read several local historical publications produced by native community members.

Fieldwork data were collected between January 1995 and August 1996 on weekly trips to the peninsula's two First Nations communities, which are about a three-hour drive from my home. I conducted a few formal interviews with non-natives in order to clarify some basic questions I had about government resource-management processes and sport-fishing interests. I followed the general principles of 'collaborative research' (see Warry 1990) or 'participatory research' (see Perez 1997; Ervin 2000) by maintaining close contact with key individuals from both communities and inviting community input during all stages of my research.

Throughout the duration of my fieldwork I worked most closely with Saugeen Ojibway Nation Research Coordinator Darlene Johnston. Our regular contact was very helpful in my effort to better understand community concerns. I also depended on her and other individuals, including Carlene Elliott, when looking for the most appropriate ways to conduct research. Feedback on my proposed research questions in itself produced useful insights into local people's perspectives on fishing conflict issues.

I planned to use formal focus group interviews as part of an initial exploration of local perspectives. However, on good advice, I opted for more informal gatherings. Community members often hold 'potlucks,' and older people in particular are more comfortable in these settings.

I hoped to include an interviewer-administered questionnaire, and spent several weeks preparing, testing, and revising questions. However, it became apparent that given the political tensions associated with the fisheries conflict, many people were uncomfortable with even the most carefully chosen wordings of survey questions. In the end, after working through several drafts, and considering feedback from various community members, I chose not to include a formal survey.

At Nawash, where preliminary negotiation meetings with the Ontario Ministry of Natural Resources (OMNR or MNR) were under way, the terms 'resources' and 'management' were particularly contentious, as they implied what was seen as a non-native approach to resource relations. At Saugeen a structured questionnaire was likewise unsuitable. There was particular reluctance to categorize fishing practices as either 'commercial,' 'subsistence,' or 'recreational,' since these terms have legal implications. Another factor in deciding not to use structured survey questionnaires is that they were seen as more threatening than less formal interviews, which would allow people to voice local perspectives in their own words. I chose an informal interview style, based on very broad open-ended questions that left as much room as possible for people to express their ideas about fishing conflict issues in ways they thought appropriate.

I took every opportunity to inform the communities about who I was and what I was doing. Posting notices, contributing articles to community newsletters, and talking about my research at community gatherings and on local radio allowed me to build trust and interact more comfortably within the communities.

I relied primarily on participant observation and in-depth interviews. There was no shortage of opportunities to learn about fishing activities, for example, by visiting fish vendors, stopping by at the Nawash fish plant, where people brought their daily catches, talking with fisherfolk at the docks, and going out on fishing boats.

I was also able to participate in community activities through volunteer work on several ongoing community projects. When I was beginning my fieldwork, Nawash was organizing a fisheries co-management conference at Port Elgin, which took place in March 1995. My first interviews were conducted in conjunction with my participation in conference planning.

At Saugeen I also got involved in a community project during the early stages of my fieldwork. Under the direction of Fisheries Coordinator Timm Rochon, local students were researching the history of the fisheries as part of a summer project. I helped them develop interview questions and conduct test interviews, and thereby built useful connections within the community.

In the early stages of my work I also collaborated with a community researcher, Clayton Akiwenzie, who was interviewing elders at Nawash for a life-history project. Though our research topics were somewhat different, sharing interviews worked well. He saw fisheries issues as relevant to his topic, and I appreciated the opportunity to see these issues in broader life-history contexts. Clayton Akiwenzie had relatives in the community, and was well liked there; so people were more willing to be interviewed than they would have been had I contacted them on my own.

I gathered information from about fifty key informants, roughly half from each of the two First Nation communities. Most of the interviewees were comfortable speaking English, but I arranged for the assistance of an Ojibway translator for two interviews.

Following established guidelines for fieldwork research, interviewees were informed that they were not obliged to participate, and they had the option of anonymity. Given the contentious nature of the topic, I expected more people to opt for confidentiality, but was pleased when things turned out otherwise, as I feel that open dialogue is productive, and people should be recognized for their contributions.

When interviews were transcribed, I gave copies back to the interviewees for review. Less than 20 per cent of the interviewees asked to make changes, most of which were minor typographic corrections. In some cases valuable elaborations were added. After the interviewees had all given final consent to allow use of their interviews in my research, and for community research and education purposes, I provided a collection of member interviews to the two communities. An explanation of the interviewee coding system I use is given in appendix 3.[8]

An important aspect of community-oriented research is returning results to the community. I worked toward this end by talking at community gatherings and on local radio, by writing short articles and reports, and by providing interview copies. Papers presented at conferences were also distributed to community representatives. In an effort to include community concerns and perspectives in these papers and in my thesis, I have maintained an open dialogue with community members and encouraged feedback. I plan to continue making my research available to the two communities. Given the proximity of this research location to my home, it is possible to maintain contacts and gather follow-up information.

The willingness of reserve community members to participate in interviews reflects the importance of fisheries issues within the communities, and the desire of community members to contribute to finding solutions to the conflicts. The assistance that I had in developing locally appropriate approaches to research also played a role here, as did a generous portion of sociability on the part of community members, offered with the more than fair expectation that local concerns be taken seriously.

2 The Fairgrieve Decision and Its Impact

The Fishing Trial

On 26 April 1993, Judge Fairgrieve of the Ontario Court (Provincial Division) announced a ruling known officially as 'Regina v. Jones [1993] O.J. No. 893 (Ont. Prov. Div.)' and less formally as 'the Fairgrieve decision.' The case is also sometimes referred to as *R. v. Jones and Nadjiwon* or *R. v. Jones et al.* In this ruling the judge dismissed charges against Howard Jones and Francis Nadjiwon, members of the Chippewas of Nawash First Nation, who had been accused of 'taking more lake trout than permitted by [the] band's commercial fishing license contrary to Ontario Fishery Regulations' (*Regina v. Jones* 1993:421). Judge Fairgrieve found that the quotas assigned to them by the Ontario Ministry of Natural Resources (MNR) 'unjustifiably infringed on [the] defendants' existing aboriginal and treaty rights' (ibid.). Applying principles set out in the Sparrow case, a 1990 Supreme Court decision, Judge Fairgrieve recognized existing rights as giving the Saugeen Ojibway First Nations 'priority [access to the fisheries] over all other groups after conservation needs [are] met' (ibid.).[1] According to Sparrow, non-native commercial and sport fisheries can be allotted access to resources only after the first two priorities (conservation and an existing native food fishery) are satisfied. Though it is a lower court ruling, Judge Fairgrieve's decision is seen as a 'highly significant precedent' (Notzke 1994:72). As evident from the tone of his decision (see his excerpted conclusion in appendix 4), Judge Fairgrieve had little doubt that the government's actions toward the aboriginal community – their quota allocation process and regulation enforcement decisions –

failed to recognize aboriginal and treaty rights as required by section 35(1) of the *Constitution Act*, 1982.

Local perspectives on the conditions leading up to the fishing trial were articulated by several people whom I interviewed. David McLaren, a non-native researcher who is married to a Nawash band member and has long been employed by that band, noted that

> there were charges laid ... by the MNR every year that the Band had to apply for a licence. Nawash applied for the licence every year under protest because they figured that they didn't need a licence to practice their rights. One of the charges was laid in connection with fishing too many splake, over their quota. And again it was a sting operation by the conservation officers. They set up a truck outside of the reserve and bought fish ... Well, finally the First Nation just let some of the charges stand, took them to court. (CP-DM)

McLaren suggests that the quota system in place prior to the court decision discriminated against native community members:

> As I understand it the quota system came in 1984. The MNR took all the commercial users at that time, and for each one they took an average of their yearly takes over the previous six years for each species and based their quotas on that. The MNR did that for all of the ten or fifteen non-native fishermen, and when it came to Nawash, it was a communal licence; there were ten or fifteen Native commercial fishermen operating under that one licence. (CP-DM)

Within this one communal licence the band's level of reliance on fish was not fully accounted for when quotas were calculated:

> So when the MNR added up the Nawash catch, they did not include the fish that was given away in the community, or sold in the community, or sold off of the back of a pickup truck. They counted only the fish that was registered through the fish buyers. Before 1984 there was no requirement to register all the fish sold through the fish buyers, or all the fish sold period. So the numbers that the ministry had on record for Nawash were woefully low. (CP-DM)

The licensing system is also seen as problematic in that it did not account for the kind of fishing that reserve members practised:

The native fishery by practice was an inshore fishery, and they have historically fished for trout along the shore for generations and generations ... thousands of years. So although the licence they had included chub and whitefish, they were unable to get at the chub because the chub is a deep-water fish and the whitefish to a great extent had been displaced by the splake stocking that was happening at the same time. So although the licence shows a range of species, the fact is that there was only one species that the native fishermen had access to, and that was the lake trout, or splake in this case. Initially they only had a five-thousand-pound quota, and they probably would fish out three, four, or five times that amount in a season. So that's how the quota system was developed. By applying it equally to all the users the MNR ended up discriminating against the First Nations. (CP-DM)

Howard Jones, one of the two men charged, explains the accusations as he saw them:

I was chief before the Fairgrieve decision. When the charges came the licence was in my name. Since I was overseeing the licence, I was charged. So the charges occurred when I was chief, but the decision to fight the case was made after ... We were charged for exceeding the quota, but also for not reporting what we were catching properly. That is what ... made me determined to fight it. (CP-HJ)

McLaren sees the Fairgrieve decision as a major coup against the two groups most often identified as opponents of native fishing rights:

And that decision turned everything upside down for the sportsmen and for the MNR. It basically said the First Nations weren't breaking the law after all. They weren't bad conservators of the resource ... they had a perfect right to catch fish and sell it, and therefore the licensing requirements, including the quota system that the MNR was imposing, was illegal – illegal and unconstitutional. The judge ... basically ruled that the quota system as it applied to the First Nations was invalid. (CP-DM)

Howard Jones notes the importance of current constitutional and legal contexts for the outcome in the case:

After I heard all the evidence I was not surprised that we won. I have suffered through a history of seeing us lose on all these little charges because no one knew how to handle it properly. I think the court case was won partly through good timing. The Canadian constitution had come into play, which recognized that our rights were still existing. I think that was a big thing, and the Sparrow case. Although Fairgrieve was a lower court ruling I think the Supreme Court would uphold it because Fairgrieve used a Supreme Court ruling in making his determination. (CP-HJ)

Jones also sees the verdict as a departure from previous legal processes:

They got a change of venue to Orangeville to stay away from the media better. And we felt that local judges had handled too many cases. Actually, they found that they couldn't get a judge locally, just a justice of the peace; and they wanted a learned judge ... Fairgrieve had an open mind and wanted to be educated about the case, and he made the proper decision. (CP-HJ)

Ralph Akiwenzie, who took over as chief at Nawash shortly after the charges were laid, also sees sensitivity to local conditions as a factor in this legal decision: 'Judge Fairgrieve took the time to study the material, and made an effort to come and hear the testimony of the elders in the community here' (CP-RA). Chief Akiwenzie comments on what this ruling meant to him personally:

We were on pins and needles for nearly a year, but the outcome was exactly as we expected ... I felt exhilarated to know that all the effort had been worthwhile ... When I come to think about it now, it was the highlight of the time I have spent in political office, having been called upon to testify in Orangeville. Those ten or twelve minutes speaking at the trial was the highlight because I felt very strongly about the rights issue and the reaffirmation of the right that we do have for trade and commerce in fishing ... augmented by the fact that we have treaty rights that have never been given up even though we have surrendered land. I really felt a sense of destiny being the one to testify in court substantiating the details. (CP-RA)

He sees this ruling as very important for the Nawash community:

It was a milestone in our involvement as First Nations people. It helped to educate an unsympathetic public to our rights. I regard it as a very historic day ... It substantiated our right. It gave us a strong sense of identity and it was very empowering. And it cleared us of the accusations in the media about us always over-fishing. We use the ruling as an important guideline in day-to-day activity and long-range planning. (CP-RA)

As indicated here, recognition of fishing rights has far-reaching effects within the native communities. Along with new economic potentials, perhaps implied above as 'day-to-day activity and long-range planning,' the ruling brings recognition of personal, social, and cultural values. But these potential benefits are limited to the extent that this recognition of rights will be applied.

The Fairgrieve decision has left important issues unresolved, including the level of commercial activity it might authorize. However, it may expand the subsistence rights spelled out in Sparrow as a 'food fishery.' Fairgrieve recognizes 'an aboriginal right of some sort to fish commercially' (Woodward and Jordan 1993:2f; cited in Notzke 1994:72). A commercial right was certainly part of the focus of this case, as noted in the opening sentence of Judge Fairgrieve's ruling: 'At issue in this case is the constitutionality of a restriction imposed by the Ontario Ministry of Natural Resources upon commercial fishing by members of the Chippewas of Nawash Band' (*R. v. Jones* 1993:423).

But the full extent of this commercial right is not yet clear.[2] While some, including David McLaren (1996, pers. comm.), interpret the Fairgrieve decision as having established a commercial right, others, including Saugeen chief Richard Kahgee, see it as only a vague statement of rights to commercial fishing: 'Fairgrieve only provided a cursory review of the rights issued and didn't define rights such as subsistence and commercial' (SG-RK).[3] It is not unusual for a legal ruling to be interpreted in various ways; in fact, this seems to be part of the legal process. Issues raised in divergent interpretations can be addressed more directly in subsequent rulings.

Though Fairgrieve recognized fishing rights as applying to traditional fishing areas as well as waters adjacent to reserves, he did not depict these rights as exclusive within their full geographic range, or state exactly what that range is. There is also uncertainty about whether the gains made in this case will remain intact, or whether they will be challenged in an appeal or in a future case. Howard Jones comments on this, and raises another important issue: 'I don't think it will be overturned. Maybe the parameters will be defined more closely in succeeding court cases, should they happen ... By parameters I mean details about where and when to fish, and what "conservation" is' (CP-HJ). The importance of what 'conservation' means, in terms of potential outcomes of recognized native fishing rights, is examined as the focus of chapter 6.

Broad jurisdictional issues concerning the ultimate ownership of the fishery, and thereby authority to manage it, remain open as well: 'There has to be a change reflected not only in attitudes, but in the management of the fishery. There are still problems there: the regulation of the fishery, the management of the fishery, the various jurisdictions' (CP-RA).

Judge Fairgrieve indicated in his ruling that he expected the MNR and the First Nations to negotiate appropriate harvesting regulations and conservation measures. Several months after the trial, a 'Statement of Political Intent' was presented to MNR representatives by the Saugeen Ojibway First Nations, but negotiations soon broke down. Nawash began holding meetings with the MNR on their own, but as of mid-1999 no agreements had been reached (David McLaren 1999, pers. comm.).

Chief Richard Kahgee of the Saugeen First Nation asserted that his people's jurisdictional rights to the fisheries were never relinquished, and therefore negotiation was unwarranted. He also saw negotiation as problematic because it could be regarded as 'consultation.' The MNR's obligation to consult with native communities (as set out in Sparrow) could then be met, even if the communities opposed whatever regulations the MNR decided on. The level of distrust toward outside authorities that existed in these native communities seemed likely to have an impact on the prospects of a negotiated agreement.

On 23 September 1995, at an international conference in Duluth, Minnesota, Chief Kahgee announced the Duluth Declaration. On 2 October 1995 it was formally signed at a public ceremony at Saugeen, which I attended. The document is a claim of jurisdiction to the 'waters in their entirety, which includes the fisheries, lands and minerals, above and below the waters, including the lake bed' around the peninsula, 'to the median point in the water between the Saugeen Nation territory ... and all other national territory' (Duluth Declaration 1995).

The declaration also served notice that commercial and sport licences would be issued by the band. Shortly after releasing this declaration, Chief Kahgee stated that beginning in January 1997, licences would be enforced by Saugeen's conservation officers (*Sun Times* 3 Oct. 1995:1). Chief Kahgee's defiant stance was supported by perhaps the majority of community members at Saugeen, but a significant number were concerned that his position might worsen already tense relations with local non-natives.

In light of Chief Kahgee's stance on jurisdictional issues, and his view that Saugeen should not negotiate an agreement since an unconditional native right already existed, Nawash's decision to enter preliminary discussions with the MNR placed a strain on the Saugeen Ojibway First Nations alliance. One person involved in fishing at Saugeen suggested that Nawash tried negotiating because they were in a weaker financial position than Saugeen was. Chief Kahgee's demands were recognized by some at Nawash as ambitious but perhaps unrealistic: 'Chief Richard Kahgee's Duluth Declaration could be a good thing for the Indian. But whether it's working too fast is another thing' (CP-FJ).

Given the potential economic and social importance of establishing native fishing rights, and the historically rooted tensions connected with resource regulation, it is not surprising that there were a variety of perspectives within both communities on how to best proceed following the Fairgrieve decision.

In June 2000 agreement was finally signed by members of the Chippewas of Nawash and Saugeen and the provincial and federal governments. The two reserves gained access to all of the peninsula's fisheries and agreed not to fish in Owen Sound and Colpoys Bays, where recreational fishers are most active. As well, protocols for setting allowable catch limits, exchanging data, and enforcing regulations were outlined (Darlene Johnston 2000, pers. comm.; David McLaren 2001, pers. comm.). As important as this agreement is, it does not solve many of the conflict's underlying issues. Social tensions are still evident, and enforcement problems have already emerged. Many native community members continue to reject any level of outside interference in what they see as their unconditional rights. Though recent negotiations and developments have partially resolved tensions that were especially evident shortly after the fishing trial, there is still worth in examining events that characterized that period, as the conditions they reflected are not altogether behind us.

Conflict Issues and Incidents

> Like any court case that affirms rights it has to be recognized by the outside parties, and I don't know what degree of acceptance we are getting. (CP-RA)

There is some support from outside the First Nations communities for their assertions of fishing rights. Church groups, for example, have circulated documents that sympathized with native-rights positions. The Canadian Auto Workers also voiced support for native fishing rights, and provided a venue for a conference on fishery co-management possibilities. But many non-natives have expressed frustration over the impact native rights will have on their own access to the fisheries. Issues are debated in the local media, on the streets, and at local meetings.

The area's television station covered the conflict in a five-part series in late 1995. Around the same time a segment about the peninsula's fisheries dispute was featured on the national CBC network program *The Fifth Estate* (see *Sun Times* 29 Nov. 1995:1).

The most emphatic objections to assertions of aboriginal and treaty rights came from sport-fishing association members. They saw native commercial fishers who set gill nets near sport-fishing areas as unfairly exploiting stocks maintained by fishing association programs for hatcheries and stream rehabilitation (*Sun Times* 15 Aug. 1995:16; *Globe and Mail* 11 Sept. 1995:A6). Non-native commercial fishers had an informal agreement with the MNR to leave Owen Sound Bay and Colpoys Bay as sport-fishing areas; however, until the agreement was signed in 2000, native commercial fishers had no reason to accept such a restriction. They felt they had a right to fish there since the bays are within their traditional territory as suggested in the Fairgrieve decision.[4] Even though there was actually little (if any) native commercial fishing in Owen Sound Bay, the position that native fishers took was seen by sporting association representatives as a threat to sport fishing, and thereby to the local economy (*Sun Times* 15 May 1996:1).

The Ontario Federation of Anglers and Hunters (OFAH) supports the position of local sport associations members who oppose priority native fishing rights, and has published statements to this effect in several magazine articles (e.g., Ankney 1991).

The hostility surrounding fishing rights issues is demonstrated in acts of property damage and personal violence. Several Nawash community members claim that their nets were damaged or stolen (*Sun Times* 28 Aug. 1995:1). One Nawash member faced charges relating to alleged attempts to protect his nets by booby-trapping net lines with razor blades (*Wiarton Echo* 13 Sept. 1995:14).

In another set of incidents, a fishing boat owned by native fishers suspiciously sank while docked at Howdenvale, opposite Lake

Huron's Fishing Islands (*Sun Times* 28 Aug. 1995:1–2). Only days after it was lifted, it caught fire (*Sun Times* 5 Sept. 1995:3). These events followed a series of less direct confrontations involving use of the dock facilities at Howdenvale:

> The Reeve of Howdenvale ... he's the one that's making all the fuss. We don't pay the thousand-dollar docking fee, but non-natives have to pay. It's our inherent right. (SG-TM)

> Township decision makers were not happy with the native fishermen using the dock at Howdenvale. So after they repaired it they put in three posts. But one of my boys got wind of a law that you can't block the dock in case an emergency vehicle has to get in, and he called someone. They wanted the fishermen to carry the fish all the way down the dock. But then when the boat was set on fire the fire truck couldn't get through, and the fire burned the dock. Now my son Francis got a bill for repairing the dock, but it would not have burnt if the posts weren't there. (CP-WN)

Native community members and supporters suspect that local residents who had been actively trying to prevent native fishers from using the docks were involved in these acts of property damage. Sport-fishery advocates are also suspected. Some non-natives have suggested that native fishers themselves had something to do with at least the fire.

Several other occurrences are linked to the tensions surrounding the peninsula's fisheries. In August 1995 a group of angry citizens, including sport-fishing association members and an elected local government official, marched to the Owen Sound market, where they confronted native fish vendors. There they 'protested' against what they saw as the government's lack of support for non-native interests. From native perspectives this demonstration was a racist act – an effort to intimidate an already marginalized group.

Within a few weeks of the market demonstration, two native youths sustained knife wounds in a late-night street fight in Owen Sound. According to native witnesses, police officers were in the area and could have stopped the fight (*Sun Times* 5 Sept. 1995:1). A police spokesperson suggested that because there were other fights on the same evening, they did not have sufficient numbers of officers to break up this particular one, but many native community members see a link between the police inaction and the fisheries conflict (*Record* 5 Sept.

1995:A3): 'The police couldn't care less. Our boys get knifed in Owen Sound and the police are there and didn't see a thing. Yet there are three men knifed. Two weeks later a white guy is hit with a beer bottle and there is a native in jail within twenty-four hours' (CP-WL).

While these confrontations have primarily occurred on the Nawash side of the peninsula, hostility is also directed at Saugeen: fishing association members stated that violence could erupt if natives try to enforce their own fishing regulations as defined in the Duluth Declaration. Tensions increased as the January 1997 enforcement deadline approached, but direct confrontation was avoided, partly due to Chief Kahgee's announcement that his community's regulation of the fishery would take place gradually.

In early April 1997, Richard Kahgee resigned as chief of the Saugeen First Nation, due to conflicts within the band council (*Record* 5 Apr. 1997:F16). The seven council members who continued carrying out band business – under protest from Richard Kahgee, five other council members, and a considerable portion of the community – suggested that they may not support the approach asserted in the Duluth Declaration.

This factionalism seriously disrupted community life. Several people noted the stress on personal relations caused by this internal political struggle. One older resident indicated that the roots of this division go back several decades, and are linked to perceived favouritism in family property allotments on the reserve. The impact of past and current conditions within this disruption to community cohesion is not clear, but it is obvious that reserve life has no shortage of socially stressful situations. While the fisheries conflict initially consolidated the two First Nations and has brought each reserve community together at times, it has also brought new social and political stresses.

Fisheries conflicts on the Saugeen-Bruce Peninsula are about control of local resources, but the hostilities are also linked to broader native-rights issues. In 1995 there was more exposure of native-rights issues in the Ontario media than there had been since the 1990 Oka stand-off.[5] Several members from both peninsula reserves joined the demonstrations at Ipperwash, to protest the first killing of a native person in connection with a land claims dispute in Canada in more than one hundred years (*Sun Times* 12 Sept. 1995:11[a]). The clash between RCMP officers and natives at Gustafson Lake in British Columbia, which also occurred at this time, similarly fuelled apprehensions surrounding native rights conflicts on the peninsula (see *Sun Times* 12 Sept. 1995:11[b]). Current fisheries conflicts on the peninsula are also affected by ongoing native

The Fairgrieve Decision and Its Impact   29

land claims: 'I think some tension is also linked to the land claims. It involves all the townships of the peninsula' (CP-RA).

Tensions have seriously polarized local native and non-native groups:

I believe there has to be accommodation made, and soon. There was a situation that developed in August stemming from the derby that was planned in Owen Sound Bay. There were a number of outstanding issues raised that have not been resolved, including damage to nets, the Howdenvale incident, where a craft was set on fire, and there was an unfortunate incident when several of our youth were involved in some stabbings and some free-for-alls just at the end of the derby in Owen Sound. We are hoping these issues will be resolved. There are investigations going on but there have not yet been any charges laid, which indicates that these actions are condoned and accepted, and this will make it more likely for similar actions to keep happening. (CP-RA)

It was a poor investigation of the boat burning. And there was a big fight in Owen Sound. The cops stood there and watched. They put the natives in jail and let the others walk. But it's not just that. Everyone's attitudes have turned against natives. Some have always been like that. (SG-PS)

There is a rumour in Tobermory that the white fishermen are going to be bought out. Everyone is uptight. I am up there in the white community. Nothing is moving, they can't sell lots, everyone is afraid ... I had a lot of good friends, I used to visit in their homes. They were willing to listen before ... There is a lot of tension now. (CP-WN)

I used to have a lot of friends there. During the Salmon Derby I walked into the bar, and people I used to play pool with got up and left. It was so tense in there ... The picture of me and Miles fishing at Vail's Point, supposedly it said 'Fishing in Owen Sound Bay,' but we were out at Vail's Point. It was posted in the laundromat – like a wanted poster. People in the car parts store knew who we were right away. You just felt like you weren't wanted. (CP-WL)

When I was in high school it used to be very bad like this. It's twenty years and it's full cycle coming back. (CP-WL)

There are benefits from the Fairgrieve ruling like more people fishing, but there have been a lot more hardships ... The children feel the tension when they go to school off the reserve ... Things are bad. (CP-WL)

> Every once in a while when I was a kid there was a problem. I remember Vincent Nadjiwon setting his nets at Barrier Island. That was his area for fishing. He had fished there for years and so had his dad. In around 1939, I think, they put him in jail. The courts threw it out, but they didn't compensate him. There has always been some conflict. This last while it has been quite bad. I don't like shirts with logos anyway, but I won't wear those Neyashiingamiing shirts to town any more. You are a target for people who want to pick a fight. (CP-RJ)

Current Native Fisheries

Despite the atmosphere of resentment and uncertainty that prevailed after the fishing trial, some community members have attempted to take advantage of the opportunity to revitalize fishing activities. At Saugeen, Chief Kahgee supported the set-up of a small fisheries department, which included a newly hired non-native program coordinator, Timm Rochon; a community member, Harold Thompson; honorary fisheries guardians; and students as occasional summer staff. A boat was purchased for departmental duties such as fisheries monitoring, and a contest to name the boat encouraged community interest in the department. Harold Thompson, who is also an artist, designed a crest for the boat. Regular community fish-fry events were organized to promote community interest and serve as venues for disseminating information about the fisheries. The band council also established a fisheries committee to oversee fisheries activities.

The fisheries department purchased a few small open boats in an effort to encourage younger people to take up fishing. Some of them tried it for a while, but most did not stay with it:

> We bought seven small boats, but there is only one still in the water cause fishing is not for everyone. It's cold, windy, wet ... especially in the smaller boats. (SG-TM)

> Fishing on boats separates the men from the boys – lots wanted to in the last few years but few did. The percentage works down again. It's hard work and you are at the mercy of the elements. (SG-WK)

Community members are unsure of the economic prospects that fishing might hold: 'The last few years people are more interested in it. Don't know if they can make a good living at it, but ... they are getting more interested' (SG-CS). Reflecting on her own life, and her husband's work on non-native commercial fishing boats, Ruth Roote advises that it is important to like the work to start with and not entertain high financial expectations: 'I hope that fishing will appeal to younger people. It's something you're born into; you have to like water and have respect for water, and the weather ... I certainly wish them success. You will never get rich fishing. It's a living. We never got rich' (SG-RR).

More generally, there is a sense within the community that economic development in the fisheries is much needed in light of current limited economic opportunities:

There is not much to hunt and not much work. (SG-RA)

The community developing the fisheries is a good idea. I hope it continues ... There is not much employment on the reserve. (SG-RT)

There is good potential in the fisheries for a variety of fields of employment. Unemployment is very high ... maybe it's higher than 38 per cent. Some are on social assistance who could also be working. Some young people leave the reserve to find work, but it's not attractive or feasible to work for minimum wage, with income tax and living expenses. To compete outside you must have a good paying job or be motivated by the kind of work, or it has to be important to your career. (SG-A1)

It is important ... to develop the fisheries because what else have they got. (SG-LK)

You see in the news the welfare problems. Fishing development could help break that cycle. (SG-WK)

Some also see fishing development as having potential for improving broader social conditions: 'Developing the fisheries could be useful. We as a fishing committee might be able to develop a program for kids who drop out of school and do nothing. We could teach them how to properly do things and respect creation' (SG-HT).

Several community members became very active in re-establishing a fishery since the court case began. Lorne Mandewaub has been involved both on the water and as an organizer. Theodore Mason (SG-TM) had previous experience on larger closed boats, and was glad for the chance to fish with other native community members. Jim Ritchie (SG-JR) became part owner of two larger boats, and opened a fish store on the reserve. For those who have increased their fishing involvement, the economic potential is part of their attraction to the lifestyle. It is difficult to assess the current economic benefits that the native fishery offers. Participation is changing rapidly, and the fish market itself is constantly fluctuating:

> Right now we are going to set twenty-two hundred yards of net and out of that we will get anywhere from a ton to a ton and a half of fish, and there is only a three-man crew. And then the boat gets its share to buy all the equipment and the nets. So we make out all right. (SG-JR)

> The prices haven't changed in thirty years. They shoot up to four dollars a pound then down to fifty cents. The processor makes the money. But it's still a good living. I fished the last two years. You can make fifteen hundred dollars on a good day in the fall and the spring. (SG-TM)

> Some small boats do good. I know a guy from Cape with an eighteen-foot boat. He sometimes would get three boxes [135 pounds each] per day. At two to three dollars per pound he does all right. Then when fishing gets good the price drops. (SG-TM)

> Most of the fish go to the States or to Europe. The truck picks them up here and goes right to New York to the street market. People take the whole truckload there. We had a truck that came from Michigan last year. And we sell the spawn. We get one dollar per pound for spawn. (SG-TM)

When I asked people at Saugeen if they thought developing the fisheries could benefit the community, most interpreted the question in terms of individual versus community benefits, rather than just in terms of the community itself, which was what my question intended. Given their concern for how some individuals might benefit at the expanse of others, they regarded the prospect of building a plant that might employ several people as a way to more fairly distribute benefits:

> If it goes it will create some self-employment. There is nothing much to do on the reserve. It would be good if they could start a company, but it

should not be just for the benefit of individuals ... [They] could build storage facilities or something; create plant employment. (SG-EM)

Some people think fishing is just helping a few, not the whole community; but that will change when we get our own processing plants and bigger boats, and a few more people employed. (SG-PS)

As noted above, there was a split between Saugeen and Nawash over approaches to negotiations. Those who supported Chief Kahgee's Duluth Declaration seemed proud that Saugeen's fisheries policies were their own. But on the water, at least around the Fishing Islands, where much of the spring and fall fishing is carried out, there was considerable cooperation between Saugeen and Cape fishers:

Sometimes we fish with people from Cape. Marshall Nadjiwon, mostly the Nadjiwon boys, Philip Jones was on our boat last year, Al Podonequot was on the boat that burnt. Turtle, Marshall and Al own it. We use each other's boats if one is broke down ... If it is too rough for smaller boats we pick up their nets. No one charges anyone cause someday you will be in the same place. (SG-TM)

I've had this boat going on three years now. We just bought the other one two weeks ago. I have some partners on it cause it's too hard to come up with the money on your own. Marshall Nadjiwon is my partner. He's the one who taught me how to fish, right after the fishing protest in 1990. I didn't know the first thing about it. His brother Francis was the one charged in the Jones-Nadjiwon case. They had charged Marshall too, but his charges were dropped. (SG-JR)

At Nawash, several fisheries researchers and organizers were hired, and a fish plant that employs about a half dozen people was built. A fisheries assessment program was put in place:

Overall the program isn't too bad. The majority of the fishermen are bringing their fish to the plant. I think there has been a lot of good information obtained ... We count and weigh the fish and then we individually assess one out of every twenty. That's 5 per cent of the total, from shiners and suckers right on up to carp, whitefish, trout ... We check for lamprey wounds, tags, clippings. (CP-BJ)

Fish cages are also operated on the reserve along the Colpoys Bay shoreline. I would estimate that two or three dozen people in total are currently dependent to a significant degree on the fisheries. A more accurate figure is difficult to establish, due to the fishery's seasonal nature, and the various levels of part-time, temporary, occasional, and full-time occupation it affords. Many people see changes since the trial as positive in both economic and broader social terms:

> It was exciting to get up early, and see that people did not have to be on welfare. Like the reserve was alive again. (CP-WL)

> Economically and morally, the decision has made a difference. People are gaining back some of their self-respect because they can do work that they are accustomed to. They like the job; they like fishing. They turn themselves to the task quite vigorously. Socially, they have improved because you see a different attitude in people. They are not so worried about getting charged and having to pay fines. And it has put more money back into the community. (CP-HJ)

Some community members, including Ted Johnston, continued to fish in a small way after the trial:

> This last year I haven't done any fishing because I have arthritis in my hands and my hands are a little bit sore ... and it's easier to buy a fish from the local fishermen. But I enjoy setting the net ... This is the first year that I didn't set a net ... I usually set only one, about three hundred to four hundred feet. It's only for my own use ... whitefish, or splake or whatever. (CP-TJ)

There has also been some new growth: 'Since the Fairgrieve trial the fishing is more stable. They get enough to support a bigger outfit. There are three or four tugs here now, which never happened before. There were mostly just twelve- or fourteen-foot boats' (CP-FJ).

Howard Jones notes secondary economic benefits associated with increased local fisheries involvement:

> I have a spin-off business. I do maintenance on the tugs, mechanical set-ups and welding. If they need advice we usually do that for free because a lot of them are my customers. People have kept the work at home as much as possible with me. They have to go off the reserve to get some

work done. Sometimes they use me as an expediter to get other people to do work for them, if I don't have the tools and machines to do the job. They do not know where all the services are and what to expect. I have had a barge for quite a few years. We take machinery across to the island, and with the fish farm we do quite a bit of work. Usually it is a one-man operation here, but as we have grown we have part-time work come in on a weekly basis. (CP-HJ)

He speculates on the directions of current changes in the native fishery at Nawash:

Right now you see a lot of people fishing because they have been fishing on a smaller scale and they think that you can just buy a big tug and you go out and fish. And a lot are learning that it costs more to run. I think when we get over this hump, a lot of people who are trying to get their own crews together will be actually working for someone else. I think that the five, six, or seven tugs right now will be cut back to three or four. There will be more of an emphasis on the Lake Huron spring and fall fishery. (CP-HJ)

Some of the people think that fishing is a get-rich-quick scheme, but I don't think it is any different than any other job. It is not a lottery win or anything. Every fish you catch costs something in overhead. Some people this year replaced their gear six times. They don't have the experience that non-native commercial fishermen do, and they are playing catch-up now ... They are trying to get up to the place that they would have been now if their rights to fish were recognized all along. (CP-HJ)

That more people from Nawash than Saugeen are currently engaged in fishing no doubt has to do with economic trends that were already in place prior to the Fairgrieve decision. Though the Fairgrieve ruling provided only a tentative statement of native fishing rights, both communities have had opportunities to expand their fisheries; but expansion has been limited. As Ruth Roote and others note, precarious work is not for everyone. In spite of the low level of economic opportunity on-reserve, and even with community promotion, the fisheries have attracted only a few new people.

A few of the older community members, notably Earl Akiwenzie, continued fishing mainly for the same reasons they always had – to maintain their livelihood. People who have begun fishing more recently are similarly concerned about their livelihood, but they are also aware that native rights, and associated cultural values, are interwoven with the economic prospects the fisheries offer. The events surrounding the Fairgrieve decision have brought important values to the surface within the two reserve communities:

> We have a right to these waters, for our people to try and develop some sort of income. We have a right to it. If an outsider would do it, it would be called entrepreneurship, but not if a native person does it. (SG-CS)

> I think fishing is very important. What other job is there for us? This was our main resource from the time I was growing up, and when I was married, when my husband was a fisherman. That's what we used for everything ... And we believe as Indian people, these fish were provided for us ... like everything else ... it's the resources ... that we believe our creator gave us ... strongly believe that. (CP-WA)

> I think to be a fisherman you've got to have it in you. For us it's part of our history, something we lost. When I was nine my grandfather, who taught me how to speak Ojibway, used to make furniture. He used to make a dip net, twelve feet square. He said you've got to have fish; and he wanted me to know how to make these things. (SG-JR)

Jim Ritchie's above-noted statement that being a fisherman is 'part of our history, something we lost' reflects the cultural importance that native fishing issues have in these communities. There is a strong sense that fishing was an important part of native history and native culture, and that it needs to be reclaimed. History and cultural identity are recognized as closely intertwined with rights issues, and with this fishing conflict.

3 Fishing in the Distant Past

> Basically, we were forced out of the fishery by regulations which never contemplated aboriginal interests ... There is evidence of aboriginal interest in the fisheries prior to white contact. There are fishing sites up and down the peninsula ... you have the fact that native peoples have fished historically in the fishing grounds – they named the islands. There is a continuing use and ownership; and certainly we have historic reference to establish this. (SG-RK)

The fishing conflict on the Saugeen-Bruce Peninsula is permeated with history. Since the conflict is a cumulative outcome of past relations, a better understanding of past fisheries involvement can help in sorting through current conflict issues. But this is not a simple proposition. Historical reconstruction is about the past, but it is also about 're-counting' things with reference to current concerns and values. Native claims to fishing rights derive in large part from historical precedents, and in efforts to assert and contest those rights various interpretations of historical events have already been debated, in legal and negotiation forums as well as in more informal settings.

The term 'historical' is often applied to anything from the 'past.' In another sense, 'historical' is contrasted with 'prehistoric,' the latter being that which precedes written (historical) documents. As part of this contrasting set of terms, 'historical' is useful as an approximate indicator of time range. But one problematic consequence of these terms is the potential implication that there is a stark difference between written and unwritten sources of knowledge. Written accounts are certainly valuable, but they should not be regarded as the only valid sources of knowledge about the past. Eric Wolf (1992) argues that scholars, by privileging written sources, have too often ignored the histories of non-literate cultural groups – a practice that is both intellectually inadequate and politically suspect.

The recent decision in *Delgamuukw v. British Columbia* (1997) recognizes oral histories as admissible legal evidence – as equal in this regard to written accounts. Though clear criteria for establishing the validity of oral accounts have yet to be developed (see Lovisek 2002), this is an important step toward correcting imbalances that might result from a more limited notion of what is historically relevant.

Native people's perspectives have often been ignored in Canadian histories, and recognizing the potential of oral accounts is an important corrective step. This does not, however, diminish the value of written sources, which can allow insights into the past that are otherwise unavailable. Each form of recollection has its own strengths, which are often mutually complementary. Julie Cruikshank (1995) points out, with reference to the Gold Rush in the Yukon, that oral history is sometimes the only source of information on how native people were affected by past developments.

Researchers are increasingly aware of the need to read written sources critically. We have only begun to address the many challenges inherent in connecting written and oral accounts.

I use oral accounts in this book in the context of recent history. My depiction of prehistoric fishing is gleaned largely from archaeological and ethnohistorical studies pertaining to the Saugeen-Bruce Peninsula and surrounding areas. These include occasional fragments of verbally transmitted information. I did not explicitly seek out oral histories to complement these records. Lenore Keeshig-Tobias, a Nawash community member, has done some work in this area as part of her job at Bruce Peninsula National Park. She is currently exploring possible parallels between local Ojibway stories and recent underwater geological findings (2002, pers. comm.). Through her research oral history may yet prove to be a source of insight into the peninsula's distant, as well as its more recent, past.

Fishing in Prehistoric Times

In examining the prehistoric fisheries in the region, I consider the Palaeo-Indian, Archaic, and Woodland periods. Following this, I discuss Charles Cleland's (1982) study, which focuses specifically on the importance of the region's prehistoric fisheries.

Palaeo-Indian Fisheries

Until recently, researchers thought that the first New World inhabitants arrived no earlier than fifteen thousand years ago, when much of the North American continent was still covered with ice. But some archaeological evidence suggests that a date as early as 25,000 BP is possible.[1] A recognizable group referred to as 'Palaeo-Indians' appears to have spread very quickly across North America beginning around eleven thousand years ago. While it seems likely that the Palaeo-Indians had recently migrated from northern Asia via the Bering Strait, it remains possible that they were descendants of people who left artefacts at much older sites on this continent (see Feder and Park 1997).

Many First Nations members state that their people were here from 'time immemorial.' Some are suspicious of academic debates about North America's first inhabitants for very good reasons. Writers such as Tom Flanagan (2000), in their critiques of aboriginal rights and associated government policies, have suggested that current First Nations are themselves 'newcomers' to particular regions, if not to the continent itself: they are one of many waves of immigrants, just like non-native settlers (see also Dewar 2001). Even prehistory can be interpreted for political purposes. Another example of the political implications of our hypotheses about the distant past, concerning the impact that prehistoric peoples had on other species and environments, is noted in chapter 5. Many native community members distrust statements about the continent's earliest occupants because they are aware of the potential political implications, and because they have had little input into the system that has produced this 'knowledge.'

Native and non-native researchers alike are increasingly aware that images of prehistoric peoples are sometimes fabricated from very little evidence. But this should not be cause to reject studies of the distant past altogether. The better option is to support efforts to develop a fuller, more comprehensive understanding, and to give careful attention to how the past is brought into the present.

It appears that people first came to the Great Lakes region around eleven thousand years ago, during what is referred to as the Palaeo-Indian period. They are characterized by distinctive stone tool forms, notably large points or blades, which were remarkably similar throughout North America, as were the kinds of stone they used for making tools (Ellis and Deller 1990:37).[2] These early people may have taken fish from the peninsula region's waters.

No evidence of Palaeo-Indian occupation has yet been found directly on the peninsula, but there are sites close by. Kolapore and Fisher (see Ellis and Deller 1990:41–52; Storck 1994) are located no more than fifty kilometres southeast of the peninsula. Another site, Sheguiandah, is on Manitoulin Island, which is currently separated from the peninsula's northern tip by several miles of open water (Funk 1978:17; Julig 1985; Ellis and Deller 1990:37). Given this proximity, it is likely that the peninsula was at least visited during this era.[3]

The likelihood that Palaeo-Indians harvested fish has only recently been considered by archaeologists. Though no Palaeo-Indian fishing tools have been found, spawning fish could have been taken with a variety of wooden implements, which are less likely to be preserved than stone tools.

Given their typical large-blade tools, Palaeo-Indian people have been imagined as big-game hunters. But fishing may still have been significant, since stone tool assemblages are not precise indicators of resource use.[4] Recently, archaeologists have questioned the extent to which Palaeo-Indians were big-game hunters (Ellis and Deller 1990:38). Peter Storck suggests that because archaeologists have been preoccupied with searching for evidence of hunting, they may have ignored indicators of fishing practices (1994:39).

Evidence in support of Palaeo-Indian fishing activity in Southern Ontario comes from use-wear analysis of tool fragments, and a documented find of fish bones at a Pennsylvania Palaeo-Indian site (Storck 1994). The lakeside camp locations that they sometimes chose may reflect an interest in fishing (Storck 1994). And they may have used watercraft occasionally, which would have increased their access to fish (Ellis and Deller 1990:51–3). While the evidence is sparse, it is quite possible that the earliest occupants of the peninsula region included fish in their diet.

Archaic Fisheries

Archaic peoples differed from Palaeo-Indians in several ways, among which was a greater diversity of resource use (see Ellis et al. 1990:65–6) that included a reliance on fisheries.[5] Southern Ontario's Archaic time range covers three periods: the Early Archaic from about 10,000 to 8000 BP, the Middle Archaic to 4500 BP, and the Late Archaic to roughly 2600 BP (Ellis et al. 1990:67–9; see also Funk 1978:20).

Among the new stone tools found at Middle Archaic period sites were objects thought to be grooved net sinkers that date to about 7500 BP (see Ellis et al. 1990:65–7). The actual use of these stones is not certain, and their association with netting materials is only indicated clearly in later periods. Fishing implements make up a large portion of the bone tools found at Archaic sites.[6] These include harpoon heads, barbed points, fish hooks, gorges, and large needles that were possibly used for making nets (Ellis et al. 1990:86).[7]

The abundance of Archaic fishing artefacts suggests that in some areas fish gained importance over other resources. Population increases, a decrease in the geographic range of annual harvesting cycles, and more established settlement patterns may be connected with increased fishing activity (see Ellis et al. 1990:91–3).

Fishing was clearly important among some Archaic-period people living to the east of Georgian Bay, who camped at river rapids where spawning fish runs could have been harvested (Trigger 1976:109). A fish weir in this region, at the Atherly Narrows near Orillia, appears to have been used forty-five hundred years ago (see Ellis et al. 1990:91). Just south of the Saugeen-Bruce Peninsula bone fishing tools were found at two Archaic sites occupied prior to 3000 BP (Ellis et al. 1990:94, 111). Fish hooks made of native copper, likely mined on Lake Superior, were also discovered at both sites.[8]

Late Archaic interior winter camps have been found on the peninsula (Fox 1988:18), and Archaic activity is indicated on the west coast of the peninsula, where fishing opportunities were available. At a beach area near the top of the peninsula, archaeologists located what appears to be Archaic-period dog excrement containing fish bone (Fox 1987:3). Archaic peoples were also on the peninsula's northern islands. Stone fragments suggest a connection between these island sites and sites near the peninsula's base (Daechsel 1994). There are also possible associations between the people who came to the peninsula during the Late Archaic period and a group centred west of Lake Erie (Spence et al. 1990:137), who are known by mortuary features including exotic burial goods (Ellis et al. 1990:115).

Given the general importance of fishing for Southern Ontario's Archaic people, along with fishing artefact finds adjacent to the peninsula, and site locations on the peninsula where fish were accessible, there is little doubt that people took fish from the peninsula's waters during this period.

Woodland Fisheries

The Early Woodland period, which extends into the last centuries of the Archaic and up to about 2300 BP (see Spence et al. 1990), is characterized by the appearance of earthen pots. A net from this period was found in New York state, which supports the interpretation of notched stones as net sinkers (Spence et al. 1990:136). A net sinker, probably used for spring fishing, was found at the Ferris site, the only known warm-season Early Woodland site in Ontario, near the peninsula's southwest corner (Spence et al. 1990:132-7).

The Middle Woodland period, which extends to about 1200 BP (Spence et al. 1990; see also Fox 1990b:171-3), is marked by a new pottery impression style. Grinding techniques for tool making were no longer practised, and in some places burial mounds were built (see Spence et al. 1990:142). The Donaldson site on the Saugeen River has an important Middle Woodland component, as does the nearby Inverhuron-Lucas site. Both represent an archaeological tradition called the Saugeen.[9]

Middle Woodland fish remains found at the Donaldson site include sturgeon, drum, pickerel, channel catfish, and bass (Spence et al. 1990:151). The near absence of sinkers at the Donaldson site indicates that nets were not important here. Given an abundance of harpoon heads, found in association with burials, spearing was likely a main fishing method. At the nearby Inverhuron-Lucas site, fish remains are also found, but in less abundance. No harpoon heads were found here, but net sinkers and copper hooks have been located (Spence et al. 1990:151).

W.D. Finlayson (1977:601-2) interprets such data as suggestive of an annual cycle in which fishing played a central role. People came together in the spring to fish on the Saugeen River, mainly with harpoons. They may have brought along the remains of those who died during the winter for reburial (Spence et al. 1990:153-5). During the summer, smaller groups went to shore sites such as Inverhuron-Lucas, where, along with other subsistence activities, a variety of fish were taken with nets and hooks. In the fall, people moved inland to winter camps.

The Late Woodland period, which extends to the contact era, is identified in Southern Ontario by the introduction of agriculture and more permanent settlements, some of which had palisade fences. Archaeologists have been interested in connections between Late Woodland peoples and contact-era groups, especially links to historically known Algonquian and Iroquoian speakers.[10] Much of this analysis centres on resource-use patterns associated with each of the two groups. Algonquian speakers are typically regarded as highly mobile hunter/gatherers, or hunter/gatherer/fishers. Iroquoians are seen primarily as settled horticulturalists. While horticultural villages have come to typify Iroquoian groups, some contact-era Algonquian groups also cultivated crops and built similar housing structures (see Waisberg 1977; Rogers 1978:762). Iroquoians also relied to some degree on fishing and hunting. While these linguistic distinctions are useful as broad generalizations, they are not to be taken as absolutes when attempting to reconstruct Late Woodland–period fishing activities.[11]

A cluster of Late Woodland–period sites below the peninsula in Southwestern Ontario, representing the Western Basin tradition (see Murphy and Ferris 1990:231–44), have been linked to later Algonquian peoples based on subsistence practices, including some reliance on fish, and housing structures (Murphy and Ferris 1990:238). But because they practised horticulture, some view them as Iroquoian peoples who were expanding into the area (Murphy and Ferris 1990:238).

There is similar uncertainty about group affiliation at a fourteenth-century palisaded village located farther north, near the peninsula's southwest corner, at the Nodwell site (see Stewart 1974; Wright 1974; White 1991:47). This village is generally regarded as proto-Iroquoian (e.g., Dodd et al. 1990:324), because horticulture was practised and because of typical longhouse building structures. But Algonquian tools and outlying fishing camps (see Wright 1974:303–5) suggest an Algonquian presence. While most regard Nodwell as a proto-Iroquoian intrusion into the area, others (e.g., Rankin 1998) view it as having evolved 'in situ' as local inhabitants took on agricultural practices. In either case, it appears to have been an active centre for trade and other social exchanges (see Wright 1974:304).

Linguists have also attempted to trace prehistoric origins by linking proto-language words to the natural resources found in particular geographic locations. Hypotheses about Algonquian origins include a 3,200 BP homeland in Southern Ontario (Seibert 1967; cited in Ellis et al. 1990:121). Ives Goddard (1978:586) notes a possible Algonquian homeland at a place between Georgian Bay and Lake Ontario. Stuart Fiedel suggests an eighth-century migration from the Great Lakes region to the Atlantic coast (1991:29), and has linked Algonquian fishing words to potential original fishing locations (1987:6; 1991:23). Similar linguistic correlations have been attempted for Iroquoian groups (see Ellis et al. 1990:121). Unfortunately, such proto-language reconstructions are not yet conclusive, as they are often inconsistent and contradict archaeological evidence (see Ellis et al. 1990:121).

A cluster at the southwest corner of the peninsula – the Donaldson, Hunter (see Prevec 1988; Fox 1989), and Chief's Point sites – is associated with the Princess Point tradition, the best-known Late Woodland complex in Southern Ontario. These sites, which appear to have served as seasonal harvesting stations, where fishing was a main activity, are all on or very near to current Saugeen First Nation reserve lands.

An 'Inland Shore Fishery'

As indicated in the above survey of archaeological sources, pre-contact fishing activity around the Great Lakes was substantial. Fikret Berkes (1990:39) claims that the northern Great Lakes fisheries were pivotal in the lives of pre-contact peoples. Harold Hickerson states that 'the importance of the fisheries for the proto-Chippewa peoples cannot be stressed too much. I should go so far as to say that without fishing there would have been no human life in the northern Great Lakes region under aboriginal conditions. Fisheries permitted settled populations; the fisheries were the villages' (1962:81; see also Lovisek 1991: 375). Richard Preston (2000, pers. comm.) suggests that Hickerson may have overstated the point here to some degree, having recently discovered that fishing was much more important than had been supposed.

Charles Cleland, in his article entitled 'The Inland Shore Fishery of the Northern Great Lakes: Its Development and Importance in Prehistory' (1982), provides what is generally regarded as the most definitive statement of the importance of pre-contact fishing activity in the northern Great Lakes. His view is cited widely (e.g., Tanner 1987:19–23; Spangler and Peters 1995:103; Koenig 1996:40). The attention Cleland brings to the region's prehistoric fishing activities is significant, but his conclusions are worth further critical assessment.

Cleland describes aboriginal fishing in the northern Great Lakes as becoming progressively more efficient through technological improvement (1982:761). He sees the gill net as the pinnacle of aboriginal fishing technology. According to Cleland (1996:1), the earliest fishing tools were the spear and harpoon, which date to about 5000 BP. The harpoon was originally designed for hunting mammals, such as seals, and was adapted for taking large fish, which people began to discover as their knowledge of the environment expanded (1982:774). Other so-called primitive fishing implements, such as gorges and hooks, were added, followed by nets: the first nets were used 'during the first millennium B.C.' (Cleland 1982; see also 1996:2). By AD 800 gill nets were made by adapting seines for use in the deep waters on the shores of the northern Great Lakes (1982:774). According to Cleland, the gill net became dominant, since it gave people access to a more secure food source. A coincidental benefit was that whitefish and trout, taken in the open waters in late fall and early winter, could be preserved by freezing.

Cleland argues that the 'unique prehistoric fishery' in the upper Great Lakes 'provides the most important single organizing concept for understanding the cultural development of this region' (1982:761). He claims that the addition of gill-net technology during the Late Woodland period led to a reorganization of social relations, based around the need for female work groups who made and maintained gill nets, and prepared and preserved fish for winter use (1982:779). This new pattern allowed large groups to extend their aggregations for several months into the early winter (1982:780), and it allowed population increases (1982:775).

Susan Martin (1989) challenges some of the assumptions in Cleland's theory. She notes that settlement types and locations do not coincide with the cultural shifts and population increases that Cleland hypothesizes: they would have better accommodated more diverse subsistence strategies (Martin 1989:594). In Cleland's rebuttal to this criticism he backtracks somewhat on his earlier suggestion of population increases, stating that while gill-netting provided the most secure food source, it was simultaneously a high-risk venture, subjecting its practitioners to periods of starvation and population decline (1989: 606–8). But he maintains that his theory of an increasingly efficient fishery best explains the region's prehistory. Martin's concern that Cleland's theory may not adequately incorporate evidence of cultural and ecological diversity seems reasonable. Technological change and increased efficiency are not necessarily the same thing. People assess potential benefits of changes, and act on these assessments, according to already established perceptions and complex vested interests. Cleland's technology-centred explanation is an interesting possibility, but more empirical evidence is required before its relevance can be adequately assessed.

The evidence needed to substantiate Cleland's theory is not easy to come by. As Joan Lovisek (1991:119–22) points out, the archaeological record of a progression in net fishing, from seines to gill nets, is not readily apparent. The difference between seines and gill nets may be more in their function than their design. Seines are pulled through shallow water to trap fish (see Cleland 1982:774). Gillnets are set in place, usually overnight. Fish are snagged by their gills as they attempt to pass through the gill-net mesh (see Cleland 1982:775–6; see also Rostlund 1952:81–100). Gill nets always have anchor stones and floats to keep them spread upright, but anchors and floats can be attached to seines as well to assist in their operation. The poor preservation qualities of mesh materials contribute to confusion between the two net types. Distinguishing fall and spring fishing sites is also problematic and has a bearing on Cleland's model (Lovisek 1991:119–22).

Another difficulty is the lack of clarity in Cleland's concept of an 'inland shore fishery.' Cleland builds this concept with reference to Erhard Rostlund's study entitled *Freshwater Fish and Fishing in Native North America* (1952). Cleland explicitly cites 'Rostlund 1952:152' as the source of his concept of an 'inland shore fishery' (Cleland 1996:1). The page Cleland sites here includes a reference to the Great Lakes as 'great inland seas,' and a comment that the fishery there was 'essentially a shore fishery,' but Rostlund does not use the term 'inland shore fishery' here. In another explanation of the origin of this concept, Cleland states: 'Rostlund made an extensive review of literature pertaining to the upper Great Lakes. Calling this fishery the "inland shore fishery" to distinguish it from the ocean coastal fisheries, he believed that in its technological uniqueness and success it compared favorably with ocean fisheries' (Cleland 1982:761). Here Cleland equates the 'inland shore fishery' with the 'upper Great Lakes.' He also cites Rostlund '1952:29–30,' which mentions a 'deep-water gill-net fishery,' but, once again, not an 'inland shore fishery.'

In my review of Rostlund's 1952 study I have found only one use of the term 'inland shore fishery.' However, the geographic context is not exactly what Cleland seems to imply. Rostlund states that the 'Great Lakes Province' is primarily a 'region of lake fishery rather than river fishery, and aboriginal fishing in the main lakes may even be called an inland shore fishery' (1952:73). Rostlund's 'Great Lakes Province,' however, is not just the 'upper Great Lakes,' which is where Cleland's 'inland shore fishery' is located. It is an approximation of the native range of a group of food fish (see Rostlund 1952:302). Rostlund's 'inland shore fishery' pertains to an area stretching from James Bay and Lake Winnipeg, in the north and west, through all five Great Lakes, and beyond. The 'upper Great Lakes' is a small area within the geographic range of Rostlund's 'inland shore fishery.'

Cleland formally defines his 'Northern' or 'upper' Great Lakes fishery as mainly the northern shores of Lakes Huron and Superior (1982:761), but historical evidence of gill-net fishing by Huron in southern Georgian Bay is prominent in his explanations. It is not clear whether Cleland uses the Huron fishery as an analogy, or includes it as part of the inland shore fishery of the northern Great Lakes (see 1982:762–9).

The concept of an inland shore fishery is also loosely defined in terms of netting methods. In places Cleland refers to an inland shore fishery and a gill-net fishery interchangeably (1982:761–2), but in other places he implies that a variety of net fishing methods are included in the former.

Rostlund (1952) depicts the gill net as a significant development, but he does not see the origin and spread of any one net fishery as readily explainable in either diffusionist or evolutionary terms (1952:92–9). He suggests that in a region that includes the Great Lakes, nets of various kinds 'must have accounted for more captured fish than any other method' (1952:85). He places the Great Lakes region within an area where 'fish was a staple food, but not more important than game or plants' (1952:304). Rostlund indicates the channels at Sault Ste Marie and Mackinac, which became famous for dip-netting activity, as the only well-known interior location on the continent where fish were the primary aboriginal food source (1952:304). While open-water fishing appears to have been important by the end of the Late Woodland period, the history of fishing methods is not yet well understood.

Prehistoric evidence from the peninsula indicates that fishing activities were indeed important at least at various times, and we can speculate that social changes may have occurred where groups were shifting toward a greater reliance on particular fish stocks (e.g., Finlayson 1977:601–2). Cleland has raised interesting and important possibilities; but without a good deal more evidence, we have only limited insight into the complexity and diversity of resource relations in the peninsula's distant past.

Fishing in Early Historical Times

There is likewise only scattered evidence of the importance of fishing activities on the peninsula during what can be called the early historical era, which covers the contact period (1615–1650), the Iroquois Wars period (1650–1700), and the French and British period (1700–1830). Though European trade, exploration, and mission activities had begun in nearby regions by the first half of the 1600s, the native peoples who came to the peninsula during the early historical period are not clearly identified through historical records.

The peninsula is vaguely represented on several maps made during the Iroquois Wars period (see Fox 1952:31–2). The most detailed map was made by René de Bréhant de Galinée, who along with his fellow Sulpician missionary François Dollier de Casson travelled by sailing canoe up the peninsula's Lake Huron shorelines in 1670 (Coyne 1903, 1923; Cruikshank 1923). Galinee's map provides previously unrecorded details of the peninsula's Fishing Islands (see Coyne 1903:xxxi). It may also include the first charting of the Saugeen River mouth (see Coyne 1903:xxvii). But, unfortunately, only passing mention of the shoreline is recorded in Galinée's narrative (see Coyne 1903:xxvi). Until a survey was conducted by Gother Mann in 1788, the peninsula was virtually non-existent in written records (Fox 1952:34).

Though there is an absence of documentation specific to the peninsula during the early historical period, neighbouring regions provide potential inferences about the importance of fishing activities here. Local and regional archaeological evidence, along with regional historical accounts, suggests that throughout most of the early historical period the peninsula's fisheries were used by native peoples. There is insufficient evidence to clearly establish uninterrupted fishing activities at any particular location on the peninsula, but it would be premature to exclude the possibility of some such continuity.

The Contact Era (1615–50)

During the Late Woodland period substantial population increases occurred in Southern Ontario (Trigger 1985:214). However, cultural affiliations during and immediately after this time remain speculative (Brose 1978:582). The contact-era peninsula is sometimes mapped as the territory of Iroquoian-speaking peoples who had villages to the southeast of the peninsula (e.g., Tanner 1987:27).[12] A map made in 1650 by Sanson inscribes the peninsula as the domain of the Petun Nation (Coyne 1903:xvi), generally thought of as Iroquoian speakers. However, many researchers regard the contact-era peninsula as the hunting and fishing territory of Algonquian-speaking peoples (e.g., Fox 1990c:459). A third perspective, equally feasible, is that the peninsula was used by both Algonquian and Iroquoian peoples (Lovisek 1991: 188). The blend of Algonquian and Iroquoian affiliations among peoples living near the peninsula supports this possibility, and is therefore worth considering more closely.

The Huron, or Wendat, as they called their own confederacy (see Heidenreich 1978:368), played an important role in the beginnings of the fur trade. Because they allowed Jesuits into their midst, historical accounts of Huron life-ways are relatively plentiful.[13] The Huron lived in villages and smaller camps around the southeast corner of Georgian Bay, and numbered perhaps thirty thousand people in the early seventeenth century (Heidenreich 1978:369). Like other Iroquoian groups in Ontario such as the Neutral and Petun, they practised horticulture, but fished, hunted, and gathered as well. When first contacted, the Huron fished more actively than their northern Iroquoian neighbours (Trigger 1976:100): their dependence on fisheries was 'second in importance only to agriculture' (Trigger 1976:31). It is possible that this strong dependence on fish reflects a shift away from hunting that accompanied declines in game availability which occurred when human populations increased during the Late Woodland period (Trigger 1985:214).

Huron fishing activities are richly described in historical literature (e.g., Wrong [1939]1968:185–91; see also Rostlund 1952:162–203; Kinietz [1940]1972:9–48). A gill-net fishery was practised in open water, and nets were also set under the ice. When fishing with spears through the ice, the Huron built small structures over fishing holes that provided shelter for at least the upper parts of their bodies and reduced the reflectiveness of the water surface, thereby making fish more visible. They speared fish from canoes at night using torch light. Weirs, lines, and various nets were among their other fishing tools. Main species harvested include sturgeon, trout, pike, and whitefish (Trigger 1976:31; Ramsden 1990:380).

While the Huron were very active fishers, they are also known to have procured fish through trade with Algonquian-speaking peoples (Trigger 1976:168, 1985:205; Barry 1978:43). There is also an account of trade with people living across Georgian Bay (see Lovisek 1991:155), though it is unclear whether this refers to nearby islands, or a more distant place such as the Saugeen-Bruce Peninsula.

Beliefs associated with Huron fishing practices are recorded in historical records as well (Trigger 1976:75–6; Lovisek 1991:153–71). A 'fish preacher' performed rituals to promote success in fishing, including a ceremony called the 'marriage of two virgins to the seine' (Lovisek 1991:167–71). There were various social feasting activities involving especially the sturgeon (Lovisek 1991:165–6). Fisheries-related ceremonies and rituals were shared between the Huron and their Algonquian neighbours, from whom the fish preacher ceremony may have been borrowed (Lovisek 1991:168–9).

The proximity of the Huron fisheries to the Saugeen-Bruce Peninsula, and importance of the Huron fisheries in both group and intergroup contexts, suggests that people who harvested the peninsula's fisheries may have been involved in these or similar practices.

The Petun were one of two groups that most likely came to the peninsula or were closely tied to those who were on the peninsula during the contact era. Also known as the Tobacco or the Khionontateronon, they lived to the west of the Huron. When the Jesuits began establishing a constellation of missions among them, their population could have been anywhere from three to eight thousand, with up to seventeen hundred people in one village (Garrad and Heidenreich 1978:395).

As historical records scarcely distinguish the Petun from their Huron neighbours, Helen Hornbeck Tanner defines the Huron and Petun as two branches of the 'Wendat' (1993:115). Petun social organization was similar to that of the Huron, but it is known that the Petun comprised two main groups, the Wolves and the Deer (Garrad and Heidenreich 1978:395). The Petun were involved in a trade network and military alliance with the Neutral to their south and Ottawa groups (Garrad and Heidenreich 1978:396). Though it is assumed that the Petun spoke mainly an Iroquoian language, many were fluent Algonquian speakers, and they had much in common with nearby Algonquian-speaking, Ottawa people, with whom they may have shared and/or negotiated access to the peninsula's fisheries.

Another group in the region, the Ottawa, appear to have covered a broad and diverse territorial range.[14] The name was applied in earliest contact times to Algonquian-speaking peoples who were met on Georgian Bay's north-east shore, on Manitoulin Island, and near the bottom of the Saugeen-Bruce Peninsula. Charles Garrad and Conrad Heidenreich state that 'Ottawa bands wintered regularly near the northern

Petun villages and in the areas farther west along the shore of Nottawasaga Bay and the Bruce Peninsula' (1978:396). They also note that on occasion Ottawa visitors had considerable influence in Petun villages. Their influence might reflect the importance of trade or military ties, but it might also indicate that some Ottawa were already living in these villages (Garrad and Heidenreich 1978:396).

The contact-era Petun are considered to be a recent amalgamation of several earlier groups (Trigger 1985:159). Since Algonquian was the primary language spoken in some Petun villages (Garrad and Heidenreich 1978:396), it is possible that Algonquian-speaking peoples (perhaps some Ottawa bands) were among the smaller groups that came to constitute the contact-era Petun.

First contact with the Ottawa occurred in 1615, when Champlain met a party of several hundred men near the French River on Georgian Bay's east coast (Feest and Feest 1978:772–5; Fox 1990c:458). Because of their distinctive raised hairstyle, Champlain named them the 'Cheveux Relevés.' The next year, Champlain visited a group located west of the main Petun villages. He suggested that these were the same people he had met at the French River. Charles Garrad (1970) surmises that this latter meeting took place at the most westerly of the Petun villages, rather than at a yet undiscovered site farther west or on the peninsula.[15]

Prior to the mid-1600s, various groups to the north-east were also referred to by the French as Ottawa: 'Seventeenth-century sources apply the term Ottawa not only to a local group ... but also to the total of totemic or local groups that together formed the tribe (Kiskakon, Singo, Sable, Nassauakueton; later others) and to all other "upper Algonquians" who came down to Montreal to trade' (Feest and Feest 1978:772). The Algonquian language and a trading lifestyle became markers of Ottawa group affiliation.[16] The Ottawa also became known as especially active fishing peoples (Feest and Feest 1978:774).

The name 'Ottawa' is currently used as roughly interchangeable with contact-era Algonquian-speaking trading peoples (e.g., Garrad and Heidenreich 1978). Given this generalized application, it is difficult to say how closely affiliated various Ottawa groups were. The absence of any definite Ottawa village sites prior to the 1660s (Feest and Feest 1978:772–4) also makes it difficult to trace connections. But several writers have attached the Ottawa name to the people who came to the peninsula's Late Woodland and early contact-era fishing sites.

At the Glen Site, located on an island at the top of the peninsula, there is evidence of substantial lake trout harvesting during the contact era. J.V. Wright (1981:45–6) suggests that this site was a fishing camp occupied by the 'Cheveux Relevés' at the beginning of the 1600s. He doubts Iroquoian occupation because of the presence of Algonquian 'pukaskwa pits,'[17] and because the level of navigational skills necessary to reach the site was more typical of Algonquian peoples. He notes that it 'appears to be impossible to distinguish between the Odawa, the Nipissings, the southeast Ojibwa or the Algonkins of the upper Ottawa Valley, [that the] ethnic discreetness of these constructs in the early 17th century is ... questionable' (Wright 1981:58). Given this uncertainty, Wright uses the name that Champlain gave to the first non-Iroquoian speakers he met in the area.

In contrast, William A. Fox (1990c:461–2) suggests that Ottawa ethnic affiliation can be confidently ascribed to late pre-contact and contact-era sites on the peninsula. He regards the peninsula's Hunter site as a camp used for fishing and hunting in the ninth and then in the sixteenth and seventeenth centuries, 'probably ... by the Odawa and their ancestors' (1989:14; see also Prevec 1988). Fox provides little support for his claim of an Odawa affiliation on the peninsula. He sees Late Woodland Iroquoian pottery finds on the peninsula as indications of trade relations between the peninsula's Odawa inhabitants and the nearby Petun (1990c:461–2), but this might as easily suggest a Petun presence of some sort.

The cultural affiliation of Late Woodland and contact-era peoples who fished at places like the Hunter site and the Glen site remains an open question. These peoples may have been Petun, who were themselves a multicultural amalgamation of other Wendat peoples and Algonquian speakers. The Algonquian speakers among them may have been Cheveux Relevés, Ottawa, or others. As well, the peninsula's northern fisheries may have been accessed across open water by Algonquian-speaking groups from Manitoulin, who were among the first to be known as Ottawa (see Lytwyn 1990:3–5). There is, however, little doubt that by the contact era the peninsula's fisheries were significant as part of the resource-use patterns of some of the region's aboriginal peoples.

The Iroquois Wars Period (1650–1700)

During the Iroquois Wars period, much of Southern Ontario was evacuated. But given the remoteness of the peninsula, it is not clear whether its fisheries were altogether abandoned during this time.

Just prior to 1650, warriors from Iroquois Confederacy groups began moving into Southern Ontario. Neutral, Petun, Huron, and Algonquian villages and camps were destroyed, and those who were not killed or captured were dispersed, many to the north and west.

If one assumes that the Petun were heavily involved in the peninsula's fisheries, then a substantial drop in fishing activity on the peninsula could have occurred. The Petun as a group vanished. Given their close ties to Algonquian peoples, some of them could have joined Algonquian groups.

The extent to which the Algonquian population was displaced during the dispersals is unclear. The Algonquian dispersal might have been sudden and thorough (Lytwyn 1990:6) or more gradual (Rogers 1978:760). In some cases, Iroquois attacks were successfully countered by Algonquian groups (Rogers 1978:760). People who had been living at Lake Nippissing returned there just before the end of this era of warfare (see Waisberg 1977:63). Many Ottawa peoples who left Manitoulin Island during the initial Iroquois incursions also returned during the following decades (see Feest and Feest 1978). After the Huron were destroyed around 1650, Algonquian bands assumed control of trade with the French (see Trigger 1985:280, 285), which might have encouraged them to maintain territorial access wherever possible.

The Iroquois were also battling the French, but during a twenty-year period beginning in 1667, hostilities between the Iroquois and the French subsided (see Coyne 1903:xxi), and this truce allowed renewed trade, exploration, and mission activity around Lake Huron (see also Tanner 1987:29–35). Such fluctuations in conflict intensity, along with the localized nature of the conflicts, make it difficult to generalize demographic changes and impacts on resource relations.

Two emerging centres that became especially important during the late Iroquois Wars period were the Mackinaw region, where the three northern Great Lakes join, and the Detroit region, where Lakes Huron and Erie connect. These places expanded because of trade, military, and later settlement activity; but they were located at fishing sites of long-standing importance (Feest and Feest 1978:774; see also White 1991:130). Some of the most detailed descriptions of fisheries activities in North America during this period come from records made by explorers, military officers, and missionaries in the Mackinaw region.

Dollier and Galinée claimed that the fisheries at Michilimackinac could support ten thousand people (Coyne 1903:73; see also White 1991:44). The Baron de Lahonton was also astonished by the whitefish and trout fisheries in the area, suggesting that the Ottawa and Huron there could not subsist without them (Thwaites [1905]1970:147-8). Sieur de Cadillac likewise recorded his impression of fish species and fishing techniques (cited in Kinietz [1940]1972:239; see also Tanner 1987:39-47). Nicolas Perrot included details of Mackinaw region fishing practices and provided rich descriptions of beliefs associated with fishing activities (Blair [1911]1969), as did Henri Joutel (see Kinietz [1940]1972:29), Père Marquette (see Repplier 1929:35-48), and Claude Dablon (see Repplier 1929:49).[18]

Toward the end of the Iroquois Wars period in Southern Ontario, dispersed peoples, mainly Algonquian speakers, also began moving into parts of Southern Ontario, some of which had been occupied by Iroquoian horticulturalists prior to the dispersals (see Rogers 1978:761; see also Schmalz 1991:18-35). The name 'Mississauga' was associated with many of these people, some of whom were originally located on the Mississaugi River, on Lake Huron's north shore. These people maintained a strong focus on fisheries resources as suggested by the locations of their new camping sites. If this was a widespread resource-use strategy, aboriginal peoples would have gathered fish on the Saugeen-Bruce Peninsula fisheries during the latter half of the 1600s whenever possible.

The French and British Period (1700-1830)

During the first half of the 1700s, and leading up to the change from French to British rule in the early 1760s, trade, particularly with the French, became increasingly important in the Lake Huron region. Native peoples in the area delivered trade commodities, including fish, to trading posts, and also provided fish directly to local markets, especially at military centres (Tanner 1987:39-43; see also White 1991:130-41).[19]

Increased contact with the French did not necessarily diminish native peoples' traditional reliance on their fisheries as one might suspect. On the contrary, the growing market for fish gave the resource additional importance (see Lovisek 1991:260; White 1991:130).[20]

The most detailed accounts of fisheries activities around Lake Huron during the period of French control are again descriptions of the vibrant fisheries in the Mackinaw region. Claude de la Potherie described the techniques, species, and local groups involved (see Blair 1969), as did Antoine Raudot (see Kinietz [1940]1972).

Edward Rogers describes the Mackinaw, or Sault Ste Marie, region and other locations around Lake Huron where the native fisheries of this period were especially important:

> The people living along the north shore of Lake Huron were migratory except for certain seasons of the year when they remained in those localities most productive of fish ... During the summer ... some ... traveled to Sault Sainte Marie. The rapids there supported an extensive fishery during September and October ... An individual had to stand upright in a bark canoe among the rapids and thrust a dip net deep into the water to secure the fish ... The Mississauga gathered at the mouth of the Mississagi River where they took sturgeon and other fish ... The Amikwa secured trout, sturgeon, and whitefish ... the Saulteax speared sturgeon. (1978:762)

Many of the settlements that grew at productive fishing areas such as Mackinaw, Chequemagon, and the Detroit areas during the early 1700s were amalgamations that included Ottawa, Huron, and an Algonquian-speaking people who came to be known as the Ojibway (Tanner 1987:29–39; see also Feest and Feest 1978:772).

Like the name 'Ottawa,' 'Ojibway' has been ascribed to various mobile Algonquian-speaking peoples, and the two are occasionally used interchangeably.[21] 'Ojibwa' once identified a village on the north shore of Lake Superior, and was later applied more broadly (Tanner 1987:62). The historical spread of the Ojibway is not clear, but the diffusion of the name itself was likely a factor, along with actual movement of people.[22]

The close of the period of French control and the beginning of British rule in the Lake Huron region corresponds with the beginning of government land acquisitions.[23] Relations between native peoples around Lake Huron and the British differed from those with the French (see Lovisek 1991:258–61). Alexander Henry ([1901]1964:29–64), who provides accounts of native fishing activity at various locations along the French River route, from Montreal to Sault Ste Marie, notes a good deal of initial resistance to British control. Relations were strengthened where native peoples made excursions to receive presents at Mackinaw, Penetanguishene, and Niagara. Presents were given as payment for land cessions, or in recognition of a military alliance. At these gatherings people depended on reliable local fish supplies (Tanner 1987:130).

An interesting historical source from the late British period is the narrative of captivity in the Sault Ste Marie area published by John Tanner. The Ojibway vocabulary that Tanner recorded ([1830]1975:311–14) offers a glimpse into the intimate knowledge of the fisheries that Ojibway people had maintained into the early 1800s. I include excerpts from his vocabulary in appendix 5.

Fishing activity became an increasingly important focus of native/non-native interaction during the British period. Fishing was already established as an important part of the fur-trade economy (Lovisek 1991:316; White 1991:491), and fishing tools, especially nets, became increasingly common trade items. Fishing activity was also a consideration in land cessions, in which quantities of seines and hooks were sometimes negotiated. New technologies, such as salt barrel packing and transportation improvements on the lakes, also accelerated fishing activity in places. With increased access to growing settler markets, Lake Huron's native peoples increasingly participated in an emerging commercial fishery (Lovisek 1991:262–323). While most native involvement was carried out at remote posts and fishing stations, native fishers also supplied fish directly to those living at expanding centres in Upper Canada (Guillet 1938:142–9; Henry and Paterson 1938:83).[24] The spectacle of natives spear-fishing from canoes by torchlight where Toronto now stands was recorded as early as 1760 (Guillet 1938:142). Upper Canada's fisheries were also increasingly harvested by non-native settlers (Henry and Paterson 1938:77–83,190).[25]

By the early 1800s, commercial fishing operations were bringing large quantities of fish into growing towns in Upper Canada, and fish were shipped to cities in the United States (Guillet 1938:151; Strachan [1820]1968:182, 216–17). During the first decades of the 1800s, the Saugeen-Bruce Peninsula was not yet open to settlement, but potential markets for the peninsula's resources were expanding.

Written accounts from the late British period provide the first documentation of native fishing on the peninsula. The earliest records of any activity on the peninsula were made in 1788 by the surveyor Gother Mann, who took shelter during a storm near a native village where Owen Sound now stands (see Armitage 1994:12). Captain Owen mapped the peninsula in 1815, and Captain Bayfield charted it in 1822 (Fox 1952:108).

Bayfield's map marks the Fishing Islands on the peninsula's Huron shore as 'Ghegheto.' Fox suggests that this is a Huron word for island (Fox 1952:108). Some of the native community members I spoke with felt that the name 'Ghegheto' was connected to the Ojibway word 'Ghego,' meaning fish. However, it appears that Bayfield named Ghegheto Island in honour of his native assistant, whom he refers to as Ogima Ghegheto – an Ojibway name indicating a position as chief speaker (Darlene Johnston 2000, pers. comm.).

Records from a Hudson's Bay post at La Cloche Island, at the east end of Manitoulin, mention some fishing activities in Lake Huron's north shore area at the end of the British period (Lovisek 1991:314), but contain little that is clearly linked to activities on the peninsula.[26]

There are brief records of trade activity on the peninsula in other sources from the early 1800s. Pierre Piche traded independently at the mouth of the Saugeen River for a few years beginning around 1818 (Lamorandiere 1904:46–8; Cadot 1920:21). Besides fish, trade items collected here from native peoples included maple syrup and venison (DeMille 1971:39).

One feature of fishing especially evident in the documented accounts noted in this section is its importance for trade. From archaeological clues it appears that fish had also been traded in pre-contact times. Exchanges between groups may have occurred in the Lake Huron region since Palaeo-Indian times (Ellis and Deller 1990:54), and by the Late Woodland period fish may have been especially important exchange items, as they certainly were by the contact era. Both economic and ceremonial aspects of fishing activity have long been integral to group and inter-group relations in this region.

Though it is difficult to clearly identify some of the groups of people in the area during the contact era, it is likely that people fairly regularly fished at various locations on the peninsula. Upheaval during the Iroquois Wars period no doubt affected aboriginal fishing activities, but the extent of such impacts is not at all clear. Emerging non-native centres and the beginnings of settler expansion provided new fish trading opportunities for native peoples throughout the Lake Huron region. While fishing remained important as part of a more traditional pattern, it can be assumed that new contact experiences entailed adjustments in the activities and social relations that occurred within and between native groups.

Annual fishing gatherings had long been opportunities for broader social activities (Rogers 1978:762). It is likely that as in other, more extensively documented areas of Canada, where new trade opportunities became available for native people, these opportunities were incorporated into seasonal resource-use patterns that had already been established. Unfortunately, there is little evidence by which to explain the extent of such adjustments. When looking beyond the end of the early historical period, into the late historical period, the ways in which contact with newcomers was affecting native peoples becomes more apparent.

4 Change and Adaptation: Late Historical Fisheries

While it is clear that the peninsula's fisheries were important for various groups of people in the distant past, it is difficult to reconstruct the details of who these groups of people were. To further complicate the situation, it is evident that an understanding of early fishery activities requires attention to group interactions as well as to the activities of particular groups themselves. In more recent historical times, during what I refer to as the late historical period (1830–1900), more information is available with which to interpret group interactions and assess the impact of contact relations on native peoples' fishing activities. In regard to the distant past, one can assume that while there were likely periods of rapid change, there was considerable continuity in fishery-resource harvesting and exchange patterns for much of the time. That is to say that, overall, adaptations involving the fishery were more gradual than in subsequent periods.

In this chapter I discuss fishing relations, beginning around 1830, when missionary-run reserves were established in Upper Canada (see Graham 1975; Smith 1987). My focus is on the rapidly changing conditions associated with demographic shifts and the newly established reserve system. I discuss population movements and land cessions, along with shifts in resource-use patterns, and the settlement of the peninsula. I then examine the swift expansion of fishing activities on the Great Lakes during this period, noting the roles that both natives and non-natives played. Finally, I describe fishing conflicts that occurred during the 1800s and discuss fishery depletions, and how these depletions, along with new fishery regulations, might have affected native people.

My description of continuing native involvement in the region's fisheries is meant in part to expand on what I see as a simplistic oppositional notion of cultural domains that is too often assumed in reconstructions of the past. In the current conflict there is a tendency to imagine past native and non-native fishing activities as entirely separate spheres. To be sure, they are unique in some respects; but if we are to gain a fuller understanding of history we must recognize the importance of cultural interaction.

Written accounts provide evidence for assessing the quality of past relationships among native and non-native groups, and how these affected changes in native peoples' access to fisheries resources. Some authors might see such evidence as sufficient for making a generalized moral assessment of settler impacts or past government policies regarding native fishing. I too see weaknesses in many government decisions, and would agree that in some cases new regulations were short-sighted and bound to have negative impacts on native communities. I do not, however, think that all past changes can be fully explained as motivated by ruthless self-interest on the part of non-native power brokers. I assume that a more complex situation existed – that within both native and non-native groups there were various positions on many of the decisions that affected native people, as there are today. This is not to excuse abuses of power wherever they occurred; but if we ignore the possibility that particular cross-cultural interactions involved good intentions as well as bad, cooperation as well as coercion, adaptation as well as enforcement, then we will gain only limited insight into past situations.

New People in Old Places

With reference to the beginning of the late historical period, Rogers states that 'as the occupation of southern Ontario ... by Euro-Americans continued, the Ojibwa had to restrict their movements and utilization of the land more and more' (1978:764). On the surface this seems to contrast with the suggestion above that native fishing activity sometimes intensified where new trade and market opportunities were presented. On the peninsula, and at other places on Lake Huron, fishing was very important for native peoples through the first decades of the late historical period. This reflects efforts to take advantage of new trading opportunities. But at the same time, as Rogers suggests, the increasing presence of settlers did bring new restrictions on access to natural resources.

Early in the 1800s both native and non-native peoples in the Great Lakes region experienced dramatic population shifts. By 1830 Upper Canada was home to more than two hundred thousand non-natives, and five times that number lived on the American side of the lakes (Robeson 1977; Tanner 1987:122). Between 1830 and 1870 the non-native population in Upper Canada increased sevenfold, and it continued to expand rapidly toward the end of the century. In contrast, during the first four decades of the late historical period (1830–70) the overall native population in Southern Ontario remained at around nine thousand (Tanner 1987:178). While the native population numbers were not changing much, there was a good deal of movement among the people represented by these numbers.

By the end of the early historical period many native groups in the southern Great Lakes region were forced by government to relocate. According to Clifton (1975:ii), about one-third of the Potawatomi expelled from American territories moved into Upper Canada between 1830 and 1850, where they joined small native groups or found their way onto newly established reserves along with other native peoples in the region.

Several groups, including the original Nawash community, as noted in chapter 1, were moved to make room for non-natives in areas increasingly populated by agricultural settlers. Missionaries were often in favour of natives relocating to more remote areas, on the grounds that isolation would protect them from the vices of contact, especially alcohol (see Cadot 1920:22). There were other possible benefits for native groups as well: more remote areas allowed better access to particular natural resources in some cases. But native groups also often lost access to local resources. As in the Nawash case, some forfeited the rewards of the considerable effort they had put into establishing farming communities. The more obvious beneficiaries of relocation policies were the non-native settlers who gained access to already productive farmlands.

The Saugeen Peninsula became a refuge for many displaced native peoples during the early and mid-1800s (Surtees 1984:100). Many of the people I interviewed, especially at Nawash, recounted stories about the arduous journey to the peninsula made by their Potawatomi ancestors. It seems likely, however, that many of the Saugeen Indians the newcomers joined had ties to the peninsula going back at least several generations.

Chief Kahgee (1995, pers. comm.) noted that opponents of native rights argue that few of the peninsula's present native people have ancestors who were here prior to the mid-1800s. They further assert that native groups were essentially nomadic and thereby had no real entitlement to the peninsula. Since the distant past many Algonquian peoples in the Great Lakes area were highly mobile, and a pattern of at least seasonal mobility continued even after the establishment of villages, which often comprised several tribal groups, during and after the Iroquois Wars period. French and British trade networks encouraged local settlement of some groups, but these opportunities also encouraged the continuation of seasonal rounds by which various trade products such as fish, fur, and maple syrup could be gathered and processed. Where small mobile groups returned to particular locations for resource harvesting and trading annually, as they often did, there is a case to be made for some sort of entitlement based on occupation.

It may be difficult to conclusively establish continuous occupation of particular geographic locations by particular aboriginal groups on the peninsula, a requirement of some definitions of native or aboriginal rights. But, in a broader context, native rights are also based on recognition of the need to address historically rooted imbalances that are the outcome of past colonial expansion pressures which often transcended territories as currently defined. Fairly broad social responsibilities may therefore have to be measured along with factors relevant to more specific questions about occupation of particular places, if aboriginal rights are to be appropriately recognized in particular situations.

Though there is little information with which we can clearly trace early historical ethnic affiliation on the peninsula, there is no doubt that some native groups regularly occupied sites on the peninsula at the end of this period. They are briefly documented as trading groups, and their presence at shoreline villages and fishing locations was recorded by the first surveyors. Indian trails that connected various occupation sites were already part of the landscape encountered by the first Euro-Canadians who came to the peninsula (Robertson [1906] 1971:19, 50). Human remains found in the 1830s at the Fishing Islands and in other places also mark the presence of native peoples prior to the end of the early historical period (see Fox 1952:70).

Land Cessions

Land cessions can be seen as having a negative impact on native people, since they lost at least some control of particular territories. But many who negotiated and signed treaties or otherwise participated in land transfers saw potential benefits as well, even where they were negotiating from politically disadvantaged positions. Assessing the fairness of past cessions in hindsight is no exact science. While some general factors could apply to most land cessions in what is now Canada, each cession had unique features. Cessions occurred fairly early in Southern Ontario, in comparison to more northerly and westerly regions. In all cases, land cessions made during the 1800s required adaptations to new social and economic conditions.

Before examining fishing activity during this era more directly I will provide a summary of cessions and agreements relevant to this area. The summary roughly follows a chronological outline presented by Darlene Johnston (1996) at a Saugeen community meeting that I attended in 1996. Robertson ([1906]1971:1–16) includes the text of some of the main treaties noted here. Other sources are also cited throughout this section.

Johnston notes two early documents on which late historical period treaties were based: the 1763 Royal Proclamation by King George III, which 'guarantees First Nations' territories,' and the 1764 Treaty of Niagara, at which the 'Chippewas of Lake Huron enter[ed a] formal relationship with [the] British Crown' (Johnston 1996:1).

The 1836 Manitoulin Treaty is the first to deal with the Saugeen-Bruce Peninsula as a separate region. Negotiated by Sir Francis Bond Head, it includes two land-cession agreements. Manitoulin Ottawa and Chippewa bands traded their claims to the island in return for its recognition as protected territory for all native peoples. A second part of the agreement involved the region south of Manitoulin Island. The Saugeen Peninsula became, like Manitoulin Island, recognized 'Indian Territory,' while the Saugeen Tract, an area of 1.5 million acres to the south of the peninsula, was ceded (Surtees 1984:89–93). In her outline, Darlene Johnston (1996:1) cites promises that the Crown would protect the Indian peninsula from encroachment and remove non-natives who were fishing in native fishing grounds.

In 1847 the peninsula's native people requested and were granted a 'Declaration by Her Majesty in favor of the Ojibway Indians respecting certain Lands on Lake Huron' (cited in Johnston 1996:2), which confirmed rights to the peninsula and its islands within seven miles of shore. In 1851 a half-mile strip that ran from Owen Sound to Southampton was surrendered.

In the 1854 Saugeen Surrender (Surtees 1984:101–5), also known in honour of its Crown representative as the Oliphant Treaty, the peninsula was ceded, apart from reserves established at Saugeen, Chief's Point, Nawash (at Owen Sound), Colpoys Bay, and Cape Croker. In 1857, just three years after the Oliphant Treaty, the Nawash reserve at Owen Sound was given up.

Several other negotiations transpired during the following decades. In 1861 the Colpoys Bay reserve near Wiarton was surrendered. In 1885 reserve territory at White Cloud Island in Colpoys Bay was ceded (Schmalz 1977:134). Also in 1885 the Fishing Islands and the Cape Hurd Islands were surrendered (Robertson [1906]1971:8; Fox 1952: 108).[1] In 1896 a sixteen-acre section of Griffiths Island, next to White Cloud Island, was surrendered. Also in 1896 the Saugeen Hunting Ground Reserve No. 60A was established (Schmalz 1977:140).

Partly due to its remote location, the peninsula was one of the last regions in Southern Ontario to be ceded. Some native resource uses were therefore not affected as rapidly as they were in the rest of Southern Ontario. But native fisheries activities were already interwoven with the broader fisheries prior to the 1836 treaty.

Changing Resource Use Patterns

Rogers summarizes the economy of Southern Ontario's native people during the late historical period as follows: 'While farming played a crucial role in the economy, the Ojibwa also collected wild rice and maple sap, hunted, and fished ... Hunting and fishing supplied the Southeastern Ojibwa with food, and trapping supplied the pelts for exchange with Whites for merchandise and sometimes food. Undoubtedly, considerable variation existed from group to group depending on the availability of game resources' (1978:765).

As in other areas where there was good fishing, the peninsula's fisheries were harvested for both food and trade at the beginning of the late historical period. The first missionaries who came to Saugeen (the village near the Saugeen River mouth) in 1828 stated that the natives there lived primarily by fishing (DeMille 1971:78–9). Two decades later Paul Kane described the same village: 'The land hereabouts is excellent, but only a small part is cultivated, as the inhabitants subsist principally on fish, which are taken in great abundance at the entrance of the river' ([1859]1974:2).

Horticulture, or small-scale farming, was already practised in the Woodland period within the Great Lakes region, so farming was not altogether foreign to late historical native peoples, but settler farming methods no doubt required some adjustment. Prior to the 1836 treaty, missionaries at Saugeen encouraged farming (DeMille 1971:78). And near Owen Sound, the Nawash band was already farming in a fashion similar to their settler neighbours.

The adoption of farming practices during the early 1800s can be understood as an example of forced acculturation. However, some native leaders saw farming as a good opportunity and chose to work with missionaries in efforts to benefit their communities. Some missionaries in the region were themselves of mixed native and non-native decent.

With the establishment of the reserve system, reliance on some traditional resources diminished. While hunting and trapping declined during this transition period, fishing did not (DeMille 1971:1). In some places throughout Upper Canada missionaries discouraged native fishing because it allowed unsupervised contact with white traders, who commonly made grog available (Morrison 1994:62; Schmalz 1991:154). Farmers were more easily supervised and protected.

There was mixed opinion, however, among Upper Canada's missionaries and government officials regarding the benefits of fishing and farming for native people. Fishing was seen by some as at least temporarily necessary, but farming was more generally recognized as in line with the work of bringing non-native life-ways to native people (Surtees 1984:90–3; Shanahan 1994:16).

There was likewise mixed opinion among native people about the desirability of farming. White education, which was tied to agricultural pursuits, was regarded as a bright prospect by some, but others resisted efforts to curtail fishing (Schmalz 1991:153–83). On the peninsula, farming was among the mixed blessings that came with increasing white influence, but its emerging importance was not enough to immediately diminish fisheries involvements.

Non-native Settlement of the Peninsula

The peninsula's fisheries were also an important focus for the first non-natives who came to the peninsula during the 1800s. They set up fishing operations on the Fishing Islands in the early 1830s, and continued to fish there through the 1800s. Fishing crews came up to the peninsula from newly established ports on the Huron shore south of the peninsula. Tobermory became a regular station for fishers from Goderich in the 1840s. Southampton was by then emerging as a shipbuilding and fishing centre (Armitage 1994:90,151). Through the 1850s and 1860s, fishing operations were developing at Kincardine as well (Fox 1952:117).[2] Over the next decades fisheries grew on the east side of the peninsula around Wiarton, at Lions Head, and at Wingfield Basin (Fox 1952:207; McLeod 1969:148; McLeod 1979:39–40; Gatis 1980:12; Wyonch 1985:18; Armitage 1994:84).

Following the signing of the 1854 treaty, most of the former 'Indian Peninsula' was put up for sale. Lumber was taken from peninsula lots several years before settlement farms were established. Most of the first settlers on the peninsula were from nearby places in Upper Canada. Many were recent immigrants from the British Isles, especially Scotland and England, and a few were of German heritage (Smith 1923:264; Robertson [1906]1971:10–37; Schmalz 1977:15–16).

Settlers on the peninsula often favoured fisheries opportunities when selecting their village locations (Robertson 1971:17; Armitage 1994:126; Wyonch 1985:17). This settlement pattern was followed in other places on Lake Huron as well, where fishing activities preceded lumbering, and the first village sites were chosen because of good fishing opportunities (Landon 1944:113–20).

Where lumbering and farming were main resource activities, fishing typically played important secondary role. Seasonal fishing was an essential part of the farming economy. At lumber-based settlements such as Dyers Bay and Pike Bay settlers combined winter logging with seasonal fishing and farming. A general shift toward a more generalized mixed economy occurred during the 1880s and 1890s, as lumber resources became less plentiful (Fox 1952:117–18). Where timber was depleted, fishing sometimes took over as the main economic resource, a pattern typified at Stokes Bay (Armitage 1994:116–17).

Land cessions were part of an effort by the government of Upper Canada to provide resource access for growing non-native populations. The growth of non-native settlements brought new economic opportunities for native people, but these opportunities were soon accompanied by diminishing access to fishery resources. Within this climate of change, native people played an important role in the expansion of the region's fisheries.

An Expanding Fishery

In 1830 Upper Canada's growing settlements, including its largest centre, York (now Toronto), were located on lakes and river systems (Tanner 1987:127). Waterways provided transportation for people and trade products, and powered mills, which were a focal point of new settlement activity. These locations also gave settlers access to fisheries.

Settlers in Upper Canada had begun harvesting locally available fish prior to 1830, and they continued to do so into the late historical period. Several studies of pioneer life in Upper Canada highlight the abundance of fish stocks that settlers encountered. Soldiers used their swords to spear sturgeon. Boys caught fish with their bare hands. Settlers used pitchforks, clubs, and flannel petticoats. Pike could be stunned by the sound of a rifle and then gathered where they floated. More typical fishing methods include the use of spears, jacklights, nets, lines, and weirs; and settlers also practised ice fishing (Scherck 1905:205–7; Guillet 1938:147–50; Henry and Paterson 1938:82–3).

Along with sturgeon and pike, settlers harvested pickerel, herring, bass, trout, and suckers. Suckers and trout were caught in largest numbers during their annual spawning runs, when they came into rivers and streams. As noted by Michael Scherck, some were especially vulnerable where they encountered new obstacles: 'In the spring of the year the sucker would swim up the rivers and creeks to spawn in the shallow running water. Being stopped in their course by the dams, people would set nets for them at this point and catch large quantities, enough to supply the whole country round' (1905:206).

The streams and rivers along Lake Ontario's north shore provided trout and salmon in great numbers (Jameson [1838]1990:169). Salmon were especially important for newcomers who had little access to winter vegetables. They often prepared several barrels of fish for winter use (Henry and Paterson 1938:83–4). Fish were also sold by settlers, who brought them to the fish market at York (Guillet 1938:144, 151) or shipped them in barrels to other markets (Henry and Paterson 1938:190). Some settlers 'paid for farms and built houses from the sale of salmon' (Guillet 1938:148).

By the mid-1800s fishing had become Upper Canada's third most important industry, after lumbering and potash production (Henry and Paterson 1938:190). On a national scale the Canadian fisheries of this period had an export value second only to lumber (Rowan [1876]1972:84). A secondary advantage of the fisheries was that it served as a school for seamen. Canada was at the time among the world's six largest ship-owning countries (Rowan 1972:84).

A substantial commercial fishery had been established in Lake Huron by the 1820s (Spangler and Peters 1995:106), but it emerged more fully during the 1830s and 1840s when the extensive use of large nets resulted in unprecedented harvests of fish (Guillet 1938:152). Using seines, typically anchored at one end to the shore, crews hauled in great numbers of whitefish, trout, and herring. Edwin Guillet (1938:151) states that as early as 1812 a thousand or more whitefish were netted at a time. These numbers grew dramatically during the 1830s and 1840s. A haul of fourteen thousand fish on Georgian Bay's east coast is recorded, and accounts from Lakes Erie and Ontario claim ninety thousand whitefish landed in a single net (Guillet 1938:151). The pound net, a kind of fish trap, was also used to harvest great numbers of fish (Landon 1944:113; Spangler and Peters 1995:110). In the Detroit River fish were driven into these nets by the 'hundreds of thousands' (Guillet 1938:151). These depictions are largely anecdotal, but even accounting for substantial exaggeration, they suggest harvests of unprecedented size.

Much of Lake Huron's harvest was sold to Americans, especially at Detroit and Chicago (Landon 1944:190; Barry 1978:56,109). Around the beginning of the late historical period American fishing companies based in Chicago and Detroit began operating along the Canadian shores of Lake Huron (see Fox 1952:119). American fishing companies maintained a presence there throughout the century. The first scheduled steamers at Tobermory belonged to the Dominion Transportation Company, a subsidiary of the giant Booth Fisheries Corporation of Chicago (Gatis 1980:25; Armitage 1994:93).

The expansion of Lake Huron fisheries was accelerated by technological innovation. The earliest use of large seines and gill nets in Lake Huron is uncertain, but their impact on production was arguably dramatic.[3] Innovations in making and operating nets also increased efficiency (Barry 1978:106–10; Spangler and Peters 1995:7–108). The expansion of the gill-net fishery is also linked to innovations in boat building that allowed easier access to open water. Huron boats, mackinaws, and later fishing tugs were adapted for working nets, and the efficiency of both fishing and shipping improved when the paddle and sail were augmented by steam power (Barry 1978:105–12; Spangler and Peters 1995:107–8). Steam tugs did not immediately reduce reliance on other modes of power. In fact, Lake Huron's sail-powered fishing fleet increased from 229 to 418 boats between 1881 and 1894, partly because newly introduced steam tugs could be used to tow them in difficult conditions (Spangler and Peters 1995:109).

Innovations in fish processing played an important role in the expansion of Upper Canada's commercial fishing industry. The American Fur Company introduced the method of packing salted fish in barrels in 1809 on Lake Huron (Guillet 1938:151; Spangler and Peters 1995:106).

Advances in other modes of transportation also contributed to the industry's expansion. The railroad reached Collingwood on Georgian Bay's southern shore in the mid-1850s and soon Lake Huron fish were shipped to Canada West's main centres via rail (Barry 1978:105). Expanded land-transportation networks also increased access to fish markets in growing American cities such as Buffalo (Wyonch 1985:14). Packing on ice became the preferred method of preservation for shipping fish to market, though salt barrelling continued to be practised for some time (Spangler and Peters 1995:108).

Native Involvement in the Growing Fish Trade

At the beginning of the late historical period many native people living on the Great Lakes relied on fishing for both food and trade. In some locations traditional practices associated with fishing were maintained, as indicated by J.G. Kohl's observations made during his travels around Lake Superior in the mid-1800s (1956:325–31). Continuity is also suggested in Frances Densmore's field observations made among Ojibway groups at the end of the late historical period at places west of Lake Huron. Densmore noted that fishing was practised there 'almost the entire year' and recorded clans named after fish, magic fishing charms, and fish symbolism in religion and myth ([1929]1970:124–5).

But there were also adjustments to new circumstances and opportunities among the late historical period's Great Lakes native peoples. Helen Tanner (1987:132) states that by the 1830s trading companies in the upper Great Lakes were focusing less on furs and more on fish products. Fish had long been an item of exchange for natives at fur-trading posts, and the growing importance of fish increased native involvement in the fisheries even more.

In the upper Great Lakes substantial native-run fishing operations were established. Preserved fish were sold along with other fish products such as isinglass, a substance extracted from the swim bladders of sturgeon and used in the manufacture of glue and other commodities (Lytwyn 1990; Van West 1990).

Anna Jameson, who toured Lake Huron in the mid-1830s, recorded natives packing fish in salt barrels for export ([1838]1990:313–14).

They participated in the shipment of eight thousand barrels of fish from the St Mary's rapids region in 1835, where the whitefish dip-net fishery was still impressive (Jameson [1838]1990:448–50). Other Lake Huron fishing activities noted by Jameson also demonstrate an increasing involvement by native people in the fish trade (Jameson [1838]1990:512–40; see also Landon 1944:103–11; Barry 1978:105–8).

Paul Kane, who travelled around Lake Huron a little more than a decade after Jameson, noted fish-trade activities as well. He remarked that at Manitoulin Island, native people, 'subsist chiefly on salmon and whitefish, which they take in such quantities as to be able to barter away a surplus beyond their own wants for other necessaries' ([1859]1974:6–16). Many native people participated in the economic opportunities that the expanding Lake Huron fisheries provided.[4]

Fisheries products had been traded by native people in the region prior to white contact, and the fish trade engaged during the late historical period can be seen as a continuation of this pattern. Natives often traded fish informally with local settlers and frequently brought fish to town markets (Jameson [1838]1990:151, 522).[5]

Upper Canada/Canada West's commercial fishery was in part an extension of activities engaged in by Lake Huron traders, who regularly arrived in southern ports with shipments of 'fish and furs and maple sugar' (Landon 1944:305). They gathered and delivered various commodities, but collecting barrels of salted fish from natives camped at fishing stations was a substantial part of their operations (Barry 1978:105).[6]

There are several examples of cross-cultural sharing with respect to fishing technologies. Wyonch (1985:7) suggests that the gill net was introduced to the peninsula's first non-native settlers by native inhabitants. This sounds possible, though the gill net would have also been widely used by this time. Fishing methods employed by settlers in other parts of Southern Ontario, including the weir and jacklight spearing, may also have been learned from native peoples (Scherck 1905:207). In the other direction, aboriginal people acquired steel hooks, net materials, and salt and barrels from white traders.

Native people benefited from the trade opportunities that accompanied the rapid settlement of Upper Canada; however, through government policies aimed at settling natives and new approaches to regulating the fisheries, they were forced to make rapid adaptations in their resource relations.[7]

Late Historical Fishing Conflicts

In 1797, in response to native concerns about non-native encroachment on fish resources, the government of Upper Canada issued a proclamation intended to protect native fisheries on Lake Ontario (Schmalz 1991:106). Similar complaints were voiced by natives in other locations (Schmalz 1991:150). Fishing conflicts around Manitoulin Island are worthy of special note because of their proximity to the peninsula and because they played a role in shaping government policies pertaining to the peninsula's fisheries.

Victor Lytwyn (1990:12–14) states that while fishing rights were not mentioned specifically in the 1836 treaty documents, a concern for protection of fisheries access was raised in preliminary negotiations and is suggested in the wording of subsequent treaties. Natives would certainly have been aware of their reliance on the fisheries. Even the large group that attended negotiations required fish, along with corn porridge, as their main provisions (Jameson [1838]1990:491–8). Native interest in maintaining access to fisheries is also implied in the fishing opportunities found at most of their reserve locations (Lytwyn 1990:14).

When the 1836 Manitoulin treaties were negotiated the island's fisheries were already coveted by non-natives (Tanner 1987:160; Shanahan 1994:25). Lytwyn (1990:15) states that by 1855, two hundred to three hundred American boats were fishing around Manitoulin. In the midst of increasing competition for fisheries resources, colonial governments began regulating Lake Huron's fisheries.

Following the enactment of fisheries legislation in 1857 and 1858, William Gibbard was appointed fisheries overseer (see Lytwyn 1990:16–17). Among other duties, he travelled the lakes to issue fishing leases. During his tenure (1859–63) his encounters with natives were generally hostile.

In 1862 Gibbard and a posse of constables were forcibly expelled from Manitoulin Island by armed natives whom he had intended to apprehend because of fishing lease violations. Several months later Gibbard was drowned in the upper Great Lakes amid circumstances that remain unknown (Leighton 1977; Tanner 1987:178; Lytwyn 1990:20; Morrison 1994:63). A native man was arrested as a suspect in the drowning but was later released.[8]

Another site of conflict was the Saugeen-Bruce Peninsula's Fishing

Islands. In the 1830s the village at Saugeen, just south of the Fishing Islands, had more than three hundred native inhabitants (Lytwyn (1992:85), making it comparable in size to Goderich, which was established in 1829 and quickly grew to be the largest non-native settlement in the area. Captain Alexander McGregor came up from Goderich and began fishing at the Fishing Islands in 1831. In 1832 he procured a licence of occupation from the government, which allowed him to establish fishing stations and thereby fish the islands (Lytwyn 1992:86).

The operation that McGregor established was one of the most active fisheries on Lake Huron. McGregor erected the peninsula's first stone building at Main Station Island, the centre of his fishing operations. His company harvested trout, herring, sturgeon, and especially whitefish for several years. Large schools of fish were spotted from tall trees and hauled in with long seines. Authors cite accounts of anywhere from one hundred to one thousand barrels of fish taken in a single haul, and note that when not enough salt was on hand, or when the nets were too heavy to pull, some of the catch had to be released (Fox 1952:110–12; Robertson 1971:22; Armitage 1994:143). McGregor apparently believed he had discovered an unlimited resource at the peninsula's Fishing Islands (Robertson 1971:21; DeMille 1971:41–2). By 1834 he was shipping three thousand barrels of whitefish and herring annually from the Fishing Islands to buyers in Detroit, who paid one dollar per barrel.

A fishing company owned in part by the prominent political figure William Dunlop took over operations on the Fishing Islands in 1834. To gain a licence of occupation for his own company, Dunlop argued that McGregor's operation allowed Americans to reap the larger part of the profits from Canadian resources. However, after driving McGregor out of the area, Dunlop's company apparently engaged American trade to the same effect.

After leaving the Fishing Islands, Captain McGregor continued fishing for a time at the peninsula's northern islands and around Owen Sound and Cape Croker, where he married the daughter of Chief Wabatic (see Fox 1952:115; Robertson [1906]1971:24). He later established fishing operations at the eastern end of Manitoulin Island, and developed social and economic ties with natives there.[9]

Dunlop's licence of occupation was given on the condition that an appropriate leasing agreement be made with native representatives, which was subsequently arranged (Lytwyn 1992:87–9). But in the same year Saugeen leaders tried unsuccessfully to terminate the lease, suggesting that the company's 'harvest of fish ... proved to be excessive' (cited in Lytwyn 1992:88). In the late 1830s native representatives voiced concerns about the government's failure to protect their fishing grounds, as implied in the 1836 treaty negotiations, and they noted problems with the collection of lease money (Schmalz 1977:70–7; Lytwyn 1992:86).

Disagreement concerning regulation of access to the Fishing Islands fisheries continued. After 1840 Dunlop's operations were taken over by William Cayley. He apparently had no leasing agreement with Saugeen representatives, who gave leases to others (Lytwyn 1992:90–1). Whether the licence of occupation that Cayley had purchased from Dunlop's company took precedence over local native leases was a point of confusion. In the following decades, rapid changes in company ownership further complicated questions about whether ownership of licences of occupation could also be transferred (Darlene Johnston 2000, pers. comm.)

In 1843 four Saugeen men went to the islands to drive Cayley's men away but were themselves chased off (see Lytwyn 1992:90–1). The following year, Metigwab, a Saugeen chief, met with government officials in Kingston to resolve this dispute. Chief Superintendent of Indian Affairs Samuel Jarvis voiced his support for Saugeen's position, but encouraged Metigwab to have Saugeen sign a leasing agreement with Cayley, which they did in 1845 (Lytwyn 1992:90–1).

In 1849 Saugeen struck a lease with Alexander MacDonald, a representative for a trader from Southampton named William Kennedy (Lytwyn 1992:92). Kennedy had grown up at a Hudson's Bay Company trading post on the Saskatchewan River, with his father, the chief factor, and his mother, a native woman (Weichel 1998:21–2).[10]

Leases and licences of occupation continued to change hands. Lytwyn (1992:92–5) notes the consecutive involvement in the fisheries of persons named Hamilton, Calder, and Jardin, and he states that Saugeen representatives continued to protest the actions of the government and the fishing company. Lytwyn further claims that throughout this period 'rent was rarely paid to the Saugeen Nation' (1992:95).

People from Saugeen were themselves fishing in Lake Huron for food and trade. During the 1840s and 1850s some leaders saw potential for expanding their fish trade, but they encountered obstacles (Lytwyn 1992:90–4). Saugeen leaders complained in 1850 that Kennedy's men were depleting the area's timber, which was needed for making barrels. In 1851 Saugeen's commercial operations were apparently set back by the late arrival of government trust funds needed to buy salt for preserving fish in barrels. Similar problems were encountered in 1856, and the government denied the purchase of other fishing equipment in 1857. In spite of such difficulties, Saugeen sold one thousand barrels of fish at five dollars per barrel in 1857 (Lytwyn 1992:94).

Because of the importance of the Fishing Islands fisheries, native leaders demanded rights to the Fishing Islands in the 1854 treaty negotiations (Lytwyn 1992:93). Following the 1854 surrender, fishing disputes persisted and native representatives continued to voice concerns about encroachments (Schmalz 1977:80-9; Schmalz 1991:220).

In 1859, following the enactment of fishing legislation and the establishment of a government leasing system, Saugeen leaders met with William Gibbard, the fisheries overseer, and demanded that the Fishing Islands not be leased to non-natives. They unsuccessfully offered to bid on the lease themselves (Lytwyn 1992:95). Because of their dissatisfaction with the leasing system, fishing stations were sometimes destroyed by natives, as reported by Gibbard in 1861. Lytwyn notes that in 1864 Saugeen unsuccessfully applied to lease Whitefish Island, one of the Fishing Islands; but the Indian agent advised that Saugeen already had more fishing opportunities than it needed (1992:96). There is evidence that Saugeen requests for leases were ignored; however, this was not always the case. By 1862 the 'Saugeen Indians' had been issued a lease for some of the islands, and fishing leases were likewise issued to bands on the other side of the peninsula (NAC 1859).

It is difficult to draw conclusions from historical documents about the costs and benefits of these new fishing arrangements for native people. However, it is clear that government involvement in leasing operations was a turning point in the story of fishing relations on the peninsula. Between 1830 and 1870, amid regulatory confusion, the Saugeen community's control of the fisheries shifted substantially. When this period began, they were issuing leases, and when it ended, leases were being issued to them. Evidence of native resistance to diminished control indicates that government regulatory authority came at some expense to native community members. This situation set a discordant tone that was echoed in future relations (Darlene Johnston 2000, pers. comm.)

Around the beginning of the late historical period, fishing conflicts were likewise building on the other side of the peninsula. Prior to the relocation to Cape Croker in the 1850s, the cape appears to have been already occupied by a small group, who like the newcomers no doubt recognized the value of fishing opportunities there. When community members were starting farms, local fishing was still a major activity, as it was when the government began issuing leases.

During the late 1850s there were fishing disputes at the newly established Nawash reserve. Of particular concern was the area around the islands south of the cape, in Colpoys Bay, where cases of tampering with non-native nets and threatening white fishermen were recorded (Schmalz 1977:119–20). It is not surprising that when Gibbard visited Cape Croker on his leasing rounds he met hostile threats there (see Lytwyn 1990:18).

Records from the 1890s likewise suggest considerable tensions. In 1890 the band protested overfishing by American crews and requested that the Indian Agent give a 'history of the decrease of the Indian fishing at this place' (cited in Schmalz 1977:187). In 1891 band leaders submitted an unsuccessful request to have what they saw as unfair fishing restrictions relaxed; and they raised a similar matter again in an 1893 council meeting held jointly with Saugeen (Schmalz 1977:186–7; 1991:221–2). The following year native representatives asked the local parliamentarian for assistance in easing restrictions, but with no luck.

Around the turn of the century tight restrictions and encroachments were major concerns for Nawash leaders (see DeMille 1971). In 1897 the Nawash fishing territory was reduced as a result of disputes with residents from nearby Hope Bay. Nawash officially protested this in 1902. In 1903 they noted hardships caused by reductions in their fishing territory when requesting permission to cut timber. They stated that with fewer places to fish they were forced into rougher water, where a greater number of nets was lost (Schmalz 1991:222–3).

Fisheries Depletions

In some areas of Upper Canada the growth of settlements and the expansion of fisheries operations had negative impacts on fish stocks during the late historical period, and thereby on the resource options available to native peoples. By the end of the early historical period once-abundant fish stocks in Southern Ontario were already threatened by settlement activities. It was common knowledge through the 1800s that fish had been driven away from many rivers, and that dams and lumbering debris obstructed spawning beds (Scherck 1905:207; Henry and Paterson 1938:82; Rowan [1876]1972:377). Other threats included the intensity of fishing, the vulnerability of spawning species at dam sites, and disturbances caused by steamboat and other traffic on water systems. Many salmon fisheries on Upper Canada's river systems were destroyed (Guillet 1938:147).

As elsewhere in Upper Canada, the peninsula's first settlers built dams and mills soon after they arrived. Brenna Wathke (1987:20) notes that after 1844 the Saugeen River alone powered 156 mills. Though there is no record of their exact impact, it can be assumed that at least some species fared poorly on the Saugeen River and its tributaries during this period. This may have had an impact on local native peoples, who continued to depend to some degree on fishing.

It is very probable that fish stocks were also affected by the intense level of commercial fishing that began around the beginning of this era. Guillet suggests that within a few decades of large-scale seining some of the coastal fisheries were depleted and commercial operators had to fish farther offshore with gill nets and other open-water nets (1938:152; see also Landon 1944:113; Spangler and Peters 1995:106).

Technological innovations that made deep-water fishing more feasible may have also played a role in this shift, but given the large numbers of fish taken some negative impact on particular stocks is likely. The most vulnerable Southern Ontario fish stocks were used for more than just food. For example, Lake Ontario whitefish were sold to farmers in the 1860s for crop fertilizer (Guillet 1938:152). By the end of the 1800s it was apparent that sturgeon stocks were greatly depleted throughout Lake Huron.

James Barry (1978:110) notes that there are no accurate statistics for Lake Huron fisheries production through the 1800s. But giving a general picture, he estimates the annual catch between the mid-1870s and the end of the century for whitefish, lake trout, and pike combined at between two and seven million pounds. The harvest of other species such as herring and sturgeon would put the annual figure much higher.

W.S. Fox (1952:116) suggests that a gradual decline of stocks on the Fishing Islands coincided with the sale of the leases to Spence and Kennedy, but he also indicates some recovery following this. Native fisher opportunities on Lake Huron may have been reduced due to commercial overfishing in some places, as suggested by Lytwyn (1990:3, 25; 1992:97) and Schmalz (1977:186; 1991:150, 221). But given the lack of harvest records, the level of depletion in particular locations remains speculative. Since native people were themselves involved in increased fishing activity, resource depletion cannot be ascribed totally to outside forces. But such depletion is clearly linked to new patterns being established within the broader society.

Though it is difficult to confidently state the extent of suggested fisheries depletions around the peninsula, natives on the peninsula during the late historical period recognized large commercial fish harvests as a threat to their fisheries options. Fisheries depletions throughout Upper Canada were also of concern to government officials, who were developing the first fisheries-management policies and regulations.

Regulating the Fisheries

The first laws aimed at curtailing the destruction of local fish stocks had already been made prior to the late historical period (Rowan [1876]1972:47). In an unsuccessful attempt to stop the overexploitation of salmon, an 1806 regulation was enacted forbidding their netting in some creeks (Guillet 1938:147). In 1857 Canada's first *Fishing Act* restricted certain nets and river obstructions, and set closed seasons for some species (Forkey 1995:54). In the following year the governor-in-council was granted the authority to issue licences and leases, and to appoint fisheries superintendents (Forkey 1995:54). Anglers were also subject to this regulation (Rowan [1876]1972:381, 417–18). In a broader context, the fish trade was already regulated in international treaties such as the Treaty of Washington, which stipulated a duty-free trade between Canada and the United States (Rowan [1876]1972:47).[11]

In 1858 Fishery Act amendments approved the establishment of sanctuaries, and an 1865 law gave fisheries officers the power to enforce regulations by seizing illegally caught fish. In the following decades, provincial governments were given the responsibility of administering fisheries regulations, while the federal government maintained legislative authority (Forkey 1995:54).

In an attempt to rehabilitate depleted salmon stocks, hatcheries were established on several rivers around mid-century (Rowan [1876] 1972:415–16). Samuel Wilmot played a leading role in developing hatchery programs. In 1867 he set up the first government-run hatchery in North America, and was appointed overseer of fisheries in 1868 by the new federal government (Forkey 1995:55; Guillet 1938:148).

Nawash cooperated in some of these early restocking efforts. In 1889 they provided parent trout for a hatchery at Newcastle. Under regulations and rehabilitation programs developed during the late 1800s, some depleted stocks became plentiful again (Scherck 1905:207; Guillet 1938:152).

As already suggested in the discussion of conflicts on the Fishing Islands, government positions on native fishing rights during the 1800s were ambiguous. Native approval for leases was not consistently negotiated, and native leases were not effectively enforced by the government. The government responded to native concerns by offering rights to fish for food, but these did not fully recognize native ownership of fisheries resources (Lytwyn 1992:97).

Amendments to the *Fishery Act* in 1865 included the first references to native peoples (Lytwyn 1990:22). In an attempt to clarify government jurisdiction and responsibility regarding native fishing activity, several reports were commissioned during the 1860s and 1870s. Within government, there were differences of opinion on how to regulate native fishing. Not all government officials were as confrontational as Gibbard. For example, William Plummer, a superintendent with Indian Affairs, recorded his concern for the government's neglect of native fishing rights (Lytwyn 1992:97). However, reports generally gave colonial notions of common law precedence over obligations apparently implied in treaties. Given this ambiguity, no clear definition of the government's authority over native fisheries was established during this period (Lytwyn 1990:18–23).

Not all native people were opposed to government fisheries leasing programs (see for example King 1994:47), since these were a potential source of band revenue. But during the 1800s it became clear that there were many unanswered questions about fisheries jurisdiction.

The conflicts of this era, and the acts of resistance that characterize them, occurred in conjunction with government efforts to increase their control over the fisheries. We should evaluate government policies and actions critically, but a sound assessment of government decisions, and government indecision, requires careful analysis of the complex situations that were created during this period. We need to recognize abuses of power, but we should also acknowledge the growing interdependence of native and non-native fisheries, and the roles that native people played in support of the emerging fisheries economy.

5 Mixed Economies: Twentieth-Century Fisheries

The Early 1900s

During the first half of the 1900s, the peninsula's native people continued to adjust to changing fishing opportunities in ways that reflect the strong influence of their relationships with non-natives. These adjustments were part of a larger pattern of mixed economic activity that characterized the peninsula during this period, and they were shaped as well by dramatic changes that began around the end of the Second World War.

Several published portrayals of non-native fishers around the peninsula provide interesting insights into fishing activities at the end of the late historical period and throughout the following decades. Such accounts are anecdotal and should be read carefully if one is looking for reliable information, but they allow us to imagine fishing as part of people's everyday life.

W.S. Fox's (1952:117–18) sketch of William Simpson characterizes the economic blending of fishing and lumbering that was common on the peninsula prior to the turn of the century. He also describes Gilbert McIntosh, who built a local shipping business that was later taken over by a large American company (Fox 1952:117–18). Jack McCauley, who ran a fish house in Wiarton in the early 1900s, is described by local historians (Gatis 1980:61; McLeod 1979:38), as is Orrie Vail, a Tobermory fisherman, museum keeper, and storyteller (Armitage 1994:95–7, 117–18).

In a local historical publication, Vincent Elliott (1987), a non-native, has recounted local fishing operations on the peninsula's Huron side prior to mid-century:

A typical day for a fisherman would be to get up at 4 a.m. and leave by 5 a.m. and run out into the lake in a certain direction for a certain time. (a boat went 10 m.p.h.) They lifted nets by hand at first and later used rollers and net winders. When the fish were taken out of the nets they would be put back in again unless they needed to be treated or mended. The fishermen had lunch on a gas stove or baked whitefish on the hot engine. A gang of nets, four boxes, about 1000 feet, would be set by early afternoon and the fishermen would be back in about 4 p.m. Hook lines were used up around Fitzwilliam Island sometimes. At Stokes Bay the nets were put out in 7 to 8 feet of water around Gobbler shoals or Goodrow shoals S. of Lyal Island. This was risky as a sudden storm could roll the shallow nets up in an impossible mess. (38)

The water was so deep in 1920 that sailboats would come across what is now sand flats and up into the 'river.' Nathan Doran, from Southampton was setting pound nets in Stokes Bay and so many fish were caught that a barrel factory (cooper) was built on the river and fish were salted in these barrels and sent to the big cities. (37)[1]

While the peninsula's native community members also fished during this century, there are few written accounts of such activities. The information provided by those whom I cite in the following sections and throughout this book contributes to a more comprehensive picture of twentieth-century fishing activities around the Saugeen-Bruce Peninsula.

After several decades of settlement expansion, which peaked around the end of the 1800s, the resident population of the Saugeen-Bruce Peninsula stabilized. In contrast, most nearby areas of Southern Ontario were settled earlier and their populations showed marked growth during the early to mid-1900s. The peninsula did, however, begin to attract growing numbers of seasonal visitors during the early 1900s, some of whom came primarily to fish. Though particular fish stocks were being depleted, fishing was still important during the first half of the 1900s. Despite adjustments to changing social and economic conditions, many of the peninsula's native people maintained an interest in fishing.

My reference to the first part of the century as a time of mixed economies indicates several areas of overlap. In both native and non-native communities fishing was blended with other economic pursuits. Overlap is also seen in the mix of several kinds of fishing activities carried out at different times of the year. Especially on the reserves, the term 'mixed economy' further implies the integration of commercial fishing and less formally structured activities. Finally, the fishing economy was mixed through the interactions of natives and non-natives. All of these kinds of blending were to a large extent continuations of earlier patterns, but new economic opportunities and pressures make this era unique.

Tourism and Recreational Fishing

By the beginning of the 1900s the peninsula's fisheries were being harvested by well-established commercial fishing concerns, but many of these were fairly small operations, sometimes involving only one or two people. As in the previous era, fishing was incorporated into broader economic patterns that varied according to local opportunity. The growing tourist industry brought new fisheries-related opportunities for many of the peninsula's inhabitants.

Fishing as a leisure activity was part of the cultural repertoire of Europeans long before settlement of the Great Lakes region. Seventeenth- and eighteenth-century writers, including Father Joseph Lafitau ([1724]1977:187), commented on the availability of fish and game around the Great Lakes, as did nineteenth-century writers such as John Rowan ([1876]1972), who promoted outdoor sporting opportunities as an attraction for Ontario's prospective immigrants.

Guidebooks and brochures advertised southern Georgian Bay's fishing opportunities prior to 1880 (Barry 1978:148). By the turn of the century, sport-fishing enthusiasts and other vacationers were travelling by rail and boat to the shores of the Saugeen-Bruce Peninsula. Such 'retreats' were becoming popular, partly as rewards for submitting to the routines of work patterns in industrializing cities and towns (see Jasen 1995). The growth of tourism on the peninsula also reflects the efforts of local residents, who were looking for ways to replace resource-based economies that were being depleted.

Recreational fishing opportunities on the peninsula were long known to local residents who enjoyed 'the angle' (Fox 1952:208). At Pike Bay, sports enthusiasts arrived by 1900 to fish perch and pickerel (Armitage 1994:123). Vacationers began arriving at Dyer's Bay in the 1920s to fish and camp (Armitage 1994:80).

Andrew Armitage suggests that patterns of commercial and recreational fishing on the peninsula show an inverse relationship. At Stokes Bay, increases in recreational fishing corresponded with downturns in commercial fishing (1994:118). He depicts a similar pattern of recreational fishing replacing or heavily supplementing commercial fishing along the beaches between the Saugeen and Sauble Rivers, where summer visitors first arrived in the 1890s and started building cottages in 1904 (Armitage 1994:149). The first tourists would have seen fishing shanties along the beaches. During the early decades of the century cottagers and fishermen coexisted, but as the number of cottages increased, the number of fisherfolk declined. The largest boom in cottage building came just after the Second World War (Armitage 1994:149), when the most dramatic depletions in the peninsula's fish stocks occurred.

This correspondence between increasing tourism and depleting fish stocks seems paradoxical at first. Recreational and commercial fishers targeted some of the same fish stocks, so where depleted stocks account for commercial fishing declines, one would expect that recreational fishing opportunities would be declining as well. However, there were also differences in the range of species the two sectors targeted, and while commercial fishing decreased, tourist fishing gained an increasingly important role within the peninsula's already mixed local economy.

Before mid-century, recreational fishing had come to rival the peninsula's commercial fishery in overall economic importance (Wyonch 1985:20–1). This entailed some heated resource competition, which is discussed below; but for many of the peninsula's local fisherfolk, the two were quite compatible. Some incorporated tourist fishing within an annual cycle of various fishing activities: 'In the spring the nets were usually set on sand bottom in 10 to 20 fathoms (100 feet). In summer they guided parties of tourists or caught tullibees (ciscos, freshwater herrings) or chub (deep-water cisco). Fall was a good fishing season again for trout or whitefish and then herring again last of all' (Elliott 1987:38). Similar adaptations to changing opportunities were made among reserve community members.

Fishing Economies at Cape Croker

Though they had less access to the peninsula's fisheries than in previous eras, Nawash community members continued to fish throughout the first half of the twentieth century. Many of the people I interviewed remembered the people, places, and community interactions associated with fishing on the reserve during this time:

Way back when I was a child, my grandma's nephews were all fishermen ... there was a lot of fishing done. I remember them talking about fishing ... talking about their boats and their gear and what have you. I've seen them maybe coming in from the waters of Georgian Bay ... coming into the harbour ... and all landing there and cleaning their fish. (CP-WA)

Fishing activity continued alongside other occupations, some newly introduced, and some that had been long part of economic life:

Oh yes, there were a lot of them that used to fish; everybody used to fish, at some time. Old Mike Lavalley used to fish; and the Akiwenzie boys all fished; my brother Edgar fished. But there were other types of employment going, such as farming. My brother was a plasterer, and there were other trades. A lot of them used to work in the bush all year around. (CP-FJ)

Now it's a good life. We used to go on horse and wagon trading crafts, like axe handles and boxes, for food and clothes. 'Do you want to buy baskets?' That's what I learned in English. (CP-R4)

While some were essentially full-time fisherfolk, others fished to a lesser extent. Some fished for only a few weeks of the year, when fish were most readily available:

Prior to Dad joining the army in 1940 or so, he'd fish twice a year on a commercial basis, in the fall and in the early spring. He had a little rowboat that was parked down along the shoreline here. The catch wasn't all that great as I recall because I think he only had one or two nets that he would put in. There were two different types of net. The herring net was about a two-and-five-eighths mesh. And there was the large four-inch mesh that they used for whitefish and lake trout. Dad was a farmer, and he had the farm to look after, so this fishing thing only took him twice a year. (CP-TJ)

Vincent Nadjiwon outlines various fishing methods that were employed according to the season:

I started fishing when I was young, you see ... trolling line. That's the lake trout. There was nets too. I did trolling in the summertime. In the fall and spring there was whitefish and trout ... We went ice fishing for lake trout and whitefish. Trolling we would use some long and some short lines. Ice fishing was about thirty fathoms. That's how the people lived long ago ... ice fishing. (CP-VN)

Though gill nets were most widely used, seines were also employed, especially for whitefish in the fall. Gill nets were set when the elements permitted:

We would go out to fish up at about five in the morning, and we'd be out till about ten. That was called before breakfast. We would come in and they would have breakfast ready. They would have a meal and then clean the fish, then patch the nets and get them ready to set in the evening. (CP-RJ)

We would set in the evening and then we would watch the weather. If a storm came up we went out to grab the nets, even in the middle of the night. The water pressure would rip the nets in a storm, cause this was before they had the nylon ones – just ordinary cotton. They would get tangled up. I've seen nets after a storm that just had the top and bottom lines left. We would have to clean those up and repair them. (CP-RJ)

For some, the annual cycle included trolling and then gill-netting: 'We would troll until late fall and then use nets until it got too cold' (CP-GK). In some cases, the two fishing methods were practised at the same time:

We used to set our nets on the shoals this time of year. The first run would be the lake trout. They called them the 'Red Fins'; their fins were all red by this time of the year. They would come onto the shoals to spawn. We would set nets alongside the shoal and during the day we would troll that shoal, with about four or five fathom of line and a spoon on the end of it. We could see where the nets were by the corks and we went alongside. (CP-RJ)

Locations as well as fishing methods varied according to the season:

We used to go halfway to Rabbit Island, then to Benjamin Point. We followed the fish. When I fished with my father we started in the spring, and by June we moved toward Rabbit Island. Then we'd move again, to Cove of Cork. You know where to set ... When fish were getting scarce there, we'd move over again toward the lighthouse. It took about two and a half hours to row from the harbour where the government dock is now to the lighthouse. At six in the morning the water is calm so we would row along the shore. We had a fish camp, two shacks, at Rabbit Island and anyone could stay there if they got stuck. They could come back the next morning. (CP-EA)

The end of November till about the eighteenth of December we would move from Pine Tree Point to Clay Banks. Clay Banks used to be an old log skid. We would set on the shoals there for whitefish. The whitefish come in fast and furious and then they dry up quickly. When there were only one or two fish in the nets we would clean the nets up and put them away for the winter. (CP-RJ)

Given the various kinds of fishing practised and the different degrees of involvement, it is difficult to characterize fishing by reserve members during this period as a particular type of economy. Since fish provided an important food source the term 'food fishery' can be applied, but fish were also part of broader economic activities. Fish were distributed informally and marketed. They were both a subsistence and a commercial resource.

Where particular fishing activities fit between these two economic poles is not always evident. During economically difficult times forms of reciprocity, or sharing, were common:

Before the war, during the depression, things used to get pretty tough. I used to get tired of salted fish and potatoes, but that was what we had. My dad had a small farm. We always had a lot of potatoes, carrots, beets, and turnips. When people got hard up on the reserve he would go around and take them food. He also put down pork in the fall of the year, two or three pigs. (CP-RJ)

In her description of the 'livelihood' that fishing provided, Winona Arriage interconnects various kinds of economies:

I married a fisherman ... and some of the family there were fishermen. He loved fishing. And that was our livelihood. He'd either trade fish on the outside for vegetables, if we didn't have enough ... or eggs, butter ... all these essentials. People out there took fish. And then sometimes when there was a good catch, he'd sell to fish buyers. There was always fish buyers around ... So that gave us our extras, like our clothing. At this time of the year, planning on Christmas, it was just something extra that he made money on ... He didn't have any other job. That's the only thing we had ... the fishing. (CP-WA).

Philomene Chegahno uses the term 'bread and butter' to indicate fishing as a way of obtaining basic necessities, either through direct resource harvesting or through a market transaction:

My first husband fished too ... He fished in ... Gravelly Bay they call it. They didn't have outboard motors at that time. They only had rowboats ... He only had a few nets ... He must have had two or three nets. That's all they could afford. Everything was expensive. That's the only bread and butter they had, from fishing, that's all they got. (CP-PC)

We sold a few just for our bread and butter like I say, or things that we need. There was no income coming in. Fishing is all we had; but we farmed too ... A lot of people had cattle ... little farms. (CP-PC)

Ted Johnson explicitly refers to his father's seasonal fishing as 'commercial,' in contrast to the small-scale farming economy, which was more informal: 'Between 1935 and 1940, I remember Dad fishing commercially. It was one of the only means of income that there was around the farm because everything seemed to be on a barter system. You raise a cow and you trade with someone else for eggs and potatoes' (CP-TJ).

Fishing provided an opportunity for reserve members to participate in the broader market economy especially at times of the year when large catches could be taken. High returns for fishing effort were often achieved when seining for whitefish:

Did you ever see a seine? They used to throw it out along here ... One pull I've seen enough to fill a good-sized boat with whitefish ... Yes, pulling that is hard work. They'd wait for the wind. The wind blowing from the east. And the fish seemed to be in the harbour. I bought a seine for the boys, something for them to do when they're out of school. I supplied everything and would get half the fish. (CP-DK)

We would start in the spring by pulling a seine. We would watch the waters, cause you could never tell. We could see these ripples on the calm water, indicating that the fish are more than likely coming in. Then we would go out and pull a seine. It is a deep net, very heavy. We watched in the spring. If we only got a few whitefish we would watch and try again. They would run for one or two weeks. There was a lot of whitefish at that time of the year, mostly whitefish. We would seine night and day. There were people down on the beach cleaning the fish and loading up the boxes with ice, and we had trucks coming from Toronto, Detroit. I think we were selling fish at that time for about fifteen or twenty cents a pound. (CP-RJ)

A few reserve members also fished commercially on boats owned by off-reserve relatives or neighbouring non-native fishermen:

When I was fishing back in the thirties, I went across to Parry Sound and fished over there. A cousin of mine, who I was fishing for, used to run the fish back here and sell them in Wiarton. It's only fifty miles across there. (CP-FJ)

We fished right around here; and we went up as far as Tobermory, fished up that far ... In the thirties I fished for Hepburn, at Hope Bay. We used to fish up to Lions Head and up further. (CP-FJ)

When I interviewed Ainsley Solomon, a resident of the nursing home in Wiarton, and asked him how important fishing used to be, he stated: 'You could not eat without fishing' (CP-AS). His comment made more sense to me when I learned that there were local stores on the reserve where people could sell or trade fish. Within the local economy fish were, in effect, a form of currency. If one had no other means, one could buy other food with fish:

Tommy Jones had a store, and everyone had a bill there; and if you had a fish he would weigh it and take so much off your bill, so you could get food. (CP-EA)

We sold what we could catch, maybe three or four a day. We sold them at Tommy Jones's store across from the community centre. He was my mother's uncle – Uncle Tom. He was a fish buyer. Uncle Tom's store was at the crossroads between the community centre and the Anglican church. And Lennox Johnson had his store on the other corner. (CP-TJ)

Local ice was used by store keepers to preserve the fish that they traded for:

88   Cultures and Ecologies

> There were two or three ice houses they called them, and they put some of those fish in there for their own use or the use of the community. (CP-WA)

> I used to have an ice house for fish. I used to buy fish, near the dock. I cut a lot of ice for Tom Jones. You use a certain kind of saw. It looked like an ordinary cross-cut saw but it was made different, about six feet long. The ice used to be thick there in the harbour. (CP-VN)

Along with the two local stores run by reserve members, and some peripheral buying activity such as Vincent Nadjiwon describes above, there was another store where people could trade fish, run by Donald Cameron, a non-native. Donald Keeshig showed me the place where Cameron's store once stood, and recounted the economic activities carried on:

> That used to be our regular store. The guy's name was Donald Cameron. Very few white people would come here, back in the twenties and thirties. He used to play soccer with the kids. I was named Donald after him. That was a damn good house, the best one around, stone and plaster with a big veranda. Two of my sisters worked for him. He had no kids. He had a big barn. All this here was covered with rowboats. The Indians made them and he bought them and then he rented them back. If you owed him money you fished and he also rented you the boat. I was old enough to talk to him man to man and he told me how much it cost him to build it. It was quite lively here when Cameron did business with Indian people. (CP-DK)

Outside buyers took fish when they could be harvested in large numbers:

> Tom Jones bought them at his store over by the monument. And Lennox Johnston had another store. White fellows would come in to buy them. They would compete for the highest prices. But most kept to Tom and Lennox cause you never knew when the others would quit buying. We got seven or eight cents for a trout in the 1930s. Some time we would get a lot of fish at Rabbit Island in the fall, and we'd bring them across and take them to Wiarton by wagon. Finally the fellow from Wiarton came out here to buy them, mostly trout. (CP-GK)

> I just remember John McCauley from Wiarton. If the fish was over five pounds, he would cut the head off and then weigh it. The old people col-

lected the heads and brined them – salted them. Then they would soak the salt out and make soup for the winter. We got four cents a pound for fish. We had to catch a three-and-a-half-pound trout to buy a loaf of bread. (CP-VJ)[2]

As George Keeshig notes above, extra fish were taken to Wiarton by wagon. They were taken as well by boat or sleigh, and later by motorized vehicle. There are also accounts of people skating to Wiarton with fish to sell (DeMille 1971:215). Along with this trade value, fishing on the reserve had secondary economic benefits associated with boat building and equipment making (DeMille 1971:211–14).

Reserve members traded with people 'on the outside' informally and dealt with outside buyers when they had large surpluses, but they appear to have preferred dealing with buyers from their own community. They were suspicious of off-reserve buyers, as noted by George Keeshig and Verna Johnston. Donald Cameron was not a member of the reserve, but because his store was adjacent to the reserve he developed closer social and economic relationships with community members than did other buyers. Tom Jones is fondly remembered as a fish buyer. He was a community leader and a trusted member of the community. His store is remembered for its social as well as its economic functions: 'I worked at Tommy Jones's store. People used to come out and sit there and tell their stories' (CP-DK).

These various reflections on early-twentieth-century fishing activities at Cape Croker suggest that social relations were regarded during this period as important aspects of economic activity. The evidence of this is only anecdotal, but it matches insights derived from various anthropological studies – that social relations are not altogether separate from economic transactions. Even where social relations are obscured within market systems, forms of reciprocity, which more explicitly entail close social relations, are often maintained. In recollections of this era's fishing activities, economic and social references are intertwined. The descriptions provide examples of the importance of social relations as part of economic exchanges in the past. Recalling these examples gives them current value – gives them a potential role in the negotiation of current practices.

Tourist Fishing at Cape Croker

During the late 1930s and early 1940s Nawash became an active centre for tourist fishing. Native fishers were already engaged in rowboat trolling in the summer months, and during the 1930s they began taking out non-native tourists who were eager to land the area's renowned lake trout. 'A lot of people from the States came for trolling' (CP-AS).

By the early 1940s dozens of trolling boats set out daily from the reserve's government dock (DeMille 1971:215). Angus Elliott, who trolled for trout in two-person rowboats in the 1930s at Cape Croker, estimates that about fifty rowboats could be seen out on the water at one time (CP-AN). Others recall similar numbers: 'I was involved in the trolling some. I was farming then. But it was nothing ... There were about sixty rowboats along the shore there. And they used to go out and troll all day for a living' (CP-FJ). George Keeshig indicates that the period of the lake trout trolling fishery was a memorable time. He 'fished with Ely Chegahno in the trolling season, during the big boom' (CP-GK).

Tourist fishing continued into the war years: 'During wartime, to make a little extra money, a lot of ... the young people that didn't go into service ... there wasn't many people left here ... they used to take the tourists out ... trolling ... in their small boats ... So they made so much an hour for going out there ... They called it guiding. They were Indian guides, they called them' (CP-WA).

Nawash residents began to use outboard motorboats during the 1940s. Angus Elliott notes Peter Desjardin and George Jones as among the first to have motor boats (CP-AN). Ainsley Solomon mentions that he and the storekeeper, Lennox Johnston, also used gas boats during the trolling boom (CP-AS).

Peter Schmalz (1977:189; 1991:223) portrays this tourist fishery at Cape Croker as a last-gasp effort on the part of native people to gain a living from a fishery that was being rapidly destroyed by non-native commercial fishing. His depiction of reserve members as merely victims in a resource squeeze raises concerns that are worth considering, but it does not account for the initiative of reserve members who participated in this new economic opportunity, nor does it recognize potential impacts that natives had on fish stocks.

Some reserve members with whom I spoke were guarded about their involvement with tourists, noting the inconvenience of taking out people who were inexperienced: 'Yes, lots of tourists. For about twenty years. When we started we used to pull in a cotton line, then we decided on wire, galvanized wire. And we had big reels inside the boat. The tourists would tangle the wire all up, cause they didn't know how to handle it, so we would put plastic on, and when the fish were biting we'd pull the plastic tight' (CP-VN). Several also stated that they could make more money trolling on their own than they could taking tourists out:

> Some people turned out to be better trollers than others. The ones selling fish did better. If you were guiding, two or three a day was alright. (CP-WN)

> After I didn't take people out because I could catch more fish by myself. I got just one dollar an hour for trolling, but for one fish I could get two dollars. (CP-AS)

> Just after the war, if you got a dollar an hour, you were right up in the money. But it was nothing for these fellows out here to go and catch twenty fish a day. And each fish would be worth anywhere from three to five dollars. And if you caught twenty fish a day you were in the money. (CP-FJ).

Since so many community members did get involved in this tourist fishery, some of its advantages must have been apparent. Recalling tourist fishing as inconvenient may in part be a mechanism to maintain cultural boundaries. Like outside buyers, tourists were not as quickly trusted as local people were. This local/non-local dynamic still exists. However, people I spoke with about the tourist trolling fishery often recalled the community activities it entailed with considerable enthusiasm.

Fishing in general at Nawash during the first half of the century is recalled as an important part of the community's history. People remember the period prior to mid-century as an economically difficult time, but still it is viewed as a better time in some ways: 'People weren't as unhealthy as they are today. Because we ate those foods, we ate the fish and the wild meats' (CP-WA).

When local fishing history is recounted, it extends social links into the past. The places where people fished are closely associated with the people who fished there:

> I used to help my brother-in-law fish at Benjamin's Point, lifting nets. There were a lot of fishermen. Bob Nadjiwon had a camp at Benjamin's Point. That was his livelihood. (CP-GK)

> Uncle Willy had a fishing camp down at Prairie Point and they would stay right down there when the season was on. In 1940 ... We used to go down and catch enough fish for our personal use. (CP-TJ)

Family connections and broader social structures are often central themes in recollections of past fishing activities:

> I learned to tie my own nets when I started. My dad taught me everything. We caught a lot of lake trout. Today you can get out there in fifteen minutes, when it used to take us two and a half hours to row out there. (CP-EA)

> The old people told us where to fish. (CP-VN).

> I fished with my father and quit when he died, but then fished with my partner Harvey Ashkewe for one fall season. (CP-R1)

> We come from a strong fishing family. My dad was of that generation where fishing was a mainstay of his livelihood, and as a boy he used to accompany his dad and uncles fishing in the nearby waters. (CP-RA)

> Everyone had a little camp there, and would watch the sky at night. If we saw a cloud with a big line across it we knew there was a wind coming. Just cloudy with a low ceiling was all right. A line is an indication of high pressure. Or they would watch the sunset. The older fellows could tell if there would be a storm just by the atmosphere. (CP-RJ)

Summer fishing camps, which were set up at various reserve locations around the cape, were recalled with particular fondness as places where families and relatives gathered and participated in a common activity. The nostalgic recollection of summer fishing camps might be seen as not much different from a typically Canadian appreciation of past summer holidays. But it may also show a connection to traditional native patterns of seasonal resource harvesting, through which social ties were established and maintained, and during which useful knowledge was shared.

Fishing during this era is also remembered in connection with tensions over the enforcement of fishing restrictions. Native fishery conflicts continued to surface during the first half of the 1900s. The fishing-licence system was seen as restricting native fishing opportunities, and some resisted such restrictions. In 1913 Nawash boats were confiscated for fishing out of season (Schmalz 1991:222).

Seines were occasionally used even though they were forbidden by regulations from outside. And Nawash members occasionally set gill nets in areas that were off-limits to natives at the time:

We used to fish in Colpoys illegally, set four or five nets for trout when they spawn on points in shallow water – shoals. Three or four boats fished there but hardly went off the reserve, except for those with nerve. We set nets when it was getting dark; then we slept in the woods. Game wardens had searchlights. We'd drag the boats right into the bush. Then we would lift the nets on the way back – get back by daylight. That was before we knew that those were our waters ... The Martin boys got picked up once and got put in jail. They took everything, the boat, nets ... MNR must have known it was our water but wanted to scare us. Wardens used to pretty well hunt the Indians ... We would paint the boats grey so they did not see us and we put grease on the oar – had to be quiet when setting corks. Couldn't smoke or they would see you. (CP-R4)

This era's fishing restrictions are remembered in connection with broader negative relations with people from the outside. Ross Waukey recounted times when he went into Wiarton with the reserve's brass band and was treated poorly by some non-natives (CP-R5). He noted that these experiences were still with him. Outsiders who enforced fishing rules on natives were no doubt regarded with suspicion, as were other outsiders who assumed superiority over native people:

They would take everything if we got caught. (CP-R1)

We caught just enough suckers to last you. Because we were always afraid of white people. If they'd catch us ... if we'd get too much they would put us in jail. That's what my grandmother used to tell us. And we were never let to catch more than we need.' (CP-PC).

Fishing at Saugeen

At Saugeen, fishing activity was greatly reduced by the beginning of the twentieth century. Hunting and trapping is remembered as the main local resource-use activity:

No, they didn't talk much about fishing. Our dad was a hunter, mostly for deer. We got raised on that when we were kids in the forties. (SG-EM)

No, I don't remember anything about fishing. My parents used to hunt ... beaver ... *amik*. Beaver are still around over here. They hunted rabbit, groundhog, porcupine, deer, raccoon ... *asibim* ... deer is *wawashgesh* ... and muskrat ... *shashko* ... partridges ... *pne* ... They are still around. They are just like a chicken. We would have one per person ... They sold furs in Owen Sound ... all kinds of furs ... muskrat, weasel, minks. (SG-RA)

The Saugeen reserve has never had a dock suitable for fishing boats, and only a few people from Saugeen fished as a main occupation during the 1920s, 1930s, and 1940s. They worked out of the nearby Southampton docks and were thereby in close contact with other fishing operators. Saugeen community members have only vague memories of pre-war fishing activities:

The only one I knew that was fishing was ... Bill Johnston. He used to work on a boat. (SG-EK)

There has always been someone working at it ... I remember my father talking about people fishing. (SG-CS)

Maybe eight, ten, or twelve worked on boats. (SG-LK)

I don't know much about fishing, but my mother and father told me some. My father worked on fishing boats out at Southampton. He would get up at two a.m. to go to Southampton on bicycle. (SG-LK)

A couple of uncles used nets ... There was a group of people that used to fish. A boat used to sit at Ruth Roote's fathers place. In the thirties they used it. (SG-AS)

Chief Mel Roote (1998, pers. comm.) suggested that for a time his father, Isaac Roote, was one of the few left at Saugeen who still fished independently. Ruth Roote recalls an older member of the family who did a lot of fishing, but it is unclear whether he worked on his own or was employed on a non-native fishing boat, as her husband later was: 'My husband was a born fishermen. His grandfather used to fish. He took after his grandfather – learned to fix nets from him. His grandfather was James Roote. He fished out of Southampton in the twenties and thirties' (SG-RR).

It appears that apart from those who found work on non-native fishing boats, fishing was disappearing as a primary occupational option for Saugeen community members during the first half of the century; however, fishing did continue on a more informal scale:

Times changed and along the way fishing was dropped except for angling. (SG-AS)

My father didn't fish, outside of a little line fishing – a lot did that. And in the spring and fall there is a traditional way of fishing with the spear. (SG-CS)

We just fished the river ... People waited for the break-up and then the suckers would come in. That was a treat – to get the first suckers. Who would think of eating those things now? ... My brother made his own spear. He used to go back to Stoney Creek ... When I was a child they used dip nets – a square net – and they would lower it into the river and get suckers and the odd steelhead ... They used to smoke the suckers to preserve them. I remember when I was a kid I used to see them hanging on the clothes line to be smoked and dried ... My dad used to have a regular smoke house for meat and he smoked the fish in it. He built it himself. My dad was a farmer, I guess you would say – had pigs, cattle, horses, chickens, even geese. (SG-EK)

When we were kids we fished with spears. We also caught smelt ... just enough for dinner. We fished at Stoney Creek ... We used to spear spring rainbow, sometimes suckers. We used to eat the suckers too. They have a lot of bones. We'd boil them. (SG-EM)

I have taken fish with a spear, when I was ten or twelve years old. We would walk to the lake, following the creek up and down, hoping to scare up a trout. (SG-LK)

The limited amount of involvement in fishing by Saugeen reserve members may reflect the impact of fishing restrictions imposed on them during earlier decades. It also suggests that the economic benefits of whatever fishing options remained were overshadowed by other economic opportunities that existed because of the reserve's close proximity to Southampton and other towns.

Fish taken from the Saugeen River and small streams had some importance as a food source, and some local fishing continued, especially during spawning seasons. Apart from this, the fisheries here appear to have been less significant for reserve members during the first half of the century than they were in previous decades.

Mid-Century and Beyond

The lake trout went away so fast; we never really knew why they disappeared. (CP-VJ)

Mid-Century Fisheries Depletions

There are indications of serious stock depletions around the peninsula before the middle of the twentieth century, most notably affecting sturgeon at the beginning of the century. But the most dramatic devastations occurred at about mid-century. During the early 1950s herring stocks dropped nearly to the point of extinction (Spangler and Peters 1995:114), and a less dramatic, but also serious, drop in whitefish stocks followed (Wyonch 1985:23). But most notable was the almost complete loss of indigenous lake trout.

Prior to mid-century the indigenous lake trout was a major species within Lake Huron's aquatic ecosystem. It was prized by the peninsula's commercial and recreational fishers alike. By 1936 significant stock declines had become noticeable, and numbers continued to diminish through the 1940s (Wyonch 1985:20; Spangler and Peters 1995:112–14). By the mid-1950s the lake trout had all but disappeared. Currently, indigenous lake trout stocks exist precariously at only three isolated locations on Lake Huron, none of them around the peninsula.[3]

Pollution may have been a factor in mid-century depletions of fishstock, as there was considerable industrial activity during this time at some Lake Huron port cities. Sewage run-off may have already become more detrimental to the water systems than industrial waste by mid-century, as it has been since then (see Barry 1978:158). One of the people I interviewed suggested that garbage from nearby towns was regularly dumped from barges into deep water (CP-RJ). Logging debris on Lake Huron rivers might also have been detrimental to fish spawning. But water-habitat quality is rarely regarded as a main cause of mid-century fish depletions.

Overfishing is suspected as a main cause of these depletions, but the most frequently cited explanation is that the lake trout were vulnerable to the sea lamprey, which made inroads into the lakes after expansion of the Welland Canal in 1932 (Fox 1952:120; McLeod 1969:4; Barry 1978:111; Gateman 1982:38). Another suspected intruder is the Atlantic smelt, which may compete with trout for food and may even have toxic effects when eaten by trout (Wyonch 1985:22–4).

As with previous eras, there are no precise harvest figures available with which to accurately assess the impact of overfishing on fish stocks leading up to mid-century, but there are rough estimates (e.g., McLeod 1969:5). James Barry's (1978:110) general picture of Georgian Bay's fish harvests indicates that figures for the main commercial stock harvest fluctuated between two and seven million pounds annually for about eighty years, and then plummeted at mid-century to under one hundred thousand pounds. They rebounded in following decades, but only to a small fraction of pre-war levels. Figures for all of Lake Huron published by the Great Lakes Fishery Commission (1995a:13, 1995b:18) suggest that during the first half of the century annual harvests of all species averaged about twenty million pounds, with a drastic decline beginning around 1940.

There is little doubt that the quantities of fish harvested placed considerable pressure on particular stocks. G.R. Spangler and J.H. Peters (1995:112) suggest that Lake Huron maximum commercial catches for all species were reached by 1915, and that subsequent technological innovations did not provide access to new resources, but instead allowed for increasingly efficient harvesting of existing target stocks. Vincent Elliott notes various mid-century innovations:

> It was not until the 1950s that scientific fishing was done with depth recorders. Ken McLay got a maximum-minimum thermometer from a malting company and started to record temperatures. He found that trout like about 50 degrees Fahrenheit or colder best and whitefish like 54 degrees Fahrenheit. Later the fishermen used Loran C equipment ... to locate their nets ... Later plastic corks were used. The amount of nets put out each day was measured in 'boxes.' A net-box would hold about three nets of 325 ft. each. The first nets were only about 14 meshes (6 feet) deep but by 1940 they were making meshes of about 36 meshes deep and by 1950 some nets were 60 meshes (20 feet) deep ... After about 1950 when all-nylon nets were used the nets could be left in the boxes, and the big drying reels along the shores fell into disrepair. (1987:37–9)

By 1950 nylon nets that were about three times as efficient as cotton ones were commonly used, as were mechanical net lifters (Barry 1978:110).

Commercial fishing is primarily implicated when overfishing is considered as a factor in the depletion of the lake trout. However, recreational fishing also exerted pressure on particular stocks. The boom in tourist fishing on the peninsula, in which both native and non-native fishers participated, coincides with stock depletions. Cathy Wyonch (1985:20) notes a marked increase in sport fishing during the 1930s, when lake trout numbers were becoming a concern for commercial fishers.

Competition between commercial and recreational fishing groups is noted prior to the 1930s. In 1928 recreational fishing representatives requested that commercial fishers only be allowed outside a three-mile limit so they would not harvest stocks along the shore (Wyonch 1985:20). As with the commercial fishery, there are no detailed catch figures by which to assess the impacts of pre-war recreational fishing.

The rapid spread of the sea lamprey is highlighted in most non-native explanations of the lake trout's demise. Overfishing is typically regarded as merely a secondary factor. However, the assessments made by most of the native fishers on the peninsula invert the emphasis – they see the lamprey's impact as only part of the picture:

The lamprey weren't that bad. (CP-VN)

I don't think it was so much the eels. They over-fished them. (SG-EK)

At one time lake trout were indigenous, but the lamprey took care of that ... so they say. But it was overfishing. (SG-TM)

The MNR says the lamprey was a major cause in wiping out the trout. So you would think that it would be mostly trout that you would see them on, but they are on all the fish – whitefish, you even see wounds on suckers. (CP-BJ)

There was quite an abundance of lake trout at one time. And I guess people never ever thought of them disappearing. And somewhere, between the commercial fishermen and other fishermen ... and pollution took the weaker fish ... they fished them out to the last one. They weren't satisfied ... the trout were the first to go. Then the herring went ... Lamprey had something to do with it, no doubt ... But those lampreys weren't a problem till the trout got down in numbers. They try to tell me that the lamprey came from the ocean. Well, maybe it did or maybe it didn't. But the lamprey was always here in the Great Lakes. When the lake trout were in abundance, they probably kept the lamprey population down, because the lake trout is quite a predator. He will eat snakes and all kinds of stuff like that. So without a doubt he kept the lamprey population down. And then when he got down in population, why, then the lampreys came up with nothing to stop it. So he took the rest of the trout, or whatever he could. (CP-FJ)

Lamprey were always here. No doubt, a lot of them came in the canals, but the species was always here. When I was a kid we caught racers (nothing but skin and bone), and you could see a scar where the fish had been bit by an eel of some kind – so that's what makes me think that the lamprey was always here ... If one of the lampreys stuck to a fish, another fish would come along and eat the lamprey. That way they kept the species from running out. But when the lake trout got down and the lamprey increased, they didn't have a hope. (CP-PT-FJ)

Native community members link questions about mid-century fisheries depletions to current fisheries issues because of current accusations that natives are depleting the resources, which I discuss in a following chapter. They are defensive about their community's possible role in local stock declines during the 1950s:

We caught a lot of lake trout. Toward the end of the fifties they were all fished out. When we used rowboats there were lots, but the whiteman had more nets, five hundred yards, and gas-powered boats and lifters. They fished close to here and caught ten to fifteen boxes a day while we were getting three to four boxes with our gill nets. That's how they were fished out ... They fished it out with bigger nets, thousands of yards of net ... You just need little boats, not the big fish tugs. (CP-EA)

Like Earl Akiwenzie, many people on the reserve equate native fishing with smaller-scale fishing and see non-native operations as more technologically advanced, and thereby more detrimental to fish stocks: 'When commercial fishing got going after the war I noticed the fish going. It wasn't Indians that caught the most. Just lately, since the court decision we are taking more' (CP-R2).

When I was interviewing Vincent Nadjiwon at an old-age home in Wiarton, a non-native fellow from Hope Bay, a small community near the reserve, came into the sitting room. When he realized that I was interested in the history of the fisheries he immediately offered an opinion on the mid-century depletions of local stocks, suggesting that they occurred because big boats out of Lions Head were setting thousands of yards of nets in the 1930s.

To provide a realistic assessment of local stocks in the decades during and just after the war, the potential impact of native fishing activities should be considered. A few native fishers were already using powered boats and net lifters, as noted earlier. Some were also working on non-native commercial boats that were harvesting large quantities of fish. And some of the spawning run harvests at Nawash were substantial. Still, the impact of native involvement was no doubt very small compared with overall commercial and recreational fishing efforts. Winona Arriaga is generous in her evaluation of this: 'When I hear the arguments about fishing, if anyone depleted the fishing of lake trout ... I would say it was on both sides. We got our fish, and everybody else got their fish' (CP-WA).

There was a great deal of confusion in the commercial industry as to the causes of the decline in lake trout (Wyonch 1985:21). The crisis led to an alliance between the government and the fishing industry (Fox 1952:120). In 1943 the Ontario Federation of Commercial Fishermen was formed, and a representative from the Lake Huron/Georgian Bay Fishermen's Association became its vice-president (Wyonch 1985:21). At the federation's insistence, the government's fisheries department agreed to stock millions of trout fingerlings, but lake trout continued to decline in Lake Huron, Georgian Bay, and the North Channel at Manitoulin Island. Tensions between the fisheries department and commercial fishers rose: fishermen claimed that the department was not planting enough fish, and the department blamed fishermen for overfishing and not observing closed seasons (Wyonch 1985:21).

Fish had long been stocked around the peninsula. Norman McLeod (1969:148–51) notes that in 1909 a hatchery at Wiarton planted fourteen and a half million fingerlings. Around mid-century a major effort was made to improve the effectiveness of fish-stocking techniques, and otherwise improve fish habitat.

New fisheries research (especially work done by Harkness, cited in Richardson 1974:69, 113) has improved ways of recognizing the suitability of particular streams as trout habitat. Habitat clean-up and restoration projects were engaged by newly formed organizations such as the Saugeen Valley Conservation Authority (McLeod 1969:116; Richardson 1974:70). Fish ladders were built to provide access for fish to spawning beds (Richardson 1974:70–3), and new dams aimed at creating ideal fish and wildlife habitats were constructed (McLeod 1969:119;

Richardson 1974:45–9). Efforts to deal with stock depletions continue today.

Economic Shifts on the Reserves

> Everything changed after the Second World War here ... everything. (CP-WA)

The mid-century depletions of fish stocks affected native community members as well, and their responses to diminishing fisheries opportunities were intertwined with broader social changes. Schmalz (1977:210) suggests that the Nawash community deteriorated because of lost mid-century fishing opportunities; however, various social and economic shifts were already under way, and it is difficult to discern the specific impact of declining stocks on the reserve communities. Stock depletions no doubt had some consequences:

> Lake trout left us ... Well, the herring left, that's what they eat. They disappeared too. Big herring and small ones. That's when I quit fishing. (CP-VN)

> People were pulling their boats up on the shore and just leaving them. I remember this Lennox Johnson used to have a couple of gas-driven boats down at the dock, and he had taken them out of the water and not put them back in. They sat in behind his little store and they rotted there. (CP-TJ)

Since the whitefish were not drastically reduced, there were still gill-netting opportunities when the trout were declining. But the recently expanded trolling fishery at Nawash was focused on lake trout, and many who were involved in this rapidly diminishing fishery looked to different livelihoods.

Economic opportunities outside the community were becoming increasingly apparent, especially for reserve members who made social contacts and received training through participation in the military. Some tried fishing for a while just after the war, but they eventually opted for other work:

> He bought a motorboat when he returned. But lake trout were going, we didn't get any lake trout, and it wasn't too good then, so he went to work out. (CP-WA)

I joined up because there was no other way to make money ... After the war everyone had money and got boats ... there were no fish left. (CP-AS)

After the war I went to the Department of Veterans Affairs and they set us up with a new set of nets, and I went out and paid for them that first year, but the fishing was really bad. It took all fall to pay off the nets. It was about five hundred dollars. That would be about five thousand dollars now. We just pulled them up and set them aside and went out looking for work. (CP-RJ)

In the decades after the war, native fishing activity at Nawash reached its lowest levels. Most interviewees seemed reluctant to depict this decline as a complete collapse, perhaps because of concerns about the political implications of admitting a discontinuity in reliance on the fishery. But it appears that very few continued to pursue fishing as a main economic activity:

They never quit fishing as far as that goes. They just didn't do it as big. Maybe the fish weren't there; I don't know. But they never gave up fishing. (CP-WA)

Maybe the younger ones went off the reserve to work more after the war, but not my two husbands anyway. In 1965 or '67 my second husband got a custodian job, looking after the school, and that's when he quit fishing ... He still had one net he was setting ... The odd time if we wanted to have some fish he would go. (CP-PC)

I was the only fisherman at one time on Cape Croker. It was right down but nothing else to do. In one week you were lucky to get one hundred pounds. (CP-WN)

While fishing all but disappeared, farming, which had become a main occupation prior to the war, seems to have collapsed even more completely. Since fishing provided a supplemental income for some farmers, the fisheries depletions could have played a role in the abandonment of farming. Another factor was likely more central to this shift: jobs that were increasingly available on the outside began to appear more attractive than subsistence farming, which provided only a meagre living even when combined with seasonal fishing. Beginning in the 1960s some took work at a nearby nuclear plant, which employed a large workforce (CP-DK), and a variety of other outside jobs were also taken (CP-R5).

At Saugeen fishing was already a greatly diminished occupation prior to mid-century. Here too the availability of off-reserve work was likely a factor in reduced fishing involvement. Some natives had already taken factory jobs in nearby towns, and after the war the trend toward off-reserve jobs continued. But some followed in the footsteps of those who worked on commercial fishing boats:

My husband worked on fishing boats out of Southampton, and Lake Erie – a place called Erieau, near Blenheim, Ontario. He started when he came back from the war overseas, in 1946, until he retired at sixty-five – almost twenty years ... We moved down to Lake Erie ... He worked on a boat out of Southampton, and a boat at Tobermory; and on the North Shore at a place called Britt. (SG-RR)

Commercial fishing was not an easy job, but it was a living:

I was a commercial fisherman ... worked on tugs for ten years ... Southampton, Meaford, and on Erieau, near Blenheim – mostly perch there. On Huron we fished chubs (tullibees) and white fish ... five hundred pounds of whitefish a day was a good catch ... Chubs went for smokers ... There was a little smoke operation here ... There seemed to be a dollar if you went after it. Sometimes we left Southampton at two-thirty in the morning and got back at eight at night. We'd see the sun come out of the water in the east and watch it set in the west the same day ... You needed weather, fish, and a market. Something would go wrong. One spring I was fishing on Lake Erie ... We were getting seventeen cents a pound for perch. We got lots, but by the time we got back to the dock, the price went down to three cents. That ended my fishing that spring. I could not support my family and work down there. (SG-WK)

They just had commercial fishing or factory work. It's better than factory work. (SG-TM)

More broadly, the number of fisheries workers around the peninsula dropped significantly at mid-century, and many who remained devoted less time during the year to fishing (Barry 1978:111). The number of fishing tugs operating out of the peninsula's harbours has fluctuated since 1950, according to harvesting opportunities (David Loftus 1996, pers. comm.). Greater efforts have been made to record commercial fishing harvests around the peninsula in the last five decades, especially since the inception of a quota system in 1984; however, the complete picture is certainly far from clear. Since the sharp mid-century stock declines the fisheries around the peninsula have supported only about ten or fifteen small commercial fishing boats at the best of times (each employing two or three people). Tobermory, once a thriving fishing port, had less than a handful of full-time fisherfolk remaining by the mid-1980s (Wyonch 1985:23). In the early 1990s, after the Fairgrieve decision, the MNR began buying back quotas, which further diminished the number of commercial non-native fishers on the peninsula. By the late 1990s there were no more licensed commercial non-native fishers on the peninsula.

While commercial fishing has been declining, recreational fishing has increased around the peninsula. Though recreational fishing is by no means the main focus of the peninsula's tourist activities, it is a significant part of it. Anglers are especially active during annual fishing derbies hosted by local sporting associations. In keeping with their emergence as a vital fishery sector, the sport-fishing industry is increasingly involved in fisheries management issues. This parallels the more assertive role that natives have recently taken with regard to the peninsula's fisheries. The peninsula's current fishing conflict is in large part a clash between these two groups, who have emerged as the main players in the local fishery.

Within this competition for resources, the focus is on group distinctions that serve as the basis for asserting group rights. The historical interdependence of native and non-native fishing activities and the cooperation that, along with tension and conflict, was part of this relationship are only rarely remembered.

6 'Conservation'

Conservation has become a focus of attention in the peninsula's fishing conflict. Both advocates and opponents of native fishing rights support their positions through appeals for appropriate conservation measures. Conservation also has political implications that stem from the Sparrow ruling, which puts native fishing ahead of non-native commercial and recreational activities but establishes conservation of fish stocks as the first priority.

The concept of 'conservation' has abstract philosophical dimensions as well as real-world implications: its ambiguities contribute to the confusion that surrounds the peninsula's fishing conflict. A better understanding of the range of meanings it encompasses for the various interests may contribute to a resolution of the conflict.

Using an ethnoecological framework, I attempt to clarify conservation's range of meanings and the implications of those meanings. I explore the various notions of conservation that are held among particular cultural groups, and also among more specific segments within groups.

I begin by examining two sets of meanings that are increasingly distinguished in environmentalist discourse: anthropocentrism and ecocentrism. I then use these sets of meanings in analysing assumptions and positions held by environmental organizations, government fishery regulators, and sport-fishing association leaders. Throughout, I explore how ideas about conservation link with notions about native ecological relations.

Ecological Principles: Anthropocentrism and Ecocentrism

From an anthropological perspective, the concept of 'conservation' can be seen as historical and cultural construct. It is most commonly associated with efforts to mitigate the negative environmental impacts of increased human activity that have occurred in industrializing and modernizing countries over the last century or more. We often use the term 'conservation,' and associated concepts such as 'environmental sustainability,' with reference to situations involving other ('non-Western,' for lack of a better word) cultural groups, but its meanings may not translate directly outside of the cultural settings in which this notion came into being. Further ambiguity arises from the fact that conservation can have a range of different meanings within a particular cultural setting. This multiplicity can be seen in mainstream 'Western' contexts.

A central debate in current environmentalist literature concerns the relative strengths and weaknesses of two approaches to conservation: anthropocentrism and ecocentrism (see, for example, Pepper 1993; Eckersley 1992). Anthropocentric conservation (a human-centred perspective) is founded on instrumental value and is typified by the American conservationist movement that began around the mid-1800s (Worster 1977); here, resources are viewed in terms of how they can best fulfil human needs. This 'classic conservationism' has much in common with a more recent 'wise use' approach. It is a kind of utilitarianism, as it embodies the ideal of the greatest good for the greatest number of people.

Ecocentrism (an ecosystem or environment-centred perspective) is premised on intrinsic, rather than instrumental, value. Intrinsic value is the worth something has in and of itself, apart from human purposes. Ecocentrism is typified by the 'preservationist' approach, which is often traced back to John Muir, the nineteenth-century American poet/naturalist and founder of the Sierra Club. In broad usage, the term 'conservation' may include anthropocentric and ecocentric approaches, but according to the terms of this environmental debate, 'conservation' is anthropocentric while 'preservation' is ecocentric. Muir rejected the conservationist focus on productive exploitation of resources and envisioned ecological relations that transcend human interest.[1]

A revised approach to resource management articulated by Aldo Leopold is a commonly cited example of the ecocentric perspective. Leopold's lifelong career in wildlife management parallels changing notions about conservation in North America during the past century. In the early 1900s he championed the ideals of efficiency and productivity, and wrote the standard American wildlife management text

(1933) in the classic conservationist style. Leopold's 'land ethic' ([1949]1989:201–26; see also Worster 1977:205–12) marks a shift from conservationist to preservationist principles. He envisions a historical progression of moral obligation that has begun to include plants and animals, and even the land, water, and air. The 'land ethic' proposes that people become 'members' of the 'biotic community,' rather than resource 'conquerors' as assumed in the classic conservationist approach.

Writers who follow Leopold's ecocentric vision see recognition of nature's intrinsic value as key to developing appropriate environmental relations (e.g., Taylor 1986; Callicott 1989, 1993; DesJardin 1993; Griffin 1993). But the notion of intrinsic value is problematic where it implies that the interests of the ecosystem or any non-human member can be regarded above or altogether apart from human interests. One can envision a moral or social bond with the environment wherein non-humans are given human values; but where decisions about conservation or preservation are made, they are inevitably made by humans, in social, cultural, and political contexts (see Eckersley 1992:61–5).

Without some human instrumental priorities there is no basis for deciding in particular cases which species might receive consideration. Ecocentrism, in this eco-egalitarian light, might protect disease-carrying insects and perhaps even viruses. Some 'deep ecologists' have in fact proposed that we devote less effort to countering epidemics, famines, and refugee disasters, because these are the ecosystem's way of dealing with human overpopulation (see Merchant 1992:175). Some writers suggest that the willingness to sacrifice people for the greater good of the ecosystem is a sort of environmental fascism (e.g., Regan 1983, cited in DesJardin 1993:201–2). Ecocentrism's focus away from human affairs is also rejected by socially conscious eco-feminists, who distrust the dissipation of unique female perspectives in deep ecology's submission to the ungendered eco-community (e.g., Spretnack 1993).

A related problem with the ecocentric position is that it often assumes a stark separation between 'human' and 'natural' domains. Nature is imagined as that which is untouched by humans – by culture. But this view is itself constructed in social, cultural, and political contexts – by people. Where they adopt the view of wilderness as untouched by humans, ecocentrics are suspected of being environmental elitists, hoping to 'preserve' nature to suit their own particular lifestyles and leisure activities.

Given such problems, environmentalist writers present various alternatives to ecocentrism. David Pepper (1993) suggests an explicitly anthropocentric approach. He objects especially to ecocentrism's political naivety, pointing out that without a direct focus on the human interests underlying resource uses, we cannot hope to counter environmental resource abuses. Ecocentrics, in return, point to the ecological destruction that has resulted when governments, be they capitalist, socialist, or other, have engaged efficiently organized anthropocentric efforts to benefit their citizens.

When anthropocentrism is defined in classic conservationist terms, or as all past efforts aimed at benefiting people through resource extraction, its lack of environmental friendliness is obvious, and ecocentrism becomes a hopeful alternative. But given attention to the historical contexts in which these two approaches were constructed, ecocentrism and recent anthropocentric perspectives, such as Pepper presents, are not necessarily in total opposition. They have both provided important insights into the limits of our ecological relations.

Current anthropocentric approaches and the anthropocentrism of classic conservationism were developed in different historical contexts. Ecocentrism, especially as articulated by Leopold, has served as a valid warning against the short-sightedness of classic conservationism. But recent anthropocentrism has also made important contributions by pointing to the need to re-evaluate ecocentric assumptions along with earlier anthropocentric ones.

In debates on environmental ethics, ecocentric and anthropocentric approaches are typically seen as conflicting: the former is focused on environmental well-being and the latter on social benefits. But when viewed as more than timeless abstract concepts, when seen in historical sequence, the two can be regarded as part of the same effort to find solutions to problematic aspects of society's environmental relations.

From an ecocentric perspective informed by recent anthropocentric critiques, society and nature can be understood as part of the same dialectical relationship: human and environmental well-being are ultimately interconnected. In the long term, instrumental and intrinsic values are not so different. When thinking about conservation, in the context of the fishing conflict or elsewhere, it seems reasonable to consider issues in both ecological and social contexts.

While we can see these two approaches as historically interconnected in a potentially positive way, we can also explore how each is used to support the agendas of particular groups.

Environmentalism

Alliances between native groups and environmentalists can benefit all sides. Especially in western Canada, the value of joining forces in activist causes is increasingly evident. Such cooperation has occurred on the Saugeen-Bruce Peninsula as well. For example, environmental organizations and native representatives worked together in hopes of curtailing a construction project on an island adjacent to Nawash (Darlene Johnston 1996, pers. comm.). Typically, preservationist approaches are at the forefront of these shared efforts. A potential difficulty for native groups in these situations is that where ecocentric notions of conservation are highlighted, social dimensions can be obscured.

It is not uncommon for people interested in environmental well-being to associate native people with the alternative ecological relationships they envision – as 'ecological Indians' (Krech 1999). Images of native people living harmoniously with nature are easily linked to Leopold's view of eco-communities. The ecological Indian has thereby become something of a spiritual leader for many environmentalists (see Jacobs 1980:57–8; Vescey 1980:35–6; Wilson 1991:318).[2] Though this image serves well in critiques of dangerous environmental practices within the broader society, environmentalists may be unintentionally contributing to problematic notions about native people and their ecological relations.

Jennifer Reid (1995) suggests that settler societies in Canada have produced images of aboriginal people that suit their own imported ideological assumptions, and ignore already existing local conditions and histories. Images of 'noble savages' who just need to be taught civilized ways, along with more derogatory images, can be produced as part of this process. Reid suggests that the potential for 'discovering' interesting culturally interactive experiences, and building integrative social structures, is diminished where such images are simplistically adopted.

Not everything about early contact relations can be explained with reference to ideological factors, but connections between a group's ideological assumptions and their 'images of the other' should be kept in mind when trying to understand native people's environmental relations.

In more modern contexts, Eva Mackey (2002) examines how images of native people are shaped in Canada today, in conjunction with ongoing efforts to establish national identity: they play roles in the narratives of nationhood we tell ourselves. Many writers analyse identity politics as a process of increased domination and oppression, as ideological control. Mackey's work is exceptional in its attention to the more complex and often ambiguous ways that cultural images are produced and employed within Canada's nation-building project. Images and assumptions are engaged strategically at government program and policy levels. They are also reproduced at various local levels, as part of 'community' celebrations and other activities. In both cases, assumed cultural values and traits can be selectively highlighted to suit political purposes.

Canada provides an especially interesting example of cultural politics, given that tolerance of cultural difference has itself become an assumed feature of our historically constructed national identity. This allows us to pursue ways to equitably accommodate cultural diversity, but we may also refer to this core value in ways that ignore or rationalize existing inequalities.

Both environmentalists and native groups can benefit by combining their efforts, but if indigenous people are seen only in ecocentric contexts, such alliances are limited.

In recent global documents, indigenous people's environmental relations are given attention as potential models of ecological sustainability. The Bruntland Report promotes the inclusion of indigenous peoples' traditional environmental knowledge in international development projects: this could improve the plight of people in developing countries and at the same time reduce stress on the environment (see Jull 1991:452; Miller 1991:447–67).[3] Members of the 1992 Earth Summit restated the Brundtland Report's theme of working to improve both social and ecological conditions through attention to traditional environmental relations. Some ecocentric environmentalists criticized the Earth Summit resolution because its inclusion of human concerns appeared to threaten their vision of ecological well-being (see Miller 1991:78; Pepper 1993:27).

Ecocentric environmentalism also has local implications for agreements on management of the Saugeen-Bruce Peninsula's fisheries. Both the Federation of Ontario Naturalists (FON) and the World Wildlife Fund (WWF) of Canada released discussion papers concerning native resource rights in Ontario following the Sparrow ruling. Conservation is defined in these papers in ecocentric terms. The FON paper, entitled 'Putting Nature First' (1993), explicitly acclaims Muir's preservationist approach, and highlights the welfare of an other-than-human nature in its list of conservation principles. The WWF mission statement likewise indicates an ecocentric focus. It proposes 'conservation of the planet's biodiversity by ... ensuring that the use of ... resources is sustainable ... for the benefit of all life on Earth' (1993:39). This articulation of conservation concerns could imply an instrumental use of resources, but the last phrase, 'for the benefit of all life on Earth,' tips it toward ecocentrism. This phrase is an obvious reworking of the utilitarian motto, 'For the benefit of all people.'

Both naturalist organizations suggest that they share a conservation ethic with aboriginal peoples (WWF 1993:3; FON 1993:25), and both see an opportunity to pursue common interests, such as slowing the spread of urbanization. But in these documents, neither the WWF nor the FON downplay the discontinuity between their goal of protecting nature from human intrusions and native people's assertions of rights to harvest resources without interference.

The preservationist definition of conservation is central to these position papers and their warning against human impact on the natural world. Where native people are envisioned as separate from the dominant society, their environmental relations can be viewed as an alternative to society's destructive tendencies. But if native people step out of the ecocentric community, for example, by using fishing technologies that are not regarded as traditional, they are no longer part of the natural world: they are members of the utilitarian society and part of the problem.

During the summer of 1995, members of Greenpeace, the international environmental organization, came to the peninsula by boat to hear native people's views on fishing issues. A statement made at the time by Greenpeace representative Jeanne Moffat seems to support native positions: 'Aboriginal culture has a long tradition which respects the intricate balance of all living things and the fact that every part of nature has an intrinsic value outside of its economic potential. This approach is essential to the survival of the planet' (*Bruce Peninsula Press* late September 1995:9). Most people in the native communities were not as enthusiastic as I expected about the visit from these environmentalists. Their guarded response is perhaps linked to the cautious assessment of outsiders that is typical here. But it may also reflect an awareness that the view of native life environmentalists supported does not represent the full range of native interests in the peninsula's fisheries.

Given the wide press coverage that fisheries-conservation issues received after their visit, Greenpeace representatives were successful in their efforts to bring attention to the ecological dangers of human-resource-use activities, which is the forte of ecocentric environmentalism – an important contribution. But their ecocentric perspective may have limited their concern about the complex social realities that permeate environmental conservation and resource-management issues on the peninsula.

Government Fisheries Management

Notions about conservation play a role in how native fishing rights accord with government approaches to fisheries management. While there has been a recent shift toward concerns for the 'ecosystem' in fisheries management, this shift could have both positive and negative implications for the recognition of native fishing rights.

Much of the resentment surrounding the current conflict is linked to uncertainty over how a balance can be achieved between native fishing rights and public rights, and how this balance can be reflected in government policies and regulations. As noted with regard to fishing conflicts during the 1800s, a lack of clarity about native rights has long been evident in government decisions about access to the peninsula's fisheries.

Soon after the colonial government introduced the 1857 Fishery Act 'conservation principles ... became paramount' (Hansen 1991:1). In 1866, the federal Fisheries Branch took over the responsibility of dealing with native fishing issues from the Indian Department (Lytwyn 1990:23), thereby linking the issues of native rights and fisheries conservation.

Assumptions about what conservation means may have had an impact on how governments viewed resource rights that native people retained under treaties. As in the United States during the 1800s, Canadian notions of conservation were closely tied to the classic conservationist ideal of achieving the maximum benefit for all citizens through the efficient use of resources. Because native resource rights are not the same as the rights held by all citizens, they pose special problems for classic conservationists. This difficulty may account for some of the ambiguity in the way native resource rights were regarded during the 1800s.

From a distance, the increased restrictions on fishing that native peoples experienced during the 1800s might be seen as an inevitable outcome of colonial expansion, which had positive and negative consequences for both native and non-native people. But from inside the current conflict, many native-rights supporters see the history of fisheries regulation and the accompanying erosion of their access to resources as a clear example of injustice: 'Some of those regulations ... which restricted access for Saugeen fishermen were unilateral actions that fundamentally changed the treaties' (SG-TR).

Victor Lytwyn's (1990:24) depiction of the introduction of fisheries-management policies in the region supports this more critical assessment. He suggests that the government's claimed interest in 'conservation' was a disguise for its efforts to deprive natives of their resource rights; after all, the depletions of the fisheries in the nineteenth century demonstrate that governments were not actually interested in conservation.

It is possible that government concern for the conservation of fish stocks was not the entire focus of early regulations, but dwindling stocks do not necessarily indicate this. The extent of mid-nineteenth-century fisheries depletions in Lake Huron is still unclear.[4] Even if we accept major stock failures, can we assume that nineteenth-century fisheries managers could have conserved stocks if they had wanted to? The condition of the early fisheries can only hint at government motives.

It is doubtful that the first fisheries regulations were enacted simply as a way to take ownership of the fisheries away from native peoples, but Lytwyn's more general concern is certainly valid – regulations had serious implications for native resource rights. We are still grappling with these implications.

During the early and mid-twentieth century in Ontario, government regulations likewise indicated a focus on common social benefits typical of the classic conservationist approach. Conservation projects were initiated in order to create employment for returning soldiers. The deadly storm of 1954 known as Hurricane Hazel inspired conservation projects, as a way to protect people against nature's unpredictable force (Richardson 1974:ix, 29). Common security is a priority when working for the 'benefit of all.'

Ecocentric ideas about resource management were only occasionally voiced in Ontario prior to mid-century. However, ecocentrism has become increasingly evident in definitions of conservation and in the principles and approaches adopted by resource managers.

During the late 1970s and early 1980s, a Draft Agreement on Ontario Native Fisheries was developed by native, federal, and provincial negotiators in an effort to incorporate native rights into resource policy

(Berkes and Pocock 1983). After aboriginal fishing rights were recognized in the 1990 Sparrow decision, several definitions of conservation came to be articulated in related Ministry of Natural Resources (MNR) documents. A Fishing Agreement (OMNR 1991) and then an Interim Enforcement Policy (OMNR 1992) were developed as temporary measures to allow for differences in the application of resource regulations to natives and non-natives.

The first document states that 'conservation embraces the protection, maintenance, use, and rehabilitation of the natural environment in a manner that insures its sustainability for the benefit of the people of Ontario' (OMNR 1991). The latter agreement (OMNR 1992) breaks away from this predominantly instrumental approach, using the same definition minus the phrase 'for the benefit of the people of Ontario.' It notes 'nature's inherent value' as an element of sustainability, and claims 'an ethical responsibility to share the planet with millions of other life forms.' This indicates a shift away from classic conservationism toward ecocentrism.

Stephen Bocking (1997) suggests that there was a general shift in Ontario's fisheries-management strategies over the last few decades, away from maximized harvesting approaches and toward principles of ecosystem protection. He sees this shift as a positive one because it indicates a growing recognition of human impacts on the fisheries. But as noted above, ecocentrism is not in itself well suited for dealing with all aspects of environmental relations. Since social and political issues are integral to fisheries-management policies, especially where native rights are involved, the trend toward ecocentric management may bring challenges along with potential benefits.

C.H. Olver et al. (1995) argue that the Ontario MNR should adopt a less utilitarian conservation approach to fisheries management. They call for an ecological approach explicitly modelled on Leopold's land ethic. But they attempt to avoid ecocentric dilemmas by distinguishing their management principles from early anthropocentric and ecocentric ones.[5] They regard their view as 'less constrained by the cultural biases' (Olver et al. 1995:1587) that impeded these previous approaches. With 'current science' as a foundation, they feel they can determine the value of other-than-human species; their approach does not suffer from the lack of information typical of the 'pre-ecological' sciences that inspired classic conservationism, and it avoids the 'quasi-religious' implications of Muir's preservationism (Olver et al. 1995:1587).[6]

The claim that 'modern science' can provide solutions where other approaches have failed is worth closer consideration. Though the authors assume they can avoid the pitfalls of ecocentrism, it is not clear how they might do so, since they share the assumption that ecosystems exist apart from human affairs. Their approach seems to ignore the importance of social, political, and economic interests as part of resource management, and is thereby limited.

The view that a more 'scientific' approach can solve problems in fisheries management may be well intended, and of course it makes sense in theory, but such claims can allow for a potential manipulation of interests (see Nader 1996). By presuming a separation from social and political concerns, 'science' can be used to silence positions that are not part of its own agenda, which it does not define as social or political. The notion that 'scientific' research has no agenda is increasingly seen as problematic. 'Objectivity' is more likely attained in my view by more fully recognizing and trying to better understand the social and political contexts in which 'science' is engaged.

The need to include human factors in approaches to fisheries management is noted by Arthur McEvoy (1988). He suggests that in the last two centuries, North American resource management has been based on four visions that 'incorporate a gradually more inclusive view of the essence and genesis of environmental problems' (McEvoy 1988:229). The first vision was the laissez-faire approach of the nineteenth century in which both natural resources and market forces were seen as essentially uncontrollable. Second, during the era of progressive conservation that followed, an interrelationship between harvesting and resource productivity was recognized, and experts attempted to find sustainable yield levels as the solution to resource crises.

The third vision, which coincides with Leopold's ecocentric writings, includes greater attention to human impacts on the environment.[7] While Leopold pointed to a lack of respect for the environment, Garrett Hardin devised a 'tragedy of the commons' model that explained human competitive self-interest as the bottom line, and either privatization or government regulation as the solution to inevitable resource depletions.[8]

McEvoy's fourth vision is characterized by an awareness that resource relations are socially interactive. This view recognizes government regulation, and the scientific data it is based on, as not completely separate from the economy of resource competition. People are not purely competitive automatons as Hardin assumed; economic values are interconnected with social and cultural values.

As an example of how awareness of the complexity of human domains has been incorporated into approaches to fisheries management, McEvoy notes the concept of 'optimum yield,' which was defined by American policymakers as a management standard in the Fishery Conservation and Management Act of 1976. Optimum yield is 'maximum sustainable yield as modified by any relevant economic, social, or ecological factors' (cited in McEvoy 1988:225). This definition can be seen as recognizing that the economic interests of human beings and the survival interests of their resources are ultimately one and the same (McEvoy 1988:225).

The approach McEvoy describes here, which incorporates both ecocentric and anthropocentric qualities, seems sufficient as a basis for developing management agreements where native fishing rights are involved, since there are complex social, political, and economic, as well as ecological, issues at stake. These issues cannot be adequately addressed through either the old conservationist perspectives that focused on human benefits, and regarded environmental impacts as inevitable to social progress. Neither can they be fully addressed through new ecocentric approaches (including some 'ecosystem approaches'), if they assume we can separate human interests from decisions about our environmental relations. An approach informed by awareness of the limitations of both seems necessary.

Even where they can be comprehensively articulated, a set of ecological principles may be more useful as a guide than a goal. Several authors have promoted an 'adaptive management' approach (see Norton 1996:122–4). Berkes (1999:125–6) suggests that 'adaptive management' is especially appropriate where native-rights issues need to be taken into account. Adaptive management is not restricted to a narrow definition of conservation, or a narrow set of principles. I could include various meanings of conservation, where each has potential for clarifying particular social and political interests.

Sport Fishing and the Ecological Indian

> God never did make a more calm, quiet, innocent recreation than Angling.
> – Izaak Walton, *The Compleat Angler* (1653)

The Ontario Federation of Anglers and Hunters (OFAH) is the largest of the Canadian Wildlife Federation's twelve affiliates (Forsey 1994:22). It was established as a conservation group, but it also functions as a

'Conservation' 117

political body in promoting approaches to conservation that are understandably linked to the group's sporting interests. OFAH spokespersons see the priority recognition of native fishing rights set out in Sparrow and applied in the Fairgrieve decision as a serious threat; they see access to wildlife resources as a right they hold as equal citizens within a democratic nation (OFAH 1993).

An article entitled 'Conservation Laws Should Apply to All' (Ankney 1991:3, 44, 49), published in their outdoors magazine, was presented by then club president Dave Ankney as the organization's official policy. His position is that natives and non-natives are no different in their capacity to overhunt if given the opportunity; therefore, in the interest of conserving resources, all Ontario citizens need to give up their particular rights and interests and comply with one set of conservation laws. Ankney warns that recognizing rights that exempt native groups from universal conservation laws will open the floodgates of unregulated harvesting activity, resulting in the overexploitation and destruction of natural resources.

These concerns are noted as well in several OFAH position papers presented to government committees (1994a; 1994b). While a few conservation groups in the region (e.g., The Morden Creek Conservation Club) have voiced objections to OFAH's position in their newsletters, spokespersons from local angler associations on the peninsula have generally supported it.

The definition of conservation implied in OFAH's position papers indicates a strong connection to the classic conservationist tradition and its utilitarian ethic. OFAH's claimed goal is resource 'sustainability for the benefit of the people of Ontario' (1994b:15; see also 1994a:11). Conservation is viewed here as a framework for bringing the greatest good to the greatest number of people. Given their utilitarian definition of conservation, it is not surprising that spokespersons for angler associations see native-rights supporters, who assert historic distinction, as working against 'conservation,' which association leaders define as founded on common interest.

OFAH spokespersons state that insuring the conservation of resources is more important than recognizing historical treaty rights and obligations (Ankney 1991:44; Morgan 1991:45). This perspective bears similarities to the views held by conservationists in the early 1900s, who also attempted to supersede native resource rights by claiming conservation concerns (see Tough 1992:70). A Commission of Conservation operated from 1910 to 1919 under the motto 'Use without abuse' (Tough 1992:62). Members of this commission claimed that native fishing and hunting patterns were unregulated and unorganized. They suggested that since native people had not established territorial boundaries they could not be using resources productively. Some saw this as reason enough for expropriating native land where it might be managed more efficiently.

In this era, anthropologist Frank Speck countered the assumption that native people were not using land productively. He suggested that among Algonquian groups the productive value of land was recognized: established territories had been passed down within families since time immemorial (Speck 1926; see also Feit 1991; Leacock 1995). Speck implied some sort of 'ownership' among aboriginal groups. Later researchers, who attempted to more precisely define early Algonquian notions of 'ownership' as it pertains to land, explained it as recognition of 'use rights,' not the right to hold it as a commodity.

It is uncertain whether family hunting territories and associated conservation practices date back to pre-contact times as Speck suggests (see Bishop and Morantz 1986). They may be adaptations to resource scarcities associated with the fur trade, and some might have been introduced as trading company conservation programs.

Speck documented 'wise use' practices that were carried out within hunting territories. He noted, for example, the selective sparing of beavers, which would allow populations to reproduce and ensure resource productivity. He further documented the practice of allowing regeneration periods when resources were becoming depleted.

These wise-use management practices spoke directly to classic conservationist concerns. In this regard, Speck's work reflects the era in which he worked – the way 'conservation' was primarily understood at the time. But Speck's depictions of native-resource relations also hint at preservationist notions, especially his claim that among Algonquians 'hunting is a holy occupation' (Speck 1935:72, see also Martin 1978:113), and that Algonquians followed a natural law of conservation. Though his assertions of historical and cultural depth have a clear cultural context, they are presented as closely intertwined with the environment, and thereby evoke intrinsic values that complemented instrumental values.

Like some of Canada's early-twentieth-century conservationists, who brought reports of native overhunting and overfishing to resource-management-policy forums (see Tough 1992), OFAH representatives have recently portrayed native-resource relations as anti-conservationist. To emphasize the impending threat to resources that might accompany the breakdown of a universal conservation code, Ankney reports on recent violations of conservation law by natives and notes academic studies that imply destructive native ecological relations in earlier eras: 'One source states that Indians literally declared war on beaver in the 18th and 19th centuries' (1991:44).

The author Ankney refers to here is perhaps Calvin Martin (1978, 1981), whose 'despiritualization' explanation of past native ecological relations has stirred controversy. Robert Brightman has also attempted to explore native ecological relations and interpret historical accounts that suggest both ecological friendliness and destructiveness (1987, 1993).[9]

Martin claimed that native people in the Great Lakes region once had an ecologically friendly belief system, but after contact-era cultural collapses caused by disease and resource shortages, this was abandoned and they began slaughtering animals where they could. Brightman claims that native beliefs never did include conservative features to start with. Their traditional ethic had long predisposed them to kill as much as possible.

Martin's theory has been critiqued by several authors (see Kretch 1981), and in my view has been discredited. For example, Bruce Trigger (1981) shows, using historical records, that Martin's proposed pattern of disease epidemics, and their correspondence with shifts in resource-use ethics and practices, was overstated. Brightman's theory is also questionable. There is still a lot we do not know about the complex ways that beliefs are constructed, and that beliefs and practices are linked. Trying to understand these processes among contemporary, more familiar groups is challenging enough; doing the same for more distant ones, where information is less accessible and cultural images of the other, that serve to fill in information gaps, complicate matters at every turn, is even more so. Given a limited grasp of how perceptions are connected to (and produced within) practical domains, there are few barriers to imaginative speculation about how a particular belief could determine a particular practice. This may partly explain the stark contrast between the two theories presented by Martin and Brightman.

Both theories are further complicated by ambiguities entailed in the term 'conservation.' Martin seems to assess native resource relations with reference to a 'Western-sounding conservation ethic' (Bishop 1981:52). He depicts early native ecological relations as being in line with Leopold's ecocentric land ethic, which he explicitly refers to in several places (Martin 1978:157, 187). An ecocentric focus in Martin's view of conservation might be expected, since he is mainly interested here in beliefs and perceptions, which are often associated with ecocentric notions. He suggests that this 'ethic' can explain the mainly anthropocentric practices noted in the historical accounts of native resource relations.

Brightman's depiction of native ecology is likewise largely ecocentric, and his attempt to measure native eco-perceptions against an anthropocentric definition of conservation is even more explicit than Martin's.

Brightman defines conservation as 'limiting kills to what is needed for survival, utilizing all products of slain animals, and deliberately managing animal populations on a sustained yield basis' (1993:281). Focusing on the latter of these three wise-use principles, he states that Algonquian peoples did not practice conservation because their world view did not include knowledge that human actions can have consequences on the dynamics of animal populations (1987:130–2; 1993:368).

Several other writers, such as Berkes (1987:83–7), agree that some native groups likely did not assess the effects of human predation on whole populations, and that in this sense, it is misleading to consider them as 'conservationists.' But, as Berkes further notes, this view emphasizes only part of the current range of meanings of 'conservation': various native resource-harvesting practices fit some definitions of conservation but not others. We can also look at our own 'conservation' practices and see that each addresses only some definitions of 'conservation.'

Even earlier contexts are considered in exploring resource relations and environmental ethics among non-industrialized people.[10] Evidence from the North American continent and from other regions of the world (see Berkes 1999:148–51) indicates that plant and animal species did not always survive the impacts of prehistoric and historic human activity, especially where groups had recently spread into new areas.

We can generalize that all people are capable of having a negative impact on environments and resources. This generalization has been used by leaders of sport-fishing associations to interrogate the imaginary ecological Indian, and to support their call for universal 'conservation' laws that do not bow to 'special interests.' With its emphasis on 'common interests,' this is clearly a utilitarian view, but it shares assumptions held by some ecocentrics, and also by some who favour a more 'scientific' kind of conservation. This assumption is that within our environmental relations we can separate human interests from the 'natural' world. It seems, however, that it is only particular kinds of human interests that each would like to leave out of the equation.

7 Local Perspectives on Conflict Issues

Attending to native people's perspectives on fishing-conflict issues can help to clarify the underlying factors, which need to be more openly examined and addressed. Concerns articulated at the local level provide insights into how social and political conditions are intertwined with ecological ones – insights into the conflict's political ecology.

The Sport Fishery

> I believe the whole restocking program has to be re-examined, because we feel that it is destroying the fishery in order to create a viable sports fishery. That is where the problem lies, in the effort of the sport fishery to overtake the commercial fishery. (CP-RA)

As Chief Akiwenzie indicates in the above quote, the fishing conflict's most volatile front appears to be the clash between native commercial fishing interests and sport-fishing interests. Most people whom I interviewed on the peninsula's reserves saw 'anglers' as the foremost opponents of native interests. Social and ecological concerns are often blended in their discussions of conflict issues: 'I see policies as heavily oriented toward sport fishing. Stocking of fish not natural to the area is not the best thing as it creates competition for natural species. It could ruin their habitat. I don't know much about fish ecology ... but I would like to see more control by our community' (SG-A1). In many expressions of local concern, social and political issues appeared especially important. The activities of angler associations are interpreted in the context of historically rooted social inequalities that native people frequently feel subjected to. They strongly object to the power that angler associations demonstrate through their control of stocking programs: anglers stock fish species that suit the sport fishery, and this may impede the viability of the commercial fishery, over which natives are attempting to gain more control:

> The anglers have had the rule of the roost for so long that they just don't understand it. (CP-HJ)

> It's just providing the sports fishermen with a hobby – something to do ... I heard once that the reason the MNR [Ministry of Natural Resources] is buying out the commercial fisheries in Georgian Bay was to make it a total sports fishery lake, so it's their own little play area ... for the sports fishermen. Some of the local angler-association people were under that assumption. That may be why they are fighting so hard, 'cause they were trying to make Georgian Bay just one big bay for sports fishermen, and it's hard for them to relate that we have the right to the fisheries now. (CP-BJ)

In this context, 'conservation' has a largely social and political meaning, as noted in the following comment about OFAH: 'They bill themselves as Ontario's oldest conservation group. Well, they conserve all right, but so their members can go out and fish and hunt' (CP-DM).

Angling activities are seen in contrast to more difficult native experiences:

> Whenever there is a big issue it seems to be play versus sacred burial grounds, their leisure versus our livelihood. Oka was a golf course, and here they want to go out with their buddies to have a few drinks and catch fish. (CP-WL)

> The sports fishermen do not know what hardship is. They are running around with their expensive beautiful boats and downriggers, and they've got good jobs. They don't know what our people had grown up with. We had nothing. I'd like to see the shoe on the other foot. I did see some of that this year when the native people were hiring whites to work on the boats. (CP-WL)

Many voice their resentment of this apparent imbalance in economic terms:

> The almighty dollar ... that's the reason for stocking salmon. We call salmon 'junk fish.' They're just for sport fishing. (SG-LK)[1]

> Stocking exotics is not fair if it's going to benefit just one part of the population ... Looks like MNR and sportsmen are just in it for the bucks and the tourists. (SG-HT)

> The sports fishermen are causing all the problem. That's a million-dollar industry. They are fighting to hold on to it. It's greed. (SG-EK)

On the other hand, angler-association representatives have claimed that an increase in native fishing activity will cause economic hardship for local non-native communities, through lost revenue from tourist fishing. Supporters of native fishing rights counter this claim by stating that the local tourist fishing economy does not benefit those who need economic assistance the most. They compare the tourist economy unfavourably with the benefits that might result from developing the native fishery:

> I know that tourist fishing is a big thing, but there are people here who just want to make a living. I don't know how much money it guarantees, but they are mostly just buying meals and rooms, not much else in the communities. (SG-CS)

> They keep saying that sport fishing is a big economic interest, but I know an old bait dealer in Southampton, he don't have a Cadillac yet. The five to six million that comes in – we don't see it. (SG-WK)

> All other issues aside, the anglers are reduced to the money argument. Local anglers figure their derbies are worth a million dollars in tourism a year. Well, that's fine, but I think you have to balance that with the cost that they are imposing on the fishery by stocking with non-indigenous fish ... If you want to look at how much money is injected into local economies, you have to look at how much First Nations inject into local economies, and just in the purchase of goods and services like cars, groceries, appliances, and all that sort of stuff. I think it is about three million dollars from Nawash alone. (CP-DM)

Non-native economic concerns are also criticized as contrary to ecological well-being, in ways that bring social and ecological issues together: 'It's fine if four hundred thousand dollars comes into the local economy from having this derby for two weeks; but in the long run if the perch and all the indigenous fish are gone it's not worth it' (SG-TM).

Some suspect broader business interests as underlying the threat to native fishing rights that anglers represent: 'Anglers and hunters are the vocal ones, but it is actually the businessmen's associations that are pushing to do away with the native fisheries. Everyone is pointing the finger at the sportsman, but they don't realize who the real opposition is yet' (CP-HJ).

A close relationship between sporting associations and government resource managers is assumed by most native community members. They regarded this as a blatant conflict of interest:

> MNR bows to public pressure ... non-native pressure. We obtained different papers. Doctors and policemen belong to OFAH [Ontario Federation of Anglers and Hunters] ... people in high places. They bow to that kind of pressure. (SG-WK)

> The government keeps washing their hands of it and the sports people have a lot of money there, doctors and lawyers. They are the squeaky wheel. (CP-RJ)

> They have men in pretty near every department of the government. So how are you supposed to fight them? Maybe at election time, but there are so many sport fishermen that vote them in. (CP-FJ)

> The MPs belong to OFAH and these groups. When there is a conflict of interest they vote for their own benefit. If they are connected with a sports group they should not be able to vote. (SG-AS)

David McLaren has investigated OFAH's political connections as part of his research for Nawash. He suggests that OFAH's links to government make their anti-native propaganda more effective:

> The current [1995] minister, Chris Hodgson, was or still is a member. The Premier of Ontario was a member of OFAH. I know that the Conservative government took OFAH's message to the floor of the legislature when they were in opposition, because their questions there reflect the OFAH lobby. (CP-DM)

We got a lot of letters between the MNR and OFAH. They show a pattern of sniping away at First Nations people, making them out as criminals or poachers, or abusers of the resources ... Most, or a lot of the conservation officers, are members of OFAH, so they get the propaganda. (CP-DM)

McLaren and other native-rights supporters counter accusations of ecological damage caused by unregulated native fishing by pointing to the unregulated nature of the sport fishery:

OFAH members are hypocritical when they complain of First Nations people taking fish. Certainly, when it comes to angling, sports fishing ... that's got to be the most unregulated user group in the whole province. Nobody really has a good handle on what sports fishermen take out. There are not enough MNR agents to go around to do creel surveys. (CP-DM)

They claim they are sportsmen. The derby at Southampton allows four thousand people to take five fish; maybe now it's three. And then the ministry has a weekend where you can fish without a licence. We used to enter that derby. A handful of natives fishing does not seem to be a big factor. (SG-TM)

The thing is, the sport fishermen are never kept track of. The commercial fishermen have to keep track and account of every fish that they sell. The sport fisherman is not selling it, at least he shouldn't be, so he doesn't have to keep track of it. Now there are so darn many sport fishermen that they take as much if not more than the commercial fishermen. (CP-FJ)

I can't see how the Indian people can be depleting the fish stock. You see how many fish the sports fishermen take out of the water. Look at how many sports fishermen came through. Someone said that the amount of fish they took out would cover a football field. What the Indian people take is just a drop in the bucket. (SG-EK)

The increasing critical attention that native rights representatives from both reserves have brought to the stocking programs carried out by angler associations is part of a broader critique of non-native resource-management practices. This effort can be explained in part as a response to negative portrayals of native people's resource relations. While the battle over appropriate 'conservation' is clearly political, ecological implications are frequently the focus of debate: 'There are still problems ... the whole question of conservation ... There seems to be a gulf between what is called restocking the sports fishery versus the natural species, because some of these stocked species are overtaking the natural species and are changing the whole ecosystem, which will impact both areas' (CP-RA).

Steve Crawford, a fisheries biologist hired by Nawash, has actively participated in this critique along with McLaren. Objections to stocking practices were presented in local news articles (e.g., *Sun Times* 7 July 1996:3) and at a co-management conference organized by Nawash, which was held in nearby Port Elgin in 1995.

Debates about appropriate conservation practices are often based on lines drawn between native and non-native interests, with the 'natural species' on one side and the 'stocked species' on the other. In support of a native approach as a viable alternative to current management practices, native representatives point to scientific studies that show the ecological dangers of stocking practices.[2]

Almost all native community members that I interviewed were of the opinion that exotic species are detrimental to indigenous fish stocks. The gluttonous characteristic of introduced salmon is viewed as especially problematic:

According to a biologist who was up here a while ago, these salmon double their weight in the fourth year. Up to four years they are only 15 to 20 pounds, and the possibility of them going to 40 or 45 pounds occurs in the fourth year when they never stop eating, they eat constantly ... They probably eat their weight every day ... You put four or five million of them things out there. And everyone is putting them in. The States is putting them in and all the fishing associations in Ontario are putting them in ... There is a hatchery in Owen Sound that puts them in. There is a hatchery in Wiarton that puts them in, a hatchery over in Port Elgin that puts them in. (CP-TJ)

There is enough food to feed the fish that are naturally here, but these salmon get to be up to forty-five pounds, and they have to eat their weight in a day. So whoever puts them in should put food in for them so they don't eat the other fish. But they don't care as long as they make money selling fishing lures and downriggers and that. (SG-JR)

Salmon is killing everything now. It's black with salmon: twenty-five to thirty-pounders. There was no run of rainbow at Stoney Creek this year;

no smelt. Salmon got them ... There does not seem to be any small salmon, all big ones. Maybe the big salmon ate the small ones too. (SG-PS)

Anglers feel that they put the fish in the lake so they have a right to them. But they don't understand that they are putting a voracious eating machine out in the lake to eat the native strains. (CP-HJ)

Along with the salmon, the recently introduced skamania is known as a voracious predator:

They breed trout, like splake and skamania, which is half trout and half salmon ... Skamania are bred as a strong fighting fish. Maybe their aggressiveness is detrimental to local fish. (SG-A1)

The skamania that they put in – several different breeds, mixtures of rainbow trout, like the salmon – it is just a glorified eating machine. It never stops eating. (CP-TJ)

Ted Johnston notes that the impact of gluttonous exotic fish is coupled with stress on local species exerted by another exotic, the cormorant, a fish-eating water fowl that has recently expanded into the more northerly parts of the Great Lakes. 'There is another thing that has come about now. I don't know what prompted it, but within the past ten years all of a sudden you see a lot of the cormorants, huge flocks of cormorants ... You take the cormorant eating that much, and the salmon eating that much ... What's left for the rest? (CP-TJ)

The threat that exotics pose for other introduced species such as the trout (splake) and smelt through predation or competition is noted as an example of the inadequacies of current stocking programs:

Anglers don't fish for whitefish; the majority of their fish is the trout and salmon. The salmon is an up-in-the-air thing because they say that they are trying to bring the lake trout back, but the salmon is taking away from the trout. (CP-BJ)

The salmon is a bigger glutton than the lake trout, and they get that much bigger. So it takes that much more to feed them. Now, will our food supply feed a lake full of salmon? I doubt it. (CP-FJ)

Too many fish put into the lake. These big salmon eat the smelts up. I think the salmon will eat the lake trout, any fish smaller. (CP-EA)

The low reproductive capacity of introduced species is also seen as a weakness in stocking programs: 'The splake are the donkey of the fish world. They don't reproduce. So if you are going to spend money on putting something back in there, you might as well put money on something that is going to reproduce itself' (CP-FJ).

Most urgent for native community members is the threat that introduced species pose for indigenous fish:

> I don't like them stocking exotic species. What do these fish do to fish that are already here? (SG-RT)

> I'm not really in favour of all the stocking programs that the MNR have, particularly the ones that they let out to the sports associations, like the stocking of salmon and skamania – the fish that are not native to the waters here ... A lot of our natural fish have disappeared; our perch have practically all disappeared now. The bass are on the decline, the smaller pickerel are gone. When you turn a huge eating machine like that salmon loose in the water it just devastates the local stock, the native stocks. (CP-TJ)

As noted in several of the above quotes, indigenous species are referred to as 'native' species. They are also seen as 'natural,' as opposed to 'artificial':

> I think it would be more desirable to go to the natural-type fish ... the lake trout. (CP-TJ)

> It would be a good plan to try and get the trout back if they could figure out a way. That's the natural fish for the Great Lakes. (CP-FJ)

> The whitefish is not an artificial species, it's a natural species ... The splake ... are artificially reproducing, they are man made. (CP-RA)

The concern for maintaining nature as a balanced system is commonly indicated in critiques of stocking programs:

> It's trying to overtake nature. Fish raised by hatcheries hurt the other ones. They take away all their food so other fish have nothing to eat ...

New species don't get along ... I don't like the idea of putting different fish in one pond. (CP-R3)

It would be good to try and revitalize the lake trout. It was one of the original fish here. There must have been a reason for it to be here, to keep the system in sync. (CP-BJ)

They [people involved in stocking programs] have interrupted the natural life cycle. (CP-BJ)

Awareness of the dangers that exotic species pose for indigenous fish has grown through discussions at community meetings and other local gatherings, and some of the ideas associated with this critique were no doubt spread this way:

I am wondering about bringing these fish in. Basically we were mostly a lake trout area, and whitefish. When they started to introduce foreign fish into the Great Lakes, they overpowered the original fish that we had here. I have heard people talking at band fishing meetings, and I found it quite interesting that these strange fish that they are bringing in eat all the food that our fish would normally eat, so they are sort of overpowering their presence here. (CP-RJ)

But the widespread interest in the threat of exotic fish suggests a deeper resonance with community concerns.

In many descriptions of problematic interactions between exotic species and indigenous ones, it is hard (at least for me) to miss the analogy to people (local native community members and outsiders). In the previous quote, for example, exotics are referred to as 'foreign' and 'strange,' and indigenous species are 'our fish.' Indigenous fish are 'overpowered.' During my fieldwork I became increasingly aware of this metaphorical association between fish groups and social groups, and it was explicitly raised by Ernestine Proulx, an Ojibway-language instructor, in a conversation I had with her (1995, pers. comm.). It is difficult to assess how aware reserve community members actually are of this, or how much they think about it. But it appears to me that the relationship between exotic and indigenous fish has become an important cultural explanatory frame of reference. It allows community members to make sense of the relations between themselves and people on the outside – especially their relationship with angler-association members who oppose native fishing rights. This image is also meaningful in that it reflects, and helps to explain, more general historically rooted social-political tensions.

Attention to the historically rooted social-political dimensions of views on angler activities allowed me to sort through several apparently contradictory statements made by interviewees. At first I assumed that stocking programs of any sort were rejected by the reserve communities, because they interfered with nature; but several people thought stocking was fine under some circumstances:

Stocking is okay, but just indigenous fish. (SG-TM)

Stocking local fish is all right – lake trout, whitefish, perch, bass, herring. (CP-R3)

Whitefish is the most important fish these days. If you can keep them multiplying you can keep fishing. Stocking exotics is crazy. You don't put anything in that you have no control over. You can't teach an exotic fish not to eat small whitefish and trout. If we were to reintroduce herring it would be all right. (CP-WN)

Stocking itself is therefore not the problem, as long as the species is indigenous, and thereby fits the community's social and economic concerns, as well as a general ideological view that seems to value minimal disturbance of natural things and processes. 'Natural' processes are often explained in ecological terms, but these too are metaphorically wrapped in social and political meanings.

Even opinions about the edibility of different fish seem to reflect social-political dimensions. Some people thought stocked fish were fine to eat, but many were quick to elaborate on their undesirability:

If you've ever fished salmon, they are the ugliest fish you've ever seen. They don't taste good. They get so big. I don't know if anyone eats them. Even the rainbow trout I don't like. Splake is too strong. I like smoked chub, whitefish, perch, pickerel. (SG-TM)

You can't eat salmon. They have a strong taste. I tried to eat small ones too, but you couldn't eat it. (SG-WK)

Put a salmon in and the small fry will disappear in no time. In my view they are a garbage fish. I wouldn't eat them. (SG-AS)

My impression is that many of the people most opposed to the fisheries being controlled by 'people on the outside' were especially adamant about their dislike of the taste of 'exotic' fish. Claiming that exotic fish are not edible implies a social-economic critique, when coupled with the local assumption that the native approach is to eat fish, not just catch them for sport. If exotics cannot be eaten, stocking programs only serve anglers. Stating that exotics do not taste good expresses a real and symbolic preference. It can be seen as a form of subtle resistance against outsiders and the control they have over the local fishery.

Another apparent contradiction that became clearer in social-political contexts is that supporters of native fishing rights claim to be vehemently opposed to 'anglers'; but many are anglers themselves:

I used to fish with a pole with my dad. (CP-RA)

I do a little bass fishing once in a while. It's not as good as it used to be when I was a kid. (CP-RJ)

I have fished mostly for sport: rainbow, bass, pike, pickerel, when there was pickerel; mostly in the river, but I also fished along the lake for rainbow. I was mainly a rainbow fisherman because of my father. My dad fished for rainbow and hunted ... Four of my uncles were ... avid fishermen, mostly in the angling sense. (SG-AS)

I just do sport and hobby fishing ... I fish inland lakes and little streams for bass and pike. I camp with my daughter. We go up north on fishing trips. (SG-A1)

I used to rod-fish for my own use up in Manitoba, at Oxford House Lake. There were so many fish there that when you'd cast, you knew you were going to catch something. (CP-FJ)

I have done some fishing up in Northern Quebec. I was up there with a helicopter group ... The guests we took out included Governor General Vincent Massey. He always seemed to select me to go fishing; not that I was the best fisherman, but in his own mind he thought that I would know where all the best fish were. (CP-RJ)

Though the popularity of angling among native people seems opposed to their anti-angler sentiments, native community members have various ways of distinguishing locally appropriate angling from the angling that characterizes outsiders: 'The majority of the native commercial fishermen are sport fishermen too. Come the springtime, all the commercial fishermen will be down at the point fishing, with their rods and reels. The anglers don't see this; but their point of view on sports fishing is different' (CP-BJ). The distinctions seen as important are linked to long-standing and more urgent relationships. One example of this, already noted, is that the native approach, even when angling, is to fish for food, not just for sport:

> And through the winter a lot of the men went on the ice and fished through the ice. That was more like a sport; they liked doing it, they liked being out there. But yet that was food they brought home. (CP-WA)

> Natives are blamed for overfishing ... but there are a lot more fishermen off-reserve than on. Here people fish for food. I still ice-fish once in a while ... It's something to do with the guys. (SG-PS)

> It's interesting to look at the other side. I grew up sports fishing. I fished with my grandmother all my life ... mostly for perch and bass. But it seems that sports fishermen consider us strictly commercial fishermen. Even when we do fish for sport we don't throw it back in, we take it home and eat it. (CP-BJ)

When natives do practise catch-and-release fishing, even this similarity is distinguished from outsider approaches:

> We put them back if they are too small to eat. Some non-native fishermen take all sizes, don't know what they do with them. (SG-PS)

> But in the last few years some of the native sport fishermen are starting to catch and release. But even then they found research that says that the longer a fish is kept on a line, the more likely it is not to reproduce. The more you play it the more harm there is. (CP-BJ)

While there is considerable overlap in species fished by native fishers and outside anglers, especially at Saugeen, where rainbow trout are available, another understood distinction is that natives tend to favour fishing for indigenous species: 'If they are going to stock something they should stock perch ... or pickerel is a good sport fish ... bass ... it doesn't have the fight like the big salmon though. I don't know what it does for them to catch the big ones' (SG-JR).

Outside sport fishing is also generalized as too individualistic in comparison with the community-oriented approach that many native community members value: 'Sports clubs are just out for their own personal interest. It's got to be for the people, not individuals' (SG-AS).

Trophy fishing is seen as typical of the non-native approach to angling as well. It epitomizes the outside angler's lack of care about the food value of fish, and shows a boastful individualistic attitude that links with the economic privileges they appear to have:

> There are a lot of people that think that Indians overhunt and overfish. But we depend on it more for food not just for trophies. (CP-DK)

> The fish taken by the anglers is more big time, like for the big splake, the big trout, the big salmon, more trophy fishing. For me, fishing is for a relaxing time. I go for the bass or perch ... It seems ironic that they catch it so they can brag about it, but if they put it on the wall they can't tell stories that exaggerate its size. (CP-BJ)

> I remember some used to boast about getting the biggest deer or fish, but they never did it to get a trophy like our white brothers, who do it for the fun of fishing. We've never done it for trophies; we've done it for consumption; and they blame us for spoiling their fun. (CP-PT-DK)

> They started a sportsmen show at the CNE, but eventually it was taken over by all the commercial products. They moved to the International Centre but the same thing happened. (CP-PT-SN)

The distinction based on trophy fishing also has internal contradictions, since natives have not totally abstained from recording unusually large catches for posterity:

> My grandfather used to have his picture in the smoke shop. Also my dad. They had their pictures there with the big fish that they caught. I had my picture there too. The fish was as tall as me when I was seven or eight, a rainbow. (SG-PS)

> There is a picture somewhere of the forty-pound fish that Bert Ashkewe caught. He needed help: the galvanized wire was cutting his fingers. Norman McLeod helped land it. The biggest one I caught was twenty pounds. Ask Ella Waukey; her dad caught that forty-pound fish. Tom Jones had some pictures. Maybe it was in the Wiarton *Echo*, around 1930. (CP-GK)

But these fish likely were eaten after they were photographed. And there are indications in these 'fish story' recollections that family and community relations were not overshadowed by individual achievement as much as one might assume.

Similarities between native and outside anglers seem to be overlooked in emerging native views on fishing activities. Focusing on distinctions may help make sense of the social, political, and economic inequalities that they associate with outside anglers and resource managers.

Native perspectives on outside anglers and their activities are clearly filtered through social and political concerns. The images of outsiders that are being constructed are not well suited for appreciating the diversity of interests that 'anglers' might actually represent. They are, however, an understandable response to the aggressive depiction by some angler associations of natives as anti-conservationist.

While criticisms of the activities of angler associations by native community members have obvious political purposes, they are worth taking seriously as conservation concerns. The dangers of introducing new fish species are noted in a growing number of studies (e.g., Billington and Hebert 1991). Exotic introductions can increase stresses on indigenous fish populations through predation, competition for food sources, loss of genetic diversity, and transmission of disease. In spite of these dangers, the stocking of non-indigenous salmon and hatchery-reared trout hybrids is still widely regarded by members of angler associations as a hallmark of their conservation work. While there is a growing general concern about the potential negative ecological impacts of various 'invasions' of exotic species, the exotic ones valued by sporting associations are not seen by anglers or most other Canadians as dangerous.

Allowing angler associations to stock the lakes with whatever species suit their own purposes seems compatible with the short-sighted conservationist approaches promoted many decades ago. It is poorly matched to the more recent awareness of the complexity of human-ecological relations.

Government Regulation of the Fishery

Many of the native community members I interviewed expressed a level of distrust for government authority that matched the intensity of their concerns about sport-fishing groups. Native representatives eventually were able to negotiate a tentative fishing agreement that allows them to exercise rights recognized in the Fairgrieve ruling. But given the historically rooted tensions between government regulators and native people, the stability of this agreement is questionable.[3] It is worth considering community members' perspectives on government regulators in some detail, as the quality of this relationship is itself a factor that will shape the eventual outcomes of fishing agreements.

The general distrust of government fishery regulators that is apparent in the reserve communities has historical roots. The Fairgrieve ruling, which determined that fisheries regulations had been imposed unjustly, can be interpreted both as a sign that native concerns are now being taken seriously and as an invitation to improve relations with outside government regulators. But when subsequent negotiations were attempted, things apparently went in the opposite direction, at least initially. Native negotiators, along with many other community members, may have viewed the Fairgrieve ruling more as proof of the long-standing injustices natives have suffered than as evidence of current goodwill.

Given this sentiment, many natives suspected that fishing would continue to be regulated by outside authorities:

> We have tried and tried to get the Ontario government to sit down with us and work out something ... but to no avail. They won't sit down with us at all. The only time those people came here for a meeting ... they didn't come here to try and negotiate something. They came here to tell us what we could do and what we couldn't do. And then they left. They didn't listen to our angle of it at all. So how are you supposed to negotiate with someone that won't talk to you? And yet the Fairgrieve decision said that we were supposed to negotiate with the Ontario government and they were supposed to negotiate with us. Negotiation is a two-way street. But when you just have it going one way there isn't much sense to the negotiation. (CP-FJ)

Some suggested that the involvement of the provincial government was an obstacle to negotiating sound fishing agreements:

I don't think that the provincial government has any idea about native rights. When the federal government handed things over they didn't know much about it, and I don't think the province knows much more. (CP-RJ)

There will always be questions about provincial and federal jurisdiction. (SG-RK)

Recent inconsistencies in the various provincial political parties' approaches to native rights also made some sceptical of the negotiation process. When the New Democratic Party was in power in Ontario in the early 1990s, they developed interim agreements that temporarily allowed some native resource harvesting, in response to the Sparrow ruling; but these were no longer officially recognized when the Conservatives came to power in the mid-1990s: 'The NDP gave us a bit of a break, but then when the Conservative government got back in with such big support, they killed that. And the Liberals were not any better ... I don't like politics that much' (CP-FJ).

Another cause for concern was the OFAH lobby effort, which was suspected of contributing to the rigid stance against 'co-management' that non-native negotiators have taken:

There was a lot of hemming and hawing by the MNR on their way to the negotiating table. These things were supposed to be ironed out, but we know that OFAH, not publicly but certainly privately, was pressuring the government not to negotiate with the First Nations, or if they did negotiate, to make sure the MNR remained the manager and not to share any management responsibilities with the First Nation. They were pressuring the MNR to allow OFAH representatives at the negotiating table. Their tactics basically resulted in stalling negotiations, and they stalled them long enough for the Harris government to get in. And now the Harris government does not want to even hear the word 'co-management.' (CP-DM)

Howard Jones explained that his community's demand that the responsibility for fisheries management be shared is linked to a more general trend in Canada toward increasing political assertiveness among native peoples:

I can see they need to ensure the practice of conservation, but not unilateral conservation. I think it has to be through direct negotiation. Indian groups have to have a full voting part. Indians have gone through a long period where someone else has always imposed their rules on them. And we are at a time in our history when Indians are digging their heels in and saying we are not going to be pushed anymore. (CP-HJ)

This trend has been accompanied by a series of legal rulings that have defined native fishing interests favourably, but inconclusively, as noted in chapter 2.

Some worried that the Ontario government would attempt to counter the Fairgrieve ruling through further court action. Some were also suspicious that the MNR was planning to use its authority as defined in Sparrow to impose regulations on native fishing (in the absence of negotiated agreements) where there is a question of safety, or a 'conservation' problem: 'If they determined that the fishery is in danger, one of their options is to close the fishery to everyone; and if the Native people then continued to fish they would charge them. And I think that we are being set up for that already by the allegations the MNR and sports people are levelling against First Nations people for taking lake trout' (CP-DM).

While native representatives frequently stated that government negotiators were stalling, they were also aware of advantages they might have where negotiations are prolonged. The Sparrow priorities adopted in the Fairgrieve decision require that a native fishery be the last to have to close for conservation purposes. Ministry managers may be more interested than native negotiators in reaching an agreement that would further clarify such priorities:

> [I]t gets to the point of who is affected first. And the way it is stated it is first the sports, then non-native commercial, then native commercial that have to cut back ... It would be interesting to see what would happen if they keep pushing and pushing the lake trout and saying that the fishery is depleting. The sports fishermen are the first ones that have to leave now. I don't know if they have thought too much about that. (CP-BJ)

Under the Sparrow priorities, any overfishing might hurt other fishing interest groups more than it would the native fishery. A cynic might even point out that native fishers could turn the tables of power on the sport fishery by disregarding conservation measures. However, native fishers are not likely to jeopardize their future livelihood (and the resource that they depend on) just to spite the sport fishery.

Some native community members link negotiation failures to what they see as a general lack of recognition of treaty rights:

> I am stunned that they still don't acknowledge treaties even though they are signed ... Fairgrieve recognized native fishing rights, but we still have the MNR and anglers associations denying this. (SG-HT)

> People have trouble realizing that Indians have rights. They don't want to live up to something that happened one hundred years ago or more; but I must tell you that the Canadian and American Constitutions are very old documents that we live by every day. An Indian treaty to me is no different than a house mortgage. The government made the deal that you give us your land and resources and we will supply education and you can fish and hunt and whatever. (CP-HJ)

In the initial negotiating position held by Saugeen representatives, ultimate jurisdictional authority over resources was an explicit issue, as indicated by Chief Richard Kahgee: 'It is important to establish who has jurisdiction to control the resource ... Those issues have to be resolved in relation to whether we are capable of having an impact in the management of the resource' (SG-RK). In his view, governments have no legitimate basis for controlling native fishing: 'I see us as having ultimate responsibility. The federal or provincial governments never acquired ownership. They can't just say it's theirs by virtue of their own constitution. That does not divorce us from the resource. Our ownership of the resource goes back into pre-Confederation' (SG-RK). This perspective is assumed in Kahgee's Duluth Declaration:

> The Duluth Declaration sets the parameters of our interests in terms of what our objectives are in relation to resources, and also our responsibility. Everything we do now has to go back to that. A more positive assertion of ownership has to come from the communities because they have to start defining for themselves and for Canada how they see themselves fitting into the resources, and what the relationship is between the federal Crown, provincial Crown, and themselves as aboriginal people. So it's more or less a self-identifying process where the community takes a greater responsibility for its actions, and will be in a better position to look at key issues where they have had little or no involvement in the past. It basically puts them back into the role of stewards. (SG-RK)

As noted in chapter 2, the Duluth Declaration, and its statement of the Saugeen First Nation's sovereignty, was regarded as too radical by some native community members, notably by band council members who succeeded Kahgee's council. The issue of ultimate jurisdiction of the fishery remains a central challenge for resource-management negotiators.

In terms of jurisdiction, native fishing rights in Canada present a difficult paradox. Though they are often asserted as being intrinsic to the native community (as existing apart from outside authority), they are only fully 'recognized' from the outside, through the constitutional definitions on which the Sparrow priorities are based.

Kahgee's assumption of absolute native jurisdiction could make negotiations, which assume some level of government authority in management, appear irrelevant. His approach is an understandable political strategy, aimed at bringing attention to issues that need to be considered. But it may also contribute to already existing barriers and obstacles.

A reluctance on the part of many native-rights supporters to look beyond jurisdictional issues is encouraged by their general perceptions of social inequity. Kahgee's focus on jurisdiction as central to fishing issues seems inseparable from his impressions of past injustices: 'You had draconian laws that wouldn't even allow us to get legal counsel. And up until 1958 we weren't even classified as Canadians. There was no way to resolve treaty matters because there was no dispute mechanism built into the process' (SG-RK). Adequate fishing agreements may depend on addressing impressions of past social injustices, and they can serve as part of the process of dealing fairly with the past.

Mixed feelings toward the Canadian legal system, through which jurisdiction is officially established, affect native perceptions of prospects for sharing resources. The legal system is seen by many as not effective in addressing the injustices that native people in Ontario have encountered:

> The justice system is power. If you have power, you have your own justice system. But if you are not powerful, you are just at the whim of someone that is powerful. That's the way they display it. You take Camp Ipperwash. That is another demonstration of the justice that they are trying to hand the Indian. I remember when that camp was taken over ... The Canadian government just walked in and said, 'We are moving you out ... You'd get it back after the war.' Fifty years after the war and they still

haven't got it back yet. And that's the justice system they are trying to hand the Indian. (CP-FJ)

Some see the courts as having an impact, but an excessively cumbersome one: 'We are starting to stand up, but that makes people madder. Courts are thirty years down the road. People want something right now' (SG-PS).

Considering that only three or four decades ago the Canadian court system was not even regarded as a feasible avenue for clarifying native rights, there has been substantial progress, especially since the entrenchment of treaty rights in section 35 of the 1982 *Canadian Constitution Act*. The legal system may seem impermeable, since it applies already established rules and guidelines, but it is also adaptive. Like all cultural institutions it is responsive to changing conditions. The concerns of Native peoples were typically ignored during much of Canada's legal history, but changes are evident in many recent rulings on native-resource rights.

Yet legal recognition does not itself dictate change. As seen in the Fairgrieve decision, a court ruling is only one step toward reforming resource-management policies and practices. Newly recognized resource rights will be resisted where they 'run counter to prevailing power relationships' (Pinkerton 1992:330–8).[4] Implementing native resource rights is dependent not only on legal decisions, but also on efforts to overcome obstacles that stand in the way of negotiated management-sharing agreements.

A Native Approach to Regulating the Fishery

There have been some suggestions that a 'native approach' to regulating the fishery needed, either in place of or as part of the existing system. However, given jurisdictional complexities and the conceptual and practical challenges of management issues, it is not altogether clear what a 'native approach' might look like, or how it would work. It appears that native community members are in the process of sorting this out.

While many are suspicious of non-native fishery management, the idea of 'management' itself has not been wholly rejected. Most people on both reserves feel there is a need for regulation of the fishery at the local level. Theodore Mason states that developing such regulations is both ecologically and politically important: 'We have to start regulating ourselves. Area four/four is such a small area. We can't take out and not put back. We have to regulate it not only cause it makes us look good, but we are actually putting back for the future' (SG-TM).

People are aware that for local regulations to be effective they have to be accepted by the community at large: 'Regulating would have to be a community effort. We would need to get people together. If the community backs up the ideas there will be less hassles. The community has to be involved' (SG-HT). Some are hopeful that local regulations might evolve as an extension of already existing local approaches: 'Yes, they would need rules, bylaws, or more like a code of conduct ... simple practices that are easily followed ... more or less like tradition' (SG-AS). At Nawash, concerns about local fishing regulations are discussed at community fishing meetings, and draft bylaws, though they exist outside of government resource management programs, have been put in place. Given current uncertainties within the fishery, it remains to be seen how consistently native fishers will comply with these local regulations.[5]

At the Saugeen reserve, preliminary local regulation plans were underway during Chief Kahgee's tenure as chief: 'After we get rolling we are going to maybe set up a time to leave this area alone and let those fish spawn, maybe just let the small boats fish here for a while' (SG-JR). But following his resignation, fisheries issues were given less attention, and the fisheries coordinator, Timm Rochon, was not rehired or replaced after the term of his contract expired. With the current tentative fishing agreement in place, local regulation of the fishery remains an outstanding issue that needs to be addressed.

Incorporating community perspectives in local regulations is likely to make them more effective and more enforceable. Their success may also depend on whether there is sufficient clarity about what a 'native approach' to fishery management might be.

The political tensions within the fisheries conflict no doubt have some effect on what people consider as a native approach to managing the fishery. Local ways are sometimes articulated in what appears to be direct opposition to what is considered an established management approach. Statements about a 'native approach' might be assessed in terms of whether they are 'authentic' – true representations of a 'culture' and its core values. Overt borrowing or political positioning could be seen as diminishing authenticity, and thereby validity. But this assumes that community ideals and practices are in fact separate from political concerns.

It is increasingly apparent that social, economic, and political concerns are closely linked to expressions of group identity – who we are and what we do. We claim greater legitimacy for our patterns of acting on our interests by defining them as intrinsic to who we are, as part of our cultural identity. Both conscious and unconscious processes may be involved here. This political dimension of group identity is germane to our examination of native and non-native views on their own and each other's resource relations, and it thereby has potential to provide insights into resource conflicts where political issues are most explicit.

In the context of this conflict, articulations of a native approach appear to be limited by an established conservation 'discourse' (communicative interaction based on frames of reference and concepts that themselves legitimate particular positions). Some of the most outspoken native-rights supporters seem to borrow from ecocentric environmental notions in their attempt to explain their vision of a native approach to fisheries management:

> If I were to sum it up, what we are actually doing is giving the resource equality with us. It's an odd concept because the resource has rights as much as you do. As a living entity it has certain things that are required in terms of a relationship: respect, being conscious of its needs ... the non-native looks at things in terms of owning, conquering, and controlling. Native people don't believe that nature can be controlled, not to the extent that non-natives do ... I think we have to start looking at it again as a viable entity that requires respect like any other living being. (SG-RK)

Ecocentric discourse has clear potential for distinguishing 'native' and 'non-native' ways. Non-native approaches are easily characterized as anthropocentric – the 'controlling' part of this definition may be especially evident to native community members. Other qualities of ecocentrism and anthropocentrism may also ring true, and may help explain the conflict, conflicting positions, and native/non-native relationships in general.

Perceived differences in economic motivation seem to highlight this contrast: 'Traditionally, fishing was always done with the intent of trying to maintain the integrity of the resource. And I think these are the type of management principles that should be brought into the fisheries now; so that again, it's not just a commodity, it's a living entity' (SG-RK). But this oppositional model is limited. Native leaders are not concerned only with the ecological well-being, or the 'integrity of the resource.' They also consider fisheries-management issues in terms of the goals of their own communities, as can be expected: 'The ministry looks at the economic level, but overlooks the social implications such as job creation and how self-government fits in' (SG-RK).

Given that native representatives do not exclude social and economic dimensions from their own interest in fisheries management, an ecocentric approach appears to be only partly suited to the 'native approach' that leaders are beginning to articulate.

The partial adoption of ecocentric discourse by supporters of native rights may be linked to its potential for critiquing established conservation language. When I was developing the survey questions, I found it nearly impossible to avoid words such as 'resources' and 'management,' but these were deemed inappropriate by some community representatives whom I consulted. The terms were regarded as not part of a native way of looking at things, as embedded in non-native practices of the status quo. This is a critique of classic conservation 'wise use' notions, and an assertion that native environmental relations are more than this – that they are spiritual.

Their point is well taken, since language can define frameworks and thereby limit and control meaning: terms such as 'resources' can carry 'ideological baggage' (Notzke 1994:1). But it is difficult to find workable alternatives for much of this 'conservation talk,' and dialogue is required in order to negotiate. Introducing more native-language terms could serve to open up current frameworks. This could also provide more insights into native resource relations (Bernie Francis 2000, pers. comm.). Efforts to include the local language could be part of a long-term solution to conflict issues.

For now, we may also have to work with the language at hand. Even the most active supporters of native fishing rights rely on established terms that are linked to both ecocentric and anthropocentric approaches:

In the late seventies I got interested in the environment and I got interested in fishing through my concern for the sustainability of resources. (CP-AE)

And that's why First Nations need co-management. They need a guarantee that their old ways, their ways of knowing the resource, will have some effect on management. (CP-DM)

An integrated management plan would be most appropriate – taking both the American and Canadian data, reconciling it to the resource, working on integrated assessment programs. (SG-RK)

While it seems necessary to engage current conservation language and discourse, it would be useful to continue exploring its implications and potential.

Interpreters of past native ecological relations often depict them in stark contrast to non-native relations, as noted in the previous chapter. Ecocentric and anthropocentric notions may also be influential in shaping discourses about past fishing conflicts. With reference to the nineteenth-century Fishing Islands conflicts, Victor Lytwyn (1992) states that native people had a spiritual connection, a 'sacred bond ... with the spirits of the fish in Lake Huron' (81, 97). His juxtaposition of native 'stewardship' with the 'European notion of ownership' (1992:81) is worth considering as part of the picture. However, this might imply that economic interest, the apparent driving force of non-native activity, was absent from native relations with the land. Native economic concerns were evident in this conflict – in dealings with lease holders, and in plans to expand commercial native fisheries (Lytwyn 1992:94–5).

Lytwyn states that during this conflict 'the Saugeen people realized the health of the fish stocks was in trouble, and brought this to the attention of the government officials' (1992:95). It is possible that Saugeen fishers were concerned about the well-being of fish, in an ecocentric sense, but the petition they forwarded to government officials speaks as well of concern for the native community: 'it will be for our interest and advantage to have them for our own use' (cited in Lytwyn 1992:95). This petition is worded in classic conservationist, not ecocentric preservationist, language.

In trying to understand past resource relations through these records, we are working with not only current notions about conservation, but early nineteenth-century discourses as well. The choice of words in the above-cited petition could have much to do with the constraints of the 'conservation talk' in that era. The wording of this petition is limited as a source of insight into native cultural perspectives on resource relations at the time.

If we assign only an ecocentric perspective to these people, we may be minimizing the importance of legitimate economic concerns. By the mid-nineteenth century, native people on the peninsula were experienced in both informal and formal (market economy) fish-trading relations, as noted in previous chapters. They had already participated in the commercial fishery for several decades, and were long familiar with other European trade practices. For even longer, native groups had been trading among themselves. Ecocentrism and anthropocentrism (as typically understood) seem inadequate on their own for a more in-depth exploration of early native people's environmental or economic relations.

As in many smaller-scale contexts, it is likely that 'exchanges' here were marked by poignant social meanings and served to establish and reinforce patterns of social interaction. One might speculate on how the economic relations of past Saugeen natives compare with those practised among their non-native neighbours at the time, or among current reserve members. As with other aspects of resource relations, economic features are integrated with cultural processes in complex ways.

Lytwyn (1990, 1992) has made important contributions to what we know about the economic and political conditions related to the peninsula's early fisheries. It is difficult to assess the 'broader' meanings that the fishing economy had for this era's Saugeen community. But it is clear that the fishery was significant both within the community and as part of external relations. Lytwyn's attention to 'spiritual' dimensions of this fishery could be problematic if it encourages one to ignore important practical dimensions, but it is valuable as a challenge to narrow notions of economics and politics that we might otherwise use here.

Many of the older community members I interviewed did not seem particularly concerned about maintaining the distance between native and non-native domains, as typically defined along ecocentric and anthropocentric lines. And they were not guarded when discussing local economic interests and activities:

> The fisheries plant still has a lot of wrinkles in it. They could operate a fish market right out of there if they so desired. But in order to get a fish market going ... you are dealing with food, and you need so many inspectors and you have to meet the high standards. It isn't just anyone can afford to get into that. (CP-FJ)

> I think that what has to be done is the people have to realize that when the price of fish drops they should pull their gear out of the water. The

reason it drops is that there is a glut on the market. Catching twice as much is not going to alleviate the situation. They have to stop feeding the market till the price comes back up. In the long run they would be farther ahead. (CP-TJ)

The processing plant is a failure because there is no boss; there are five different guys running it. Business is generally a one-person dream. Once you have confidence then there is a possibility of business. (CP-WN)

We are so oriented to the white man's way that our Indian ways don't work anymore. When you are earning dollars and cents you have to keep looking for more fish. (CP-PT-FJ)

While ecocentric perspectives can draw attention to the need to guard against the excesses of economic interest, the practical view that many of these older community members bring is relevant to the development of local regulations and management approaches. Their pragmatic knowledge can contribute to an understanding of economic issues, and of ecological questions as well.

The need to address ecological issues brings special challenges. As noted earlier, there is a general consensus in both communities that stocked exotic species are undesirable. This preference may be seen as ecocentric, as it is associated with the maintenance of established ecological integrity. But it is also anthropocentric in that the preferred species are the ones most likely to benefit native communities.

The preference for indigenous species raises the difficult ecological questions about what steps, if any, should be taken to ensure and promote the well-being of indigenous species. A general non-interventionist approach to fisheries management is often expressed by native community members. But this approach is not straightforward.

Timm Rochon, fisheries coordinator at Saugeen, suggested that before a non-interventionist approach could be followed – before 'nature' could be left alone – exotic species needed to be eliminated: 'Asking whether we would try to deal with these problems the presence of exotic species is like asking whether we would try to clean up an oil spill' (SG-RK-TR). His approach to insuring the well-being of indigenous species was extreme compared to most. Typically, a non-interventionist approach seemed adequate even for dealing with introduced exotic species. Nature would eventually take care of these things too:

> I don't believe in lamprey control. Should let it take its course. Nature would balance the lamprey problem. (CP-R2)

> I figure nature will take care of its own. There is a reason for those zebra mussels being here. There must have been something wrong or they wouldn't have came. There must be a purpose, maybe to clean the water or something. There is a reason for everything ... The cormorants are sure coming back here. Everything has its purpose. We shouldn't interfere with nature. (SG-JR)

> I think all these things are subject to some kind of control. Man tries to intervene with purple loosetrife or mussels or lamprey, but nothing really happens. There are probably natural cycles and control mechanisms that we should rely on more. Like everything, these introduced species have to run their course. (SG-RK)

A non-interventionist approach has potential as a guideline for incorporating local concerns into fishing management. But this is an especially challenging area, in more than ecological contexts: 'On a practical level, though ... there is little we can do about what is happening outside of our jurisdiction in the lakes. But within our jurisdiction it might be all right to run a lamprey program at Denny's Dam, for example. Another thing is to find a use for them. People consume them, so maybe we could start a new market for them' (SG-RK). Any decisions based on a non-interventionist or any other approach are limited by the current lack of clarity in matters of political jurisdictional, and by the fact that ecosystems are interconnected beyond jurisdictional boundaries.

Likewise, issues related to the rehabilitation of fish stocks present challenges that a non-interventionist approach is only partially applicable to:

> We would try to re-establish the lake trout if we could find some that were indigenous to the area. I see fish as being adapted to particular areas ... Transplanting would have adverse effects ... because of natural selection. The food chain might not be complementary. If you could totally duplicate things it might work; but otherwise the fish is probably traumatized being out of its natural habitat. Given a chance to develop, the resource will come back. (SG-RK)

Perhaps because strict non-interventionism is closely tied to ecocentrism, it cannot be expected to offer specific solutions to complex problems.

Where ecocentric principles are viewed as central to a native approach, many other fisheries-management decisions also become problematic. For example, since shortly after the Fairgrieve decision, an aquaculture project involving open-water fish cages has been in operation at Nawash. Chief Akiwenzie suggests that this enterprise is reflective of a native approach – it is a way to add to the resource and thereby help maintain ecological integrity: 'I believe there are methods in place whereby there would be regeneration, and the First Nations people strongly favour the natural way. We have also in this last while had a natural going process established by the Nawash Fish Farm. Setting up cages in the water is one way to add to the resource that we think has a lot of potential' (CP-RA).

There are interesting possibilities here, though most of the support for the fish-cage project within the Nawash community seems to stem from its potential social and economic benefits, rather than its potential for enhancing the environment or reducing negative impacts. Some have in fact voiced concerns about ecological impacts: 'I like the idea of them running the fish farm ... I think there is potential to create employment through fish farming, but one thing that bothers me is the question of how much pollution comes from these fish. They were going to monitor the waters to make sure there was no pollution' (CP-RJ).

Others have noted the apparent contradiction between the community's criticism of sport-fishing hatchery operations and their own fish farming:

> There is a lot of concern too about the disease that comes with stocked fish. Fish coming out of a hatchery could carry some sort of a virus that could be devastating to the natural fish. This fish pond that they've started behind the fire-hall leads me to believe that we are talking in two different directions. We are talking about them stocking salmon and skamania from the fish hatcheries, and they are afraid of this virus and disease; and at the same time, we bring the same fish here and put them in the cages where they are still in the same water ... At the fishing meetings that I have gone to, concern about diseases coming from hatchery fish was one of the big things; but we turn around and do the same thing. (CP-TJ)

Given the widespread objections to sport-fishing hatchery programs, I was somewhat surprised to find a good deal of interest in establishing a hatchery at Nawash. Older community members are particularly enthusiastic about this prospect: 'They should start a hatchery to get a restocking program going' (CP-EA). The potential contributions to ecological well-being from fish farming are more difficult to see than those coming from hatchery activity: 'I think a hatchery would be worth pursuing ... As far as putting fish back in, our lakes are going to take a long time to recover' (CP-RJ).

Those concerned about accusations from the outside note that establishing hatchery operations would also be a statement of the community's concern for conservation: 'We should have a hatchery so we can put fish back and won't be accused of just taking' (CP-R2). The potential economic benefits of a hatchery are also noted by several people:

This is the lake trout country. There is no two ways about it ... We have to have a hatchery and then use all the shoals around the Cape ... The demand for lake trout could come back. The purchaser is not aware of the lake trout any more. He hears whitefish and trout, but he is not sure what the trout is so he buys whitefish. Trout was a greater demand all my life. It would grow. You could get 75 cents for lake trout and maybe 15 to 35 cents for whitefish. Now trout is 50 cents and whitefish $1.90. (CP-WN)

Ninety-five percent of the people at Cape Croker became trollers for lake trout in the summertime ... If you could develop that – maybe splake could be used the same way ... You could have guiding for tourists. (CP-WN)

I see this internal criticism of the community's fishing activities as a healthy sign, as indicating a potential for adjustment and improvement. Ted Johnston sees the community's decision not to set up a hatchery as an indication that concerns for ecological well-being have been pre-empted by short-term economic interest:

At one time I thought they were going to go into a stocking program – stocking the natural species that are in the lake; but it has not progressed yet to my knowledge. As a matter of fact, I see where one of the things noted in the Fairgrieve trial was that people at Cape used to mix eggs and milk and return it to the water. But with the economy sliding they are selling the eggs to the States instead. They have moved away from concern about what is in the lake and what should be in the lake, to monetary concerns. What is more valuable, a dollar a pound that they are getting from the States or a pound put back into the lake as a fertilized product? (CP-TJ)

Mixed local opinion might be viewed as evidence of conservation problems by opponents of native fishing rights who may still be looking for inadequacies in native resource relations as a way to distract attention from the ecological impacts of their own practices. This makes an open critical assessment of local fisheries decisions even more difficult. Where it does occur, it is a healthy step toward dealing with challenges in local fisheries management.

8 Traditional Knowledge

Traditional environmental knowledge (TEK) has important meanings within this fishing conflict as part of a critique of established approaches to fisheries management. It also has a potential role in negotiated fishing agreements. To explore these meanings and potential I further examine local perspectives on established fisheries management and science. I then discuss how notions about traditional knowledge were articulated by Nawash community representatives at a co-management conference they hosted. This is followed by an analysis of how traditional environmental knowledge is reconstructed in the context of the conflict, and as part of broader initiatives in cultural revitalization. Finally, I explore the ethical potential of traditional knowledge.

Fisheries-Management Science

I think that the whole situation has to be rethought because the ministry itself does not seem to have a real good track record as far as I am concerned. (CP-TJ)

Native fishing rights are often argued with reference to the appropriateness of apparent differences in native and non-native approaches to conservation. While stocking practices are a central focus of this debate, native community members have voiced dissatisfaction with established (non-native) management in broader contexts. Some of the people I interviewed felt that they were not knowledgeable enough to assess management science, and so they generally accepted it; but many have serious concerns about the science on which the management decisions of the Ontario Ministry of Natural Resources (MNR) are made:

> MNR aren't managing it. They don't know what's out in the water. By the time they finish their studies three years is gone by. Talk to the fishermen; they can tell you what is out there. (SG-TM)

> The perch went here within the last twenty years. And yet you try to tell MNR that they are not there. MNR insists that they know how to run the fishing and how to manage that; but they can't tell us what happened to the perch. (CP-FJ)

Scientific findings regarding stocking practices are especially likely to be viewed with suspicion. Some natives assume that biologists who provide studies in support of stocking are biased in favour of angler associations:

> There are a number of MNR bureaucrats and biologists who are OFAH [Ontario Federation of Anglers and Hunters] members, and there is a lot of cooperation between MNR biologists and OFAH in stocking programs, even though they may be harming the ecosystem. (CP-DM)

> Sporting clubs will say they have done tests, but they use their own biologists, not independent ones. They will say the salmon is not doing any harm. They can pay a man to say almost anything. (SG-LK)

At the same time, native community members readily assume that scientific research can support their critiques of stocking programs:

> This minister was applauding a hatchery that dumps two hundred to three hundred thousand fish in. There is no scientific data on these fish. (SG-WK)

> They are all hatchery raised. Even the full lake trout that they say is natural is raised in a hatchery. So that's what some people in the scientific world are studying now, whether a lake trout raised in a hatchery can actually reproduce in a natural system. (CP-BJ)

Science is also often accepted as a potential support for the approaches that some native-rights supporters see as alternatives to current fisheries management:

> We would use scientific data and use a quota system. We would have to be strict with that. It would have to be on the fishermen's minds. We can't deplete the stocks. (SG-WK)

> The preference is to let the system regenerate itself, over time. And of course that would have to be augmented by data, scientific data. (CP-RA)

These various assumptions about the validity of fisheries science are linked to political concerns.

In keeping with the oppositional politics assumed by both supporters and opponents of native rights in this conflict, 'ecological knowledge' is emerging as a dual model that supports essentialized notions of cultural difference. As noted previously, the 'ecological Indian' has been critiqued by one side. The other side has questioned the validity of established fisheries science and compared it unfavourably to 'native approaches.'

A fisheries co-management conference was hosted by Nawash in March 1995 in Port Elgin, a town just south of the peninsula. Its stated purpose was to provide a venue for comparing native and scientific approaches to fisheries management. In the troubled atmosphere that followed the fishing trial, it was clear that the conference was also part of an effort to question the credibility of 'scientific knowledge,' especially as applied in established fisheries management.

At the conference, several invited scientists presented evidence of the dangers of stocking practices – evidence that supported native positions:

> At the Nawash Fisheries Conference the University of Toronto biologists showed that if you stock with non-indigenous fish, especially sports fish, you are looking for trouble. They compete with the lake trout in the area for food; and there is evidence of salmon attacks on some of the only remaining indigenous lake trout stocks in Georgian Bay ... We know they [hybrid lake trout] don't breed well in the wild; or if they do manage to breed with wild fish then they pollute the gene pool. And they introduce disease into the wild. If the goal of fisheries managers is, first, do no

harm, as I think it ought to be, then they have to take another look at their program. (CP-DM)[1]

Scientists from the University of Toronto substantiated the impact and devastation of stocking foreign species. (CP-RA)

The Port Elgin conference was an interesting political event in that native-rights supporters were given the opportunity to turn 'science' against those seen as having previously wielded its authority. In a broader context, native-rights supporters participated in an established process of advancing knowledge through scientific debate.

Traditional Environmental Knowledge

Contrary to the stated purpose of the co-management conference, there was no apparent productive dialogue between those with traditional knowledge of the fisheries and those with scientific knowledge. The traditional environmental knowledge that was supposed to be compared with or linked to scientific knowledge was not easy to locate.

Fikret Berkes (1999) provides good definitions, discussions, and illustrations of traditional environmental knowledge, or TEK (see also Scott 1996; Sillitoe 2002). TEK generally refers to experiential understandings about the environment and its features that are accumulated and transmitted within a particular social network, or cultural group. Like the term 'tradition' in its broader meanings, the 'traditional' quality of TEK is difficult to define precisely. There is growing recognition among anthropologists that tradition does not necessarily exclude change. In fact, the absence of change might even be seen as distancing an object or practice from the traditional category.[2] TEK is sometimes interchangeable with 'local environmental knowledge.' The two can overlap, but they can mean different things as well, since local knowledge is more explicitly dependent on place than on multigenerational social/cultural affiliations.

When I was doing fieldwork, conference organizers asked me to help with preparations for the co-management conferences. I was to contact elders at Nawash and encourage them to share their 'traditional knowledge' of the fisheries at the conference. I found this task to be quite difficult, partly due to my lack of social connections within the community at the time, and perhaps because of my own uncertainty about what traditional knowledge could be.

About half a dozen elders attended the conference. A few noted some general points in the workshops, but none addressed the topic of traditional fishing knowledge in the main sessions. Instead, a younger community member described a dream in which he experienced a connection between himself as a native person and the animal world. His presentation revealed his strong personal and political commitment to native ways, native rights, and the idea of traditional environmental knowledge; but what traditional knowledge is, or how it could be relevant to management of the peninsula's fishery, remained unclear to me. Since no clear definitions of TEK were provided at this conference, it is not surprising that little dialogue between representatives of traditional and established knowledge systems occurred.

Conference organizers were working with various notions of what traditional knowledge might be. The main conference coordinator asked me and others to look for specific examples of traditional environmental knowledge, based directly on local experience and passed down within the community. He was apparently interested in both 'local' and 'traditional' knowledge. But we were all aware that TEK is also a focal point in a 'global' movement aimed at the recognition of indigenous resource rights.

Conference organizers had access to various examples of the growing body of TEK research, including Johnson (1992), Suzuki and Knudtson (1992), and Inter Press Service (1993): several of these publications could be purchased at the conference. While global examples of TEK provided clues for finding local illustrations, the ideological and political dimensions of TEK may have distracted us from our local focus, and impeded our search for traditional knowledge of the peninsula's fishery. Only a few possible examples of local TEK were located: 'I was talking to Charlie Akiwenzie. He was talking about all the people who were involved in the egg ... stuff that was going on with lake trout, and how they noticed the rapid decline in '54' (CP-AE). The first point noted here had potential as the kind of specific example of local TEK that we were looking for: if native fishermen were involved in fertilizing and planting spawn on shoals around the reserve, and these practices were passed down through the generations, then this was a good sample of the ecologically sound implications of TEK.

This example may reflect elements of traditional knowledge; but how common this practice was, and how culturally specific, is not clear. Spawn was planted in local waters prior to the mid-1900s (CP-R1); but whether this practice was tied to the past in a way that can be called traditional is uncertain. Spawn planting was more clearly linked to hatchery programs in nearby towns:

> That was back in the thirties ... I took spawn in there when I fished with Hepburn ... All you done was to take the spawn and put it in the pail. Then take the male sperm ... rub the fish on the belly and that sperm would come out in the pail and then you'd swish it around and let it set for about fifteen minutes ... drain it off and then pour these spawn on a screen. That's where you kept them damp, with just a damp cloth over them ... The hatchery there was still running when the war was on. I don't know when it finished. (CP-FJ)

The other specific example of local TEK noted by Charlie Akiwenzie in the second-last quote is an observation of mid-century fisheries depletions. Native fishers no doubt accumulated considerable 'local' knowledge on which their fishing success depended. This allowed them unique perspectives on changes in the fisheries:

> In the middle fifties, in January, Charlie Shoot asked me if I had a net 'cause the bay had not frozen up like it usually had ... As soon as we started pulling the net it was white with fish, nothing but herring ... I have never seen so many. And that was the last time I saw so many, in the middle fifties. (CP-PT-DK)

> I mostly catch splake and whitefish and chubs. But there is not many chubs left, and hardly any smelt left. You used to get a truckload of perch or chub, but now you just get six or seven. And that's what the other fish feed on, chubs and alewife, at the bottom. (CP-EA)

> The old people know the shoals. (CP-WN)

A level of local environmental knowledge is also reflected in the way that Nawash fishermen timed seasonal fishing patterns: 'When the wild strawberries ripened then the spring trout were ready, so we could start trolling' (CP-GK). The ecological benefits of such local experiential knowledge are apparent: this could be combined with less experiential scientific information and thereby contribute to more effective management. Non-natives who have also gained knowledge through their involvement in the peninsula's fisheries have something to offer in this regard as well.

Past rituals associated with fishing were of special interest because they take knowledge beyond the local into the cultural. The most notable example we found relates to the treatment of fish bones: 'They had little ways to show spiritual connections. The fisherman would boil a fish but never put the bones in the fire. They had a spiritual kind of respect for them bones' (CP-WN). Fred Jones notes specific people who practised this ritual at Nawash: 'I remember my brother Edgar. Now, he would never throw his fish bones back in the fire. He always threw them out, to feed some other thing, some other form of life. That was the Indian's way of conservation' (CP-FJ). This seems to show a traditional native environmental practice at Nawash that is linked to perceptions about resource relations. It hints at links to very old cultural rituals and world views that are described and interpreted in some of our best ethnographic studies of Algonquian speakers (e.g., Speck 1935; Feit 1973; Hallowell [1960] 1976, 1992; Tanner 1979; Preston [1975] 2002). However, it is not clear how locally specific this example is:

> That is mostly what I've seen on the West Coast, if they were fishing by the river they wouldn't throw the bones back in the fire. They would put them there by the side of the river. Some people said they believed that another fish would take that frame, and it would come back to life. Or it was put there to feed animals, and save the other fish. (CP-FJ)

These ideas about how to treat fish remains may be part of a more broadly based 'Indian's way of conservation,' but they can be seen as 'traditional' by the peninsula's reserve community members nonetheless.

In practical terms, it is difficult to see how a traditional ritual treatment of fish remains might be translated into current management activities: the remains of larger fish harvests cannot be reasonably handled in the same way that smaller catches were. However, this example suggests an ideological value that might be incorporated at some level into a new management approach. And it has political currency in that it can be used to illustrate a possible contrast between native and non-native people's resource relations and values.

George Keeshig's example of information about the fishing season (ripe berries) and Fred Jones's examples of rituals regarding spawn planting and fish bones point to the possibility of very old ecological relationships – of knowledge passed down from early times within the community. However, to my knowledge there has been no sustained effort to gather traditional fishing knowledge in a way that would allow critical assessment of particular cases or of the overall pattern. Conference planners tended to accept hints of TEK unconditionally. There was no attention given to how the peninsula's histories of native resettlement and cultural interaction might have affected the flow of traditional knowledge. Along with our unfamiliarity with this complex topic, our efforts to locate and define TEK were limited by its political implications and essentialized assumptions about native/non-native differences.

Some native-rights supporters who are engaged in efforts to revitalize native traditions seem eager to accept any ecological statements made by older native community members as 'traditional.' When I interviewed Frank Shawbedees, he began talking about the disappearance of Ontario's passenger pigeons in the early part of the century. I first thought I had stumbled on a splendid bit of TEK that was transmitted through several generations. When I asked where his information came from, he replied, 'From the Discovery Channel' (SG-FS). Since almost everyone on the reserves now has access to a wide range of information sources, including television and printed material, it would be naive to assume that current environmental knowledge or even knowledge of native traditions has all been transmitted orally.

This does not diminish the possibility that other useful examples of TEK might be located on the peninsula. But a more critical perspective may be needed if we want to gain a fuller understanding of how complex social and political situations influence TEK, and thereby have a better grasp of what it is and how it could be used.

Gathering information about other traditional resources, for example, wild plants, would not be subject to the same political pressures as collecting knowledge about fishing. TEK of this kind may be easier to pursue. Since women have likely been more involved in some of these areas, questions about how gender roles have shaped processes of information gathering and transmission could be of interest here.

The main difficulty in our efforts to locate TEK in preparation for the fishing conference was the limited time we had, as dictated by the conference planning schedule. But I suspect that all involved gained some insights through participating in this search. One thing I learned was that traditional knowledge might be more about social processes than practices or ideas.

Tradition and Revitalization

The recent interest in TEK on the reserves is connected to a global movement that links environmental issues and indigenous peoples' rights, and it is part of an emerging effort toward the revitalization of native cultures and traditions. Not all community members are enthusiastic about the potential of 'bringing back the old ways,' but many are. A kind of 'traditionalism' is emerging, especially among younger and middle-aged adults. Many of the most active supporters of native fishing rights are strongly influenced by traditionalist assumptions. They draw on various sources in attempting to articulate and value what they see as 'the old ways.'

Most reserve community members identify to some degree with native people who have become popular figures within mainstream society. These figures seem to take on a special meaning for individuals who are focused on the work of cultural revitalization and are involved in fishing issues:

> Natives teach to respect. It will be acknowledged in time. Don't have to seek glory and fame. Sitting Bull was a humble man. He only did what his people wanted him to do. (CP-AE)

> There were things that happened here long before the whites arrived. There were prophecies of the whites coming. Black Elk was a prophet. His prophecies dealt with the environment ... He was talking about pollution of the waters and how this would effect fish life. (CP-AE)

Many see questions about environmental knowledge, especially debates involving the relative values of scientific and traditional knowledge, in the light of their enthusiasm for revitalizing 'traditions':

> The thing that's been running through my mind is the difference between traditional knowledge and Western 'civilized' knowledge ... Pollution came from Western science and from Western civilization. There hasn't been any of that sort of thing introduced by native people prior to the landing of Columbus five hundred years ago ... There are some rivers now that are on the verge of dying completely. That's all Western science. It's time we start using traditional knowledge in hopes of avoiding more damage. (CP-AE)

Some see the protection of 'traditional cultures' as a necessary step toward preserving traditional knowledge: 'There are people who ... should be left untouched or they will lose the traditional knowledge that they have. People lose their identity, their culture' (CP-AE) This explicitly links cultural revitalization with environmentalism, in a kind of cultural/ecological traditionalism.

From this perspective, local community values can be defined in sharp contrast to values held by non-community members:

> I like the way native people live ... If they couldn't look after you then a relative would take care of you. With state regulations that is all gone. We are finding out now that traditional methods have a more solid ground to them. Where they still have that community contact they still learn traditional values of respect ... I was raised with values to respect others and respect elders. I have to teach my children this. These traditional values have been lost in the Western world. They teach you to take care of yourself, not to work as a team. Get an education so you can stand on your own or take somebody else's job. (CP-AE)

While many of the older community members are likewise critical of the way things are done on the outside, they seem to base their views less on differences between traditional native ways and non-native ways and more on practical purposes. For example, few would completely agree with the sentiment of the last sentence in the previous quote. They are more likely to see the beneficial possibilities of educational opportunities as outweighing the system's corrupting or manipulative potentials.

The enthusiasm some people have for trying to return to the old ways is understandable, as they see this as a solution to the unacceptable conditions they have experienced. And where 'traditionalism' affects people's outlook on life, it can be a source of 'symbolic healing' and can have very real therapeutic benefits (Waldram 1997). But in some contexts, such as the fishing conflict, it also has potential pitfalls. It can, for example, encourage uncritical acceptance of idealized assumptions that may have limited relevance to current conditions.

While there are certainly exceptions and variations, my impression is that the older generation's orientation toward fishing issues is typically more practical than ideological. People old enough to remember the war years seem more concerned about immediate conditions than political ideology. Old and young identify their community in contrast to outsiders, but while differences were once largely understood in social and economic terms, they are seen in rigid ideological contrast in the emerging traditionalist perspective.

I use the term 'traditionalist' hesitantly in reference to those most actively engaged in an ideological redefinition of their communities. I do not mean to overstate internal community differences. Several older community members are actively engaged in reviving native traditions, and in that sense have much in common with the younger, more politically active community members who first come to mind as traditionalists. Also, traditionalists and others are working toward many of the same community goals. It is worth drawing our attention to traditionalism, however, since it is an important part of the community dynamic and plays a significant role in positions concerning fishing rights and management questions.

The fact that only a few older people on the reserves are actively involved in revitalizing the more essentialized forms of 'tradition' presented a problem for me when I assisted in gathering TEK in preparation for the fishing conference. Most do not explicitly associate past fishing practices with native philosophy or native spirituality, as these concepts are typically defined by traditionalists. I asked George Keeshig in a variety of ways what special importance traditional fishing activities had for the community. He repeatedly told me about the very real economic significance fishing had, and seemed a bit confused about why it was taking me so long to get the point. When I asked him about the way that native peoples used to think about the environment and how they looked after it, he replied, 'Well there used to be a conservation officer' (CP-GK). His response to my attempt to learn the difference between native and non-native fishing traditions was, 'They had different quotas' (CP-GK).

Fred Jones is interested in tradition, but when considering sacred rituals he does not lose sight of practical contexts: 'Fishing and hunting was the native's main source of livelihood, so naturally that went with all his ceremonies' (CP-FJ). Perhaps because he does not so readily view native/non-native differences in ideological terms, Fred assesses the prospects of MNR stocking programs without rejecting them outright simply because they are non-native. He is more focused on their ineffectiveness, their lack of attention to local conditions:

And the lake trout ... when they did try to replant them ... They had those hatcheries going, and they used to hatch the frys and take them out by boat, and let them go out in the deep water. Well, if there was any predators around ... goodbye lake trout. So they never got anywhere with that reproducing. What they would have to do is let the fish go where those other fish used to breed. And then as he found his way out he would find his way back there again. That is my theory, anyway. (CP-FJ)

Fred also provided an example of how local and non-local knowledge were integrated in a fluid way in past fisheries activities:

As I first remembered the smelt, we didn't know what it was ... When we pulled up the herring net we found a small herring that had teeth ... When we took it home nobody around here knew what it was, so we sent it to Toronto. Word came back that it was a smelt. That was the first I'd ever seen of them. After ten or fifteen years or so, you could find them in any creek. (CP-PT-FJ)

Though often reluctant to trust outsiders, older community members have made the best of social and economic opportunities where they could be found, and have incorporated various sources of information and influence into their communities where they could best contribute to community needs and aspirations.

After my interview with Fred Jones, I turned my tape recorder off, and he ended up telling me a story. Looking back now, the story seems to convey a message about my efforts to locate TEK. He told me that once when he was in town some of the fellows at the car dealership he often visited asked what kind of winter they should expect. They wondered if he might have some inside information, so to speak, since he was an Indian. Fred gave a prediction, I think it was for a very cold winter, based on several natural signs such as the abundance of different kinds of berries. His prediction turned out to be way off. When they asked him the next year for his prediction, he told them, 'You better ask the guy upstairs.'

Perhaps the message was that I had my work cut out for me if I was looking for idealized notions of native ecological relations. Or maybe Fred was saying that TEK, or knowledge in general, has a lot to do with social relationships – that it is good to stay humble about what one 'knows.' Maybe this is an important bit of knowledge passed on by the ancestors. In any case, I was glad that he could joke about a topic that is sometimes taken too seriously. At the time, I took his story as a refreshing reminder that it is good to keep an open mind.

Revitalization Challenges

Since the various positions on fishing-conflict issues are influenced by the broader emergence of traditionalism within the peninsula's native communities, current efforts at cultural revitalization deserve more attention. The term 'revitalization movement' was popularized around the mid-twentieth century by anthropologists interested in questions about culture change. They focused on how people attempted to make their lives better when cultural resources became threatened or limited (e.g., Wallace 1956; see also Warry 1998:208–13). Some anthropologists were especially interested in the role personal experience played in the profound decisions people were compelled to make when faced with situations of intense cultural contact. Broader structural pressures are also seen as significant factors that contribute to the disappearance and emergence of cultural forms.

The awareness that many of the problems within native communities are linked to historical conditions – that they are part of the legacy of colonialism – inspires traditionalists to revitalize the peninsula's two communities through restoring connections to the old ways. They draw attention to traditions in an effort to regain confidence, which has been diminished through social and economic marginalization. For example, promoting the Ojibway language, especially among young children, can encourage a greater appreciation of native culture, and has potential for linking younger and older generations: it increases opportunities for older people to share their knowledge.

But there are concerns in the communities about how far the revitalization of traditions should go. It has already gone beyond what most among the older generation are familiar with. An overly enthusiastic agenda of revitalization can create difficult challenges for the reserve communities. The practical gain of greater inclusion in the broader society that the older generation made may be overlooked in the effort to re-establish essentialized native ways that could have little connection to local realities. While revitalization efforts can renew links between elders and the younger generations, they might also bring new discontinuities.

At both reserves occasional recollections of traditional belief and ritual practice can be found: 'This fellow ... used to make cedar chairs, from the bush. He used to tell us: "Every time you take something from the ground, you put tobacco there." He used to put tobacco in the stove when there was a thunderstorm' (SG-RT). But many see traditional ways as something completely new:

> There wasn't any Indian religion when I was young. They said their prayers in English every night. No ceremonies as far back as I can remember, or my father could remember. He was ninety-four when he died and he told me that he never ever saw this kind of stuff that's going on now, the dancing, the tradition and that ... I can't remember any of that. (CP-EA)

Many older people understand traditionalist efforts as an attempted correction to the suppression of native ceremonies in the past: 'Traditional native religion is coming back, but it's not quite the same. The older people are gone ... Laws were passed to outlaw drumming, singing, dancing. The government said it was non-productive (SG-FS).

Older people who as elders have developed their own interests in native traditions provide guidance for younger people. They are sometimes asked to help sort out particular traditions: 'There is always some good and some bad. That's why when people ask me about some ceremonies, if they are right or wrong, I say they are not right or wrong. How you were taught is right for you' (SG-FS). Not surprisingly, what appear to be pan-Indian themes emerge in the revitalization of native ways on the peninsula, as indicated in Harold Thompson's descriptions of his paintings:

> It comes to me when I am drawing. It's about what the elders talk about: appreciating gifts; tapping into the source; unknown spirits. (SG-HT)

> It refers to fish and native people. The fish would give itself to people and in return people would let fish multiply. My other paintings also refer to respect for animals or mother earth. (SG-HT)

The old ways can also be renewed through the incorporation of ideas from non-native sources: 'When I went to school out west I used to hang around with Chinese and Japanese, and a lot of their beliefs are the same ... the four elements: fire, water, wind ... water represents life ... water belongs to a woman ... when a woman is pregnant a child is in water, so it is life' (SG-RT). Many regard native spirituality as very flexible: 'Spiritual belief is in you; and that's what I read in scripture. Traditional people use sweetgrass, but I don't know how to do it. I'm not saying I don't believe it, but I've never done it. It would be like reading your Bible, talking to the creator' (SG-RT).

Like on many reserves in Canada, there is a high level of involvement in organized Christian religion at Saugeen and Cape Croker. Some among the older generation are sceptical about the possibilities of maintaining more than one religious conviction:

> Christianity was creeping in. It did not care if you threw the whole damn fish in the fire. Even back then Bob Nadjiwon was more prone to go to church than to his old ways. He was already in a no-man's-land, a 'nothing time' or something, neither one nor the other. Even at my age I cannot take on this new spirituality. I believe it, but I can't take it on. Although I left the church a long time ago, you still have a conflict in your head. When I was in the war, in the trench, you were praying to a God, to keep you till morning. I never seen any atheists in the front line. Now they want to go back, to get their roots. I don't blame them, but I don't know whether they can or not. If they grow up in it they'd be alright, but if they go to church one week and then the sweat lodge the next, they are going to have a tough time. (CP-WN).

> The religious beliefs that come through now would have a lot of conflict with the European religious beliefs. (CP-PT-FJ)

Some see revitalizing native ways in general as being in contradiction to current realities:

> I think they should leave it and look ahead, not look back, because those days are gone by. They don't know what it was like. (CP-EA)

> It's hard to go back to tradition: you have to wear a war bonnet to look like an Indian. (CP-EA)

Older people's scepticism about revitalizing traditions does not stem from a lack of concern about social and cultural problems. This is implied in the way Fred Jones shifts, in the following quotation, from the topic of traditional ceremonies to the subject of reserve authority structures:

I don't really remember anything like rituals or ceremonies here at Cape. The only thing I remember ... is that at that time they had the Indian Grand Council. And they were supposed to be able to talk to the government ... but nothing ever came of it ... They had the Indian agent here then, and if the Indian agent said 'shit' you were supposed to stoop and strain to the utmost. This Indian Grand Council had representatives from all the reserves, probably about fifty people. But it never went any place because the Indian agent had all the say anyway. (CP-FJ)

Past experience dealing with non-native authority figures has left a lingering mistrust, but most among the older generation seem unconvinced that the new traditionalism is the only solution to current problems. They are cautious, as they would be toward any ambitious plan aimed at changing local conditions.

Traditionalists respect elders as potential sources of tradition. But where traditional knowledge is viewed narrowly it is difficult to see what can be gained from older people who have learned about adapting to local realities, but have not generally been focused on what might be distinctly native.

Several of the older community members at Nawash were invited to a potluck dinner, as part of the preparation for the Port Elgin co-management conference. Conversations recorded there between elders and younger people who were interested in traditions provide insights into the challenges of revitalizing traditional knowledge in the peninsula's reserve communities. Members of the older generation tried to encourage recognition of the contributions made by past generations, but they also had to deal with possibly unrealistic expectations.

Wondering why community ideals were disappearing, Sidney Nadjiwon asked, 'Is it too late to change it back?' (CP-PT-SN). Fred Jones replied: 'You would have to take a person away from all the influences here' (CP-PT-FJ). Eric Johnston speculated on how one could bring about changes needed in order to revitalize native traditions: 'A lot of things shape a culture, but at the end you have to have your change in values' (CP-PT-EJ). Fred Jones might have agreed to some extent: 'It's a hard thing to talk about. I could say it in Indian: "Nah wab in ah. Cup chin wah wi yah"' (CP-PT-FJ). But I suspect that his language shift was part of his answer. It was difficult for him to discuss native values with those who speak little Ojibway.

Getting back to the discussion of traditional knowledge, Sidney

Nadjiwon noted: 'My brother says over by Parry Sound the smelt are twice as big as they are here' (CP-PT-SN). Fred answered: 'That's possible. I wouldn't want to contradict him. You see, a fish grows a hell of a lot faster after its caught' (CP-PT-FJ).

At the end of this meeting, the elders were encouraged to attend the Port Elgin co-management conference and participate in discussions of traditional knowledge. Rather than answer yes or no about whether he would attend, Donald Keeshig joked about the name of the town where the conference was to be held. He made reference to part of the shoreline at Cape Croker, also known by the same name: 'Port Elgin is on the reserve "Little Port Elgin"' (CP-PT-DK). He then added: 'Our forefathers were great storytellers and we are losing it' (CP-PT-DK). His references to a local place and to the contributions of older community members suggested apprehensions about advocating traditionalism in a broader arena – apprehensions that he shares with many older community members.

My discussion of these topics is not meant to imply that the reserve communities are rigidly factionalized along traditionalist and non-traditionalist lines. Tradition means different things to different people, and most of the people I interviewed were surprisingly flexible in their abilities to see various perspectives. But some appear to be fundamentally attached to a traditionalist (or 'nativist') ideology in a way that limits a broad view of fishing issues. Interestingly, some of the most ardent nativists are themselves non-natives who are employed by the bands.

Neither do I mean to imply that the wisdom of most older people on the reserves that is not clearly linked to traditionalist scenarios is disregarded. On the contrary, I am impressed by the high level of explicit attention and respect older community members generally receive. This suggests that the community is so far flexible enough to incorporate a substantial amount of traditionalist activity, and the rapid changes that it encourages.

Those who are engaged in revitalizing native ways, and those who are uncertain how old ways apply to the native life they have experienced, have similar concerns for the well-being of their communities. Though the knowledge accumulated by the latter is a broader kind of traditional wisdom than most traditionalists are concerned about, it is the substance of the communities as they currently exist, and will hopefully not be overlooked. The wisdom that older community members have gained may be particularly important in attempts to find practical solutions to fishing-conflict issues.

Tradition and Ethics

One dimension of TEK often discussed by researchers, and of interest to conference organizers, concerns attitudes toward resource use, and how these are passed on within communities. In global contexts this links to debates about the existence of conservation ethics among indigenous peoples, and their apparent scarcity in non-indigenous societies. Locally, it reflects on the prospects of developing and maintaining fisheries regulations within the two reserve communities.

Several people provided interesting examples of how they learned lessons about the appropriate uses of resources as children, through participation in family activities:

> The only fishing we ever did was by hook and line. We used to go down to the river; the whole family would walk down. We'd catch bass and catfish, take them home, clean them, cook them, and eat them. We'd eat all the fish we caught. Nothing went to waste. (SG-EK)

> If one family did not have as much luck they would share it. And if you caught too much you got heck 'cause you are not to overfish or waste. (CP-PT-RW)

> I remember I was taught a wonderful lesson when I was a boy. Dad left me at the lake while he went and hunted someplace else. I shot a duck but I didn't want to wait for it to come to shore because it would be dark before I got home. Dad says, 'What did you shoot?' I said, 'I shot a duck.' He said, 'Did you kill it?' I says, 'Yes.' He told me to go right back and get it. He said, 'If you don't want it, don't kill it.' So I went back in the dark to get it. (CP-PT-FJ)

Donald Keeshig claims that 'an old Indian philosophy is not to overdo what you depend on; and not make fun of what you depend on' (CP-PT-DK). As a general statement of native ethics regarding resource use, this claim could be debated according to historical or ethnographic data, as noted in previous parts of this book. But this would miss the point. Donald Keeshig's claim is not so much intended as a statement of fact. Its primary purpose is to encourage behaviour that he sees as appropriate, and it indicates his concern about practical issues of resource distribution. At the same time, his statement has implications for maintaining community stability. One's identity as a community member can be expressed by upholding such norms. Donald Keeshig's claim is 'true' to the behavioural standards and community solidarity that it is aimed at promoting.

I found several other examples of how older community members have appealed to native traditions, as a statement of community ethics. These might appear to contradict the older generation's tendencies toward practicality and locality, but their traditionalist interests also reflect practical community concerns.

Winona Arriaga was one of the few older community members who spoke at the Port Elgin conference workshops. She expresses her ideas about native traditions in an unassuming way:

> In my own way ... my age ... I still believe in the old teachings of the people ... that we will continue to fish ... we will continue to hunt. We will continue to do what our ancestors have done ... to raise families. (CP-WA)

> I know the people ... they had means of ... they did what they had to do to keep the fish going. Let's put it that way. They knew what they had to do. They were taught from generations back ... to keep the fish going. (CP-WA)

Practical concerns that she shares with her peers are evident in the above quotes: she hopes to improve the well-being of families within the community. In her role as elder, Winona Arriaga provides guidance to various younger people, including those who are more actively involved in native resource issues: 'Like Winona says, everything is connected. The water is polluted because of the air' (CP-PT-DJ).

In 1995 a sunrise ceremony welcoming the return of spawning fish was performed just outside of the Nawash reserve at Colpoys Bay. This ceremony, which was not known to have been held in the area previously, is a good illustration of how 'tradition' is being revitalized in order to express ethical positions and at the same time support political ones. The ceremony's organizer, Brad Kiwenzie, described the native perspective that the ceremony was intended to demonstrate: 'It is a way of respect; a way that sees the fish and the fishery as part of a world we all share' (*Bruce Peninsula Press*, early May 1995:1). Winona Arriaga, who performed the ceremony, stated that 'in the old days everything had a ceremony; it was a way of showing gratitude to the Creator for what he gives us. We offer tobacco to welcome the fish back. But the ceremony is not just for native people – we share it with our brothers from the four directions' (*Bruce Peninsula Press*, early May 1995).

The sacred qualities of this ceremony are explicit in these descriptions, and so are the political ones. The fish that were ritually offered were taken from a restricted area. MNR authorities contemplated laying charges, but decided not to because of jurisdictional and political uncertainties. There was some disagreement at Nawash about whether they should have taken fish from a restricted area, but among traditionalists the ceremony was likely viewed as an important political statement.

Several years later, native fishers tested the political waters without ritual association, by netting fish at a restricted spot on the Sauble River. In this case, local enforcement officers took no action because they interpreted native fishing rights as allowing them to take fish from such places for their own consumption (Owen Sound, *Sun Times*, 4 April 1997).

The example of the welcoming ceremony can be seen to illustrate the close fit between ethical and political implications of 'traditions.' As a statement of appropriate resource relations, the ceremony has normative impacts within the community. Winona Arriaga's participation as an elder extends her connections to members of the younger generation, who may seek her advice in other matters. In the politically charged atmosphere of the fisheries conflict, the ceremony conveys community values beyond the community as well, which gives them a more explicit political role.

In both of the above descriptions of the welcoming ceremony, people from outside the native community were explicitly invited to participate. Sharing in this 'traditional' re-enactment would bring them into the circle of community norms and extend the community's sphere of influence. As with Donald Keeshig's claim about Indian philosophy, the validity of this ceremony as a 'traditional' performance could be debated with reference to historical fact. But it is at least as interesting, and as relevant to the fishing conflict, to explore how 'tradition' functions within ongoing social processes, and what it means on a personal level to individuals as well.

Though Ross Waukey is reluctant to speak about traditions in public, younger community members often talk with him individually or in small groups. Ross sees native and non-native perspectives as quite distinct: 'Indians have their own thinking. They see nature differently' (CP-R3). Like many of the people I interviewed, he is careful to state that his own perspectives are not necessarily shared by all community members, as noted in the following quotes:

> When you plant a garden and put too many seeds in, once they grow you have to start thinning. Same thing with nature; it balances everything ... dead trees ... nature balances it. Indian people thought of nature as a person looking after things. That's my opinion, anyway. (CP-R2)

> Nature is alive – a living person – just like you and I. You can only do so much to nature and it will eventually give you a disappointment, just like a human being. Because if you distrust nature it will do the same back. The creator put these things here for us to use, not to disrespect. That's about all I can say ... Different people have different ideas. This is my own. (CP-R3)

Ross Waukey's descriptions of the native view of nature emphasize personal awareness of a place within the environment:

> We are part of nature but don't recognize this. It's up to the individual. All trees and animals are like humans. We have to communicate with them because they tell you something – show you something. (CP-R3)

> There has to be a regrowth for humans to live. (CP-R3)

> I think that is why humans are here, to look after trees ... help keep the balance. (CP-R3)

But his concerns extend beyond individual connections to the environment. His expression of traditional knowledge has social implications, hinted at above in his reference to not disrespecting nature and in his personification of nature. Ross links the kind of respect one should have for nature to respect within social relations: 'If you don't respect a thing, the thing won't respect you' (CP-R5). He suggests that people who discriminate against others or become too greedy are falling 'off the path' (CP-R5). The 'path' is both social and natural.

There are traces of old Ojibway ideas in Ross Waukey's expressions of TEK. He is fluent in the language and he listened to older people, particularly an aunt, when he was young. He also has ideas about the personification of thunder and other environmental features that are similar to descriptions noted in Ojibway ethnographies (e.g., Hallowell

1992). But Ross Waukey's insistence that his ideas are his own points to the role of individuals in reconstructing traditional knowledge.

The notion that individuals recreate traditions challenges the view of traditional knowledge as a fixed set of beliefs and practices passed on through generations. But the adaptive quality of tradition is as interesting and significant as its stability and continuity. Traditional knowledge may be refashioned to suit new resource opportunities or problems. And in the context of its social normative functions, traditional knowledge is bound to change according to the changing social conditions that a community needs to address. Old messages will be maintained where they are useful, though there 'usefulness' can be broadly defined.

The fact that a community's stories are sometimes passed on for long periods with little alteration may indicate that the messages they carry can address conditions that are regularly prevalent.[3] But the past is not just tradition when it is brought into the present.

Given the adaptive aspects of traditional knowledge, Ross Waukey's view that he is only giving a personal opinion does not conflict with his suggestion that he is explaining the Indian perspective. The 'Indian life' in the past century has entailed rapid changes for many, and has been different for different people. Ross Waukey begins to explain what native life is in the preceding quotes where he discusses his beliefs and links them to appropriate social relations. In the following quote he remembers economic hardship as a large part of Indian life: 'Indian life was rough. I remember times when we had nothing to eat in the house. We preserved fruits – wild apples for the winter ... We used to live on hunting and fishing: we would make sure nothing was wasted' (CP-R4). In this context, Ross's philosophical notions about relationships with nature are grounded in practical concerns. When one has the right relations with resources and with people, resources are shared and social hardships are alleviated. In this light, necessity might encourage conservation in the classic sense of not wasting resources. Ross's frequent references to notions about 'respecting nature' might also be seem as ecocentric, but he typically links the individual's responsibility toward nature to social responsibility. In his view, neither people nor resources should be taken for granted.

Sharing as a Conservation Ethic

Several of the elders who spoke at the Port Elgin co-management conference workshops noted that they have always known 'sharing' as an important value within the reserve community. They were hopeful that this value might inform fishing-conflict issues and fisheries-management questions.

Sharing is often noted as a unique quality within native communities. From my experience, I would agree that sharing is highly valued within the peninsula's reserve communities. I also think sharing may have some universal qualities, in that it is likely to emerge in particular places. Where there are obvious economic and cultural differences, sharing can take on special importance (in terms of survival) and special meaning within disadvantaged groups. While most reserve residents have greater economic opportunities than their ancestors did, many still see themselves as economically less well off than most in the broader society. A living memory of frequent informal exchanges within these native communities is frequently articulated as an important traditional value.

This tradition of sharing might be incorporated into a local fisheries-management approach. Translating values into practice is not simple, but perhaps fisheries resources have special potential in this regard. Even during the hardest times, fish could be caught and distributed to those most in need:

> If anybody came along they could have a fish. (CP-EA)

> Being that Grandma's nephews were fishermen, she'd just go down there to the shore where they landed and she'd go and get a fish or two, but she always took the heads. She had a wooden barrel, a lard bucket they used to call them at that time, and in the fall of the year, around November I guess, she would salt these fish heads down for use in the winter months. (CP-WA)

Such recollections maintain the special meanings that fish have as a focus of sharing within the community. This also extends to people in other native communities:

> I like pickerel ... they get them where native people are fishing on the Thames River down south ... Of course, there are some of the people from down there married up here, so we get the pickerel up here. They bring it up for us, just to give us a treat of their fish ... pickerel. (CP-WA)

Since this sharing ethic can operate as a mechanism of social control, it has potential for encouraging the observance of fishing regulations that the communities are establishing:

> Dad used to go down if there was a boat there that had fish, and he'd take one without asking for it, and nothing was ever said. You were welcome to take what you wanted ... Any of the older people could do that ... Well, I guess they still do that, but not too much. I would go up where those fishermen are fishing, and they will just give me what I want. Or if they had a different kind of fish that they didn't have a sale for they would offer it to me. So I guess sharing is of the same value that it was then. (CP-FJ)

In the above quote, Fred Jones suggests that today's native fishers share like they always did. But more importantly, where he hesitates in making this statement, he demonstrates the social process that helps keep this ethic in effect.

The ethic of sharing shows the goodwill of community members; it also depends on social commitment. On the two reserves there is close scrutiny of how resources are distributed: there is pressure to maintain the social commitment on which the sharing ethic is built. This became evident to me when I discussed 'overfishing' problems with community members. I introduced the topic of overfishing in several instances with the intention of gathering information about how the resource was being affected. But the term seemed to have different primary associations for most of my interviewees. For them, harvesting too many fish has more to do with people than with the resource – 'overfishing' occurs when individuals benefit from the fishery at the expense of others:

> Fishing might be the only way to earn a living for some. Not sure if it will help the reserve but some people might help themselves. We need to watch, not to overdo it. There is always someone who will overuse the fish. Natives should have their own conservation officers. (CP-GK)

Many people are very concerned about how the benefits of increased fishing activity will be distributed in the community. Reserve fishermen who own larger fishing tugs are sometimes suspected of taking too much:

> Everyone should have equal rights to fish, the same opportunity. If you have a big tug it should be the same. I sometimes get three or four boxes. (CP-EA)

Maybe more people could get involved in fishing; but not with such big nets 'cause the fish would be gone. Even now we should be careful. When we used rowboats we only got about fourteen fish each day. (CP-R2)

Oh, lots of people used to fish with rowboats, almost everybody, mostly for their own use. Not like today, just for the money. Every year we fished, we would buy something we needed for the family. When I was small they asked someone for a quarter. Now it's a loonie. I bought a freezer one year, a washer, a dryer the next. (CP-EA)

The suggestion in this last quote that some people may be in the fishery 'just for the money' is a powerful sanctioning statement: questioning a person's commitment to appropriate economic relations can be a challenge to their place within the social group that is defined in part through the sharing ethic.

Such social pressure could contribute to the effectiveness of a local fisheries-regulation system. It is likely not powerful enough to eliminate fishing tugs; however, it allows concerns to be taken more seriously than they would be if sharing was not so highly valued.

Some regard the presence of a sharing ethic in native communities as a kind of natural conservation approach: 'Concepts of conservation, although not widely publicized, are followed by most native peoples in terms of sharing resources and having a sense of community instead of living an individualistic life' (SG-RK). Sharing within the context of a reserve community is relevant as a general guideline to some local fisheries-management questions, but there are issues that may not be usefully clarified through reference to community interests alone.

While all Canadian citizens face the challenge of balancing community and individual rights, this tension is especially evident for native community members. 'Community' here is defined and emphasized through continual contrasts with the outside. The collective quality of native fishing rights in itself contributes to the identification of group difference, and of community.

Native people also participate to varying degrees within the broader society, where individual well-being and achievement often seems to be encouraged with only vague reference to social responsibilities. Shifting between contexts where social ties are valued differently can be informative, but it can also be disorienting. Each individual has culturally mediated notions of social, economic, and ecological well-being that play a role in their decisions about how to participate in various levels of community.

Since the peninsula's fishing opportunities and problems transcend reserve boundaries in both social and ecological contexts, native community members cannot avoid involvement in wider domains. How to participate meaningfully within the broader society remains a special challenge for many native people. This tension plays a role in how people understand and respond to fishing-conflict issues. Resolving this conflict can go a long way toward resolving deeper challenges.

9 Toward Dialogue

The most important issues are who owns the fishery; who manages it; whether the stocks are adequate to sustain a commercial harvest ... basically, whether or not there is a future in fishing. (SG-RK)

The current fishing conflict on the Saugeen-Bruce Peninsula involves a complex mix of social and ecological issues. Assessing these issues critically and openly can allow useful insights into the conflict. Given the political volatility of the situation, it may be difficult for representatives with various interests to look beyond the frameworks they have built in support of their positions. But some steps have been taken in this direction. A more open dialogue can clarify underlying issues and common concerns.

Revisiting the Past

The field of historical ecology has served the purpose of this book in several ways.[1] It highlights the importance of history as a context for understanding resource relations. Historical depth assists in sorting through the complex concepts and assumptions we have developed to explore relations between humans and the environment.

The relevance of history for understanding native issues is increasingly evident to researchers and policymakers, as it is to native people. Many of the individuals I interviewed were very interested in historical aspects of the fishing conflict.[2] They are aware that a lack of attention to their history in the past is part of a broader pattern of marginalization. They also see social inequalities as historically rooted, and view the rights they assert as historical rights.

Opponents of native fishing rights also recognized the importance of historical context. Differences of opinion over historical questions constitute battle fronts in this conflict. Since cultural identities are tied to historical interpretation, the very act of contesting history can accelerate tensions.

By including historical contexts in this study of fishing conflict, I too have become a participant in complex processes of cultural identity formation. I have often reflected on the seriousness of my roles and responsibilities, and I remain confident that it is better to apply what I know of anthropology in an effort to improve things than to abandon this project because of potential disadvantages for the various groups involved.

While this book is my own analysis of conflict issues, and includes my own interpretations of what local community members say about the fishing conflict, it is greatly enriched by the local perspectives that these people contributed. Their histories of the fishery and views on fishing issues bring the past into the present in especially meaningful ways.

There are other individuals and communities whose voices could elaborate on the interpretations provided here, and thereby contribute to an expanded dialogue. I feel that a focus on native perspectives is a good starting place, given the limited opportunities Canada's aboriginal people have had to speak in such contexts in the past. This book is an unfinished story of the peninsula's fisheries and its people. Hopefully, it provides some useful insights and points to questions that deserve further exploration.

Michael Herzfeld (2001:56) suggests that anthropological histories can be more relevant by not only illuminating the past, but also by including histories of the concepts and assumptions that we use to do this. Assumptions on which we base interpretations of prehistoric and historic resource relations are worth revisiting in this regard. The image of prehistoric peoples as big-game hunters is rightly being reevaluated by archaeologists, who suspect that it has diverted our attention from other subsistence practices such as fishing. This has limited our explanatory scope; it has also raised problematic gender issues.

The importance of early fishing activities in the Great Lakes region is now generally accepted, but there is still much we do not know about the complexity and diversity of past resource relations. By more explicitly recognizing and admitting what we do not know about the past, we may be in a better position to avoid investing too heavily in tentative notions.

We know more about subsistence practices and fish-harvesting patterns in the region during and since the early historic period, given the availability of written documents, but here too much is unclear. Speculating about the peninsula's contact-era inhabitants is difficult since we are unsure of the constitution of cultural groups in the area at the time. We can make educated guesses, based, for example, on typical differences between Algonquian and Iroquoian peoples – their subsistence modes and related settlement technologies (especially housing patterns). But we should not forget that 'typical' necessarily implies possible exceptions. It appears most likely that Algonquian speakers were on the peninsula during this period, but there are unanswered questions about how they were connected with other Algonquian groups and other Iroquoian people, or with 'multi-ethnic' groups that included both Algonquian and Iroquoian speakers.

Fishing activities were likely affected by population shifts (refugee dispersals and new amalgamations) associated with the Iroquois incursions into Southern Ontario in the mid-1600s. But the lack of clear evidence of continued native settlement on the peninsula during the seventeenth and eighteenth centuries does not exclude the possibility that native bands relied at least intermittently on the peninsula's fisheries.

More recent historical situations are likewise still open to interpretation. Lake Huron's commercial fishery is typically viewed as a non-native fishery, but it can also be understood as emerging through increased non-native involvement in an already existing native fishery. As the Great Lakes commercial fishery expanded, native participation did not necessarily diminish. Expanding market opportunities were pursued, and there was some benefit for native communities from fisheries leases. While the constraining impacts of changing fishery policies and settler expansion in general should not be overlooked, neither should the substantial contributions made by native people to the emergence of this industry.[3]

Fishing has played an important role in the peninsula's changing social and ecological landscapes for hundreds and likely thousands of years. The fact that there is a native commercial fishery here today attests to its special importance for the peninsula's aboriginal people. To understand the role of the fishery, and thereby the peninsula's historical ecology more fully, we will have to continue evaluating our methods and assumptions, as well as the information we use.

Rethinking the Present

Ethnoecology can be defined as the study of how people in different cultural settings understand ecological features, and how their constructed meanings are connected to other cultural domains (e.g., history, social organization, political situation, economic mode). This orientation meshes easily with historical ecology, which also recognizes symbolic and ideological domains as integral parts of human-environment relations. While much ethnoecological research is focused on gaining insights into unique ecological categories and world views, we can also recognize the construction of meaning as having moral and political dimensions. Given this broader context, ethnoecology can connect easily with political ecology. Interestingly, it also shares purposes and potentials with the approaches of discourse analysis, both being concerned with how accepted concepts and meanings might support established power relations. A broad ethnoecological framework can help clarify perspectives on fishing issues held within various groups.

The conceptual and ethical basis of native people's past resource relations has become a contentious issue in this conflict. Exploring areas such as this can be interesting, but interpretations that overlook the real-world interdependence of ideas and practical conditions are of limited relevance. Whether native people's cultural perspectives somehow predispose them to conserve nature is often debated as if it could be settled by weighing historical and factual evidence. The many faces of 'conservation' may account for some of the confusion that seems to pervade such debates.

But this is more than an intellectual exercise. When we engage with this debate, we almost automatically enter moral and political domains. The uses of such notions of 'ecological Indians' are at least as interesting as their substance. Anthropologists may be able to contribute more by clarifying the contexts in which they are used than by playing the 'role of referee in a game of truth in which there are no winners' (Herzfeld 2001:88).

Many environmentalists adopt the image of the ecological Indian in their efforts to counter forces they see as devaluing and destroying the environment. Perhaps some identify with the image because it symbolizes and expresses a deeply felt affinity they have with the natural world – a world that represents higher meanings, not found in the social world as they see it.

Ecocentric environmentalism may be an attempt to both counter negative environmental impacts and imagine a better world. In the latter sense, it has a revitalization quality that may seem familiar to some First Nations community members. Ecocentric perspectives can give meaning to one's experiences and bring much-needed attention to environmental degradation. But they are limited when it comes to finding workable solutions to complex conditions created within the inevitable presence of social, and not just ecological, order.

Though native ecological relations are often associated with ecocentric qualities, practical resource-use concerns are readily apparent, particularly among the older generation. Opinions on fisheries issues often suggest classic conservationist notions more vividly than they do preservationist ones. In this regard there is some common ground with typically conservative angler-association spokespersons. Some such overlap should be expected, since many native community members are themselves active anglers and hunters, and it is not unusual for natives and non-natives to participate in outdoor activities together.

While angler-association representatives seem to hold mainly conservative notions, they too cannot be adequately portrayed as a homogeneous group. They are regarded by many native-rights supporters as classic conservationists in the worst sense, efficiently controlling and exploiting an already endangered fishery for short-term personal gain. While some may fit this depiction, and while it is not hard to understand why native people might focus on features that threaten them, anglers also incorporate preservationist approaches in their activities to some degree. Programs for the restoration of fish habitats, for example, may be motivated by a combination of instrumental and intrinsic values.

It should also be noted that the level of anti-native rhetoric seen in Ontario Federation of Anglers and Hunters (OFAH) magazine publications during the early 1990s is no longer evident. This could reflect a response to opposition from native-rights supporters, coupled with a need to accommodate diverse perspectives on native rights within the association's membership. It might also reflect the fact that OFAH representatives are currently more concerned with other political issues. They are actively defending their group's fishing and hunting interests against opposition from a rapidly growing animal-rights lobby.

While some common ground is visible, OFAH's opposition to native fishing rights is still a central focus of the conflict. The classic conservationist doctrine of the greatest good for the greatest number remains a slogan for angler-association representatives in their promotion of what they see as the interests of their constituents. And this doctrine still clashes with approaches that would incorporate social justice and historical agreements in decisions on resource use.

Revisiting, Rethinking, Rebuilding

Political ecology further emphasizes the role political power plays within resource relations. It traces its lineage in part to the field of political economy, and it has incorporated the latter's focus on large-scale global workings of power. This focus reflects concerns about domination and oppression. Political ecology can also inform studies where more diverse and often ambiguous power positions are evident.

Political ecology links easily with historical ecology, since some impacts of power are best seen through time. It also connects with ethnoecology's potentials: political power has ideological dimensions and is maintained or contested through assertions of meaning.

Within the peninsula's fishing conflict, political positions have been formed on either side of a debate about recognition of native resource rights. Rubinstein (1994:1000) points to a common pattern seen in conflict situations. Through various means, each side depicts the opposing group as a threat. In this fishing conflict both sides have constructed images of their opponent's resource relations as part of their portrayals of threats to their own livelihoods. Some writers have referred to this, especially when regarded as a form of resistance, as a kind of 'strategic essentialism' (see Herzfeld 2001:64). This tendency makes it difficult, if not impossible, to build a dialogue aimed at reaching agreements about how to address underlying problems.

While the fishing conflict centres on fishing rights, broader social issues are involved. The feeling of marginalization prevalent in native communities filters perceptions of the way fisheries are managed and controlled by people on the outside. A better understanding of this sense of alienation may be a necessary step toward productive agreements on fisheries management.

The study of revitalization movements explores how various groups of people have dealt with cultural stresses – how they respond to such situations by constructing and following visions of a better world. The current interest in native ecological traditions within the peninsula's reserve communities may be part of a revitalization process, part of an effort to deal with social stresses associated with problematic cultural conditions.

While all people encounter stress in their lives, the reserve situation is not typical: social difference is delineated by the reserve boundary, which protects the integrity of the community but at the same time maintains a level of marginalization. Spatial distance is compounded in many cases by natives' memories of discriminatory experiences when on the outside, and by recognition of a lack of fairness in government policies, past and present. Such tensions shape feelings about current fisheries issues.

When OFAH representatives challenge the ecological Indian, and blame natives for depleting the fishery, they invite dramatic responses. Given an ever-present concern about the lingering effects of colonialism, which is part of the world view of many reserve community members, even a well-meaning or apparently neutral non-native interest in native cultural symbols can invite accusations of cultural appropriation (see Warry 1998:20–8). Debating or otherwise defining native traditions, ecological or otherwise, is sure to be contentious where colonialism is the backdrop (see Kaiser 1987; Churchill 1988; Gill 1990:131-2; Kehoe 1990).

It would seem that part of the solution to the conflict and to more general problems on the reserves is to reduce the factors that contribute to the marginalization of native people. But with escalating tensions, the native community is increasingly marginalized as differences between natives and non-natives are emphasized.

Band leaders and researchers have countered accusations of native overfishing by criticizing those who oppose native fishing rights. Non-natives are portrayed as anti-conservationist, and also as racists. The OFAH campaign is seen by some as bringing politically established anti-native sentiments from far and wide to fan the flames of local racism, which has infected both local citizens and MNR enforcement officers regulating fisheries. There are few greater dangers than racism. But given the rampant promotion of difference on all sides within this political conflict, it is difficult to know which fears are warranted and which are not.

If resolving the fishing conflict's underlying issues is a community priority, it may be necessary to also promote awareness of what native and non-native groups have in common. A shift in this direction might only be expected, however, when there are sufficient indications that non-natives are doing their share to combat racism where it does exist.

One of the few local non-native peninsula residents I interviewed runs a business that provides services for tourist anglers. When I asked him what he thought of MNR conservation programs, his answer seemed to typify a 'wise use' approach to conservation. He suggested that MNR officers spend more time working on the river instead of in their offices. They should be keeping a better eye on the number of fish caught. He regards hatchery programs aimed at increasing rainbow trout stocks as very important because he sees tourist fishing as offering the greatest benefit for the greatest number of local people.

The sense of practicality indicated here would not likely be altogether foreign to many reserve members, even though this interviewee's support for hatchery programs conflicts with the official native critique of angler associations, and native fishers value different kinds of fish. But this articulation of a utilitarian, 'wise use' approach seems to be an example of the view that sport-association representatives typically convey in their arguments about why we should not recognize native fishing rights.

Though not everything about the 'classic conservationist' approach is necessarily wrong or dangerous, it is well matched to sentiments expressed within a 'populist' movement that has emerged in Canada over the last decade or two. This movement claims to speak for a cultural majority, which it sees as 'ordinary Canadians' who have lost their fair share of political control because of concessions made to 'special interest' groups (see Mackey 2002). Within this perspective, 'governments' are portrayed as inefficient and inept managers. The comment noted above, that resource managers should be spending more time working on the river instead of in the offices, may be an example of this. Government is, more seriously, targeted for supporting 'politically correct' policies that give advantages to 'special interest' groups.

A better system, according to this populist view, would support fairness and equality. It would treat all citizens the same, and thereby achieve maximum benefits for the largest number of people. Opposing 'special interests' is thereby a rational and just measure needed to insure optimal benefits for all. It is a good 'Canadian' thing to do.

The problem with this set of notions is that it presumes the right to define what a 'special interest' is. It claims to represent 'ordinary Canadians,' and thereby attempts to privilege a particular set of preferences as 'ordinary interests,' against which all others can be known as 'special.' Should we as Canadians be concerned about who is thereby establishing our identity, and for what purposes?

This 'populist' movement may be attractive to many because it promises a simple solution to complex policy issues, including questions regarding native resource conflicts. And it seems to offer individuals an avenue for gaining and exercising some control. Given the complex social structures and processes we have created in the 'modern world,' there is no shortage of reasons to wish for more control in our social and environmental relationships, and to hope for more meaning and certainty.

Populism promises a more secure cultural identity, but what might this promise be worth, and what might be the cost of accepting a vision of 'equality' that is defined according to what it excludes? The potential negative consequences of the exclusionary possibilities entailed in populist assumptions deserve critical reflection. If we accept the populist approach, would we be less motivated to continue exploring more inclusive ways to distribute power, less interested in achieving democracy's greater potentials, less willing to do this difficult work?

Several of the native community members I interviewed felt that better communication with the outside is an important step toward resolving the conflict issues:

> Anglers are accusing the Indians of slaughtering, of rape and pillage, but they are not showing an atmosphere of trying to understand what is going on with the native fishery. (CP-HJ)

> This problem could be corrected by better communications. Whoever is on the other side, they don't know who all is fishing. If they found out more they would realize more, not jump to conclusions. (SG-PS)

> It is also important to bring people here to see who we are. There needs to be more of that. A lot of misunderstanding is created by artificial walls. (CP-RA)

> And when I see what is happening ... to me, it is unnecessary, if everyone learned to share. And that is part of our history, as a people ... to make sure you share ... Too bad today that there's anger included in dealing with fishing and land claims. And I believe why this is happening is no one knows us. That part of our history was never known ... was never even in the history books. (CP-WA)

Appendix 1 Time Frames

This chronological list of time frames is adapted from various archaeological and historical studies. These time frames are useful for organizing information about past fishing activity in my study area. Unless otherwise indicated, each time frame follows in fairly direct succession.

Prehistoric
Palaeo-Indian Period   begins 11,000 BP
Archaic Period   begins 10,000 BP
   Early Archaic   ends 8000 BP
   Middle Archaic   ends 4500 BP
   Late Archaic   ends 2600 BP

Woodland Period
Early Woodland   overlaps last centuries of the Archaic and ends 2300 BP

Middle Woodland   ends 1200 BP
Late Woodland   extends to the contact era

Historical
Early Historical
   Contact Era   1615–50
   Iroquois War Period   1650–1700
   French and British Period 1700–1830
Late Historical   1830–1900

Twentieth Century
Early 1900s   1900–45
Mid-Century and Beyond   1945–2004

Appendix 2 Information Sources: Prehistoric and Historic

As research on the Saugeen-Bruce Peninsula is limited, I make use of writings on other regions from which relevant information might be inferred. Several broad studies convey a sense of the antiquity of fisheries relations, and indicate the various ways fishing methods have been employed in the past. Radcliffe's study ([1921] 1974), based primarily on Old World sources, includes illustrations of ancient fishing activities. About half of Rau's (1884) study is focused on North America. Rostlund (1952) remains the most comprehensive source on North American aboriginal fisheries, in spite of a few tentative speculations, some of which have been subsequently refined (see, for example, Lister 1993:265). Cleland (1982) builds on Rostlund's work. Brief descriptions, but fairly extensive reference lists for aboriginal fishing and related topics, are found in White ([1913] 1969).

Jennings (1989) is a good introduction to North American prehistory. A collection of articles edited by Chris J. Ellis and Neal Ferris (1990) is among the most informative and up-to-date studies of Southern Ontario prehistory (see also Wright 1994).

Until about two hundred years ago, the peninsula was peripheral to recorded history. Some maps of the Lake Huron region were made during the late 1600s and early 1700s (see Fox 1952:27-37), but these maps are typically poor in detail, suggesting a lack of first hand familiarity with the area. A few rough survey sketches and notes were made in the late 1700s and early 1800s, but the peninsula's past was otherwise not written down until the 1800s, when the first records of resource activities on Lake Huron's shoreline were made.

Information about the Saugeen-Bruce Peninsula's native peoples has been published in a few recent historical works. Schmalz (1977) includes reference to nineteenth-century fishing conflicts. DeMille (1971) provides valuable insights into the history of the peninsula's reserve-period native people and their resource relations. Lytwyn (1992) is the only substantial article focused primarily on the peninsula's aboriginal fisheries. Polly Keeshig-Tobias, a First Nations community member, presents a local perspectives on the history of the peninsula's native fishery (1996).

Jenness's study (1935) of a nearby aboriginal group provides valuable insights into traditional native perspectives and practices in the region. The region's past is examined in a collection of articles edited by Rogers and Smith (1994).

Useful references to the peninsula's native fishery are included in studies of groups adjacent to the peninsula (e.g., Waisberg 1977; Lovisek 1991) and in broader regional studies (e.g., Rogers 1978; Schmalz 1991). Several researchers (e.g., Lytwyn 1990; Van West 1990, Hansen 1991, Wright 1994) have focused on the history of the regulation of native resource uses in Ontario. Scattered descriptions of mainly non-native fishing activities on the peninsula are included in McLeod (1969), Robertson ([1906] 1971), and in less formal local histories (e.g., Gatis 1980; Wyonch 1985; Armitage 1994; see also Fox 1952; BCHS 1967). Other references are noted throughout this study.

Appendix 3   Interviewee List

This list includes the names of people who were formally interviewed during my fieldwork. Quotes from nearly all are included in this thesis. A copy of the interviews was returned to each community with the names of the interviewees noted, and permission to include interviewees' names in my thesis was received during the interview process.

The first two letters in the interview codes refer to the reserve community (SG = Saugeen; CP = Cape Croker). The last two letters are derived from the interviewees' names. I occasionally attach a third set of initials to the main interviewee designation where I am citing a statement made during an interview by someone other than the main interviewee. A third set of initials is also used to indicate specific people within the 'Potluck' ('PT') group interview. I interviewed Ross Waukey on five occasions. His interviews are numbered accordingly. This referencing scheme does not apply to the anonymous interview conducted at Saugeen, or the two anonymous interviews conducted with non-natives that are noted at the end of this list.

Cape Croker Interviews
CP-AE	Austin Elliott
CP-AN	Angus Elliott
CP-AS	Ainsley Solomon
CP-BJ	Blake Jones
CP-DK	Donald Keeshig
CP-DM	David McLaren
CP-EA	Earl Akiwenzie
CP-FJ	Fred Jones

CP-GK	George Keeshig
CP-HJ	Howard Jones
CP-PC	Philomene Chegahno
CP-PT	Potluck Group Interview:
CP-PT-EJ	Eric Johnston
CP-PT-DK	Donald Keeshig
CP-PT-FJ	Fred Jones
CP-PT-SN	Sidney Nadjiwon
CP-PT-DJ	Darlene Johnston
CP-PT-LK	Lenore Keeshig-Tobias
CP-PT-RW	Ross Waukey
CP-PT-ED	Ed Koenig
CP-R1	Ross Waukey
CP-R2	Ross Waukey
CP-R3	Ross Waukey
CP-R4	Ross Waukey
CP-R5	Ross Waukey
CP-RA	Ralph Akiwenzie
CP-RJ	Ross Johnston
CP-TJ	Ted Johnston
CP-VJ	Verna Johnston
CP-VN	Vincent Nadjiwon
CP-WA	Winona Arriaga
CP-WJ	Wayne Johnston
CP-WL	Wilma Nowell
CP-WN	Wilmer Nadjiwon

Saugeen Interviews

SG-A1	Anonymous
SG-AS	Arnold Solomon
SG-CS	Carol Solomon
SG-DR	Darlene Ritchie
SG-EK	Emma Kahgee
SG-EM	Esau Mitchell
SG-FS	Frank Shawbedees
SG-HT	Harold Thompson
SG-JR	Jim Ritchie
SG-LK	Leonard Kewageshig
SG-PS	Perry Solomon

SG-RA	Rosa Anoquot
SG-RK	Kahgee
SG-RK-TR	Timm Rochon
SG-RR	Ruth Roote
SG-RT	Rita Root
SG-TM	Theodore Mason
SG-WK	Willard Kewageshig

Anonymous Interviews

MN-AN	Anonymous
SO-AN	Anonymous

Appendix 4   Excerpt from *R. v. Jones and Nadjiwon*, 26 April 1993

DAVID A. FAIRGRIEVE,
Provincial Judge

Conclusion

In my view, it is not the function of a summary conviction trial court hearing charges under the *Ontario Fishery Regulations* to state what scheme for allocating fishery resources might meet the appropriate jurisdictional standard. Apart from lacking the technical expertise, there are other users with claims to be made and interests to be considered who have no standing in a prosecution of this nature: see *R. v Duncan* (1991), 65 C.C.C.(3d) 546 (B.C.S.C). In the particular context of the Georgian Bay and Lake Huron fishery, there are complications arising from the fact that certain fish stocks, and lake trout specifically, currently depend on government hatcheries and plantings. It may also be that the aboriginal community derives direct or indirect economic benefit from a tourist industry that operates in part as a result of the recreational fishery available. Quantifying the benefits may be problematic. All these matters are undoubtedly appropriate subjects to be considered during the process of negotiation and consultation between the government and the Saugeen Ojibway, a process that does not involve the court.

What should be stated, however, is that a high-handed and adversarial stance on the part of the Ministry will neither meet the constitutional requirements with which, one would expect, it would consider itself duty-bound to comply, nor will it provide an enforceable regulatory scheme capable of achieving the conservation goals which it seeks. It is self-evident, I think, that s. 35(1) of the *Constitution Act, 1982*, particularly after the judgment of the Supreme Court of Canada in *Sparrow*, dictated that a new approach be taken by the government to ensure that its policies discharge the obligations assumed by its constitutional agreement. I do not think it was ever suggested that there would necessarily be no adjustments required or no costs attached.

As a practical matter, the Court cannot compel good faith or recognition of changed constitutional realities. All that can be done here is to state the conclusion that the quota restrictions do not meet current constitutional standards and are, accordingly, unenforceable against the defendants. The imposition of a prohibition against the purchase of lake trout from Band members pending negotiations and a new arrangement which recognizes the priority of their aboriginal and treaty rights would, in my view, also be unconstitutional. It would also fail to reflect the high standard of honourable dealing which the public expects its government to take in respect of the rights of aboriginal people.

Howard Jones and Francis Nadjiwon are found not guilty, and the charges are dismissed.

Appendix 5   Ojibway Vocabulary from Tanner*

Fish Species

[Ke-goi-yug]   fishes
[Nah-ma]   sturgeon
[Mas-Ke-no-zha]   maskenonge, or pike
[O-zhaw-wush-ko-ke-no-zha]   green pickerel
[Ke-no-zha]   pickerel; from [Kenose] long
[Na-ma-goosh]   trout
[Na-zhum-ma-goosh]   brook trout
[Ne-git-che]   buffalo fish
[Bush-she-to; plural, Bush-she-toag]   sheeps head
[Mon-nuh-she-gun]   black bass
[Ad-dik-kum-aig], [Attai-kum-meeg menom]   whitefish;
    from [Ad-dik]   reindeer and [Gum-maig]   water
[Buh-pug-ga-sa]   large sucker
[Mis-kwaw-zhe-gun-no]   red horse
[Nah-ma-bin]   sucker; [Mis-kwun-nah-ma-bin]   red sucker
[Ug-gud-dwawsh]   sunfish
[Sah-wa; plural, Sah-waig]   perch (yellow)
[O-ka-ah-wis]   fresh-water herring
[We-be-chee]   a fat fish larger than herring; only found in the Red
    River
[Mon-num-maig]   great catfish
[Ah-wa-sis-sic]   little catfish (The indians say this fish hatches its

*([1830] 1975:311–14)

young in a hole in the mud and that they accompany her for some time afterwards.)
[Ke-na-beck gwum-maig]   eel (water snake)
[O-da-che-gah-oon]   gar
[Shig-gwum-maig]   shovel nose, only in the Mississippi
[Kuk-kun-naun-gwi]   little toad fish, in Lake Huron
[O-gah-suk]   little dories, in Lake Huron
[O-gah]   dory
[Bug-gwut-tum-mo-goon-suk]   (These are small fishes that make their appearance in ponds having no connexion with rivers or lakes, and which are sometimes quite dry. But though they all perish in times of drought, they re-appear when the ponds are filled.)
[Shaw-ga-she]   crawfish.
[Ais; plural Ais-sug]   clam
[Ais-ainse]   little clam
[Mis-koan-sug]   red clams

Totems

[Ke-no-zha]   Pickerel, of [A-ke-win-de-ba]
[Ad-dik-kum-maig]   Whitefish, of [Wawb-o-jeeg] the white fisher
[Nah-ma-bin]   Sucker, of [Nain-no-we-ton]
[Ah-wa-sis-se]   Small Catfish, of [Matche-kwe-we- zainse] (Sometimes they call the people of this totem 'those who carry their young' from the habits of the small catfish.)

Notes

Introduction

1 See Adlam (2002) concerning native fishing issues and conflicts in Eastern Canada.
2 The historical ecology, ethnoecology, and political ecology approaches are discussed in more detail in chapter 9.

1 Getting to Know the Peninsula and Its People

1 The term 'fishery' is used to signify either a fish population or both the resource base and human harvesting activity. Unless otherwise indicated, I imply the latter. The terms 'fisheries relations' and 'resource relations' indicate broad interconnections between people and resources, including both practical use patterns and underlying knowledge and meaning.
2 I follow standard archaeological style where indicating dates, placing 'AD' before the date and 'BC' or 'BP' after it. AD 1950 is the date from which the number of years BP (before present) are counted.
3 An alternative meaning is suggested by W.S. Fox (1952:2, 3).
4 'Chi-Cheemaun' means 'Big Canoe' in Ojibway. Donald Keeshig, a member of one of the peninsula's two native communities, suggested the name in a contest in the 1970s.
5 Chief's Point, a smaller reserve located a few kilometres up the Huron shoreline, beyond Sauble Beach, is also part of the Saugeen First Nation.
6 These figures were obtained from Chief Richard Kahgee (Saugeen) and Chief Ralph Akiwenzie (Nawash).
7 I capitalize tribal and band names as well as the term 'First Nation,' which implies a specific group. For writing convenience I do not capitalize broader

categories such as non-native, native, and aboriginal. The terms 'aboriginal' and 'native' refer to pre-contact peoples of what is now North America, and those who claim ancestral ties to such peoples. I also refrain from capitalizing the term 'white,' which I use only where its generalized connotations are part of the context. I employ all of the broader categories with attention to their limits as generic references that gain much of their meaning through assumed exclusion of equally generalized opposites.

8 When I was not certain about whether individuals were capable of giving informed consent, I obtained consent from close relatives as well. In three cases, interviewees passed away before I got final copies back to the community. I also obtained consent from next of kin to use these interviews.

2 The Fairgrieve Decision and Its Impact

1 Regarding interpretation of the Sparrow ruling, see also Boldt (1993:32–8), Crystal (1996), and Sharma (1998). This ruling helped clarify how 'the constitutional recognition of treaty and Aboriginal rights works' (Crystal 1996:120). More specific to fishing rights, it established a priority order for groups wanting to fish. Sparrow also defines government responsibilities for actions that might be taken in the name of conservation if such actions could infringe on native rights. This responsibility includes consultation with native representations.
2 Regarding legal attempts to address the question of whether aboriginal fishing rights include a right to 'commercial' fishing, see Wilson (1993). The challenge of defining the commercial extent of native fishing rights has recently come to the forefront in light of the 1999 Supreme Court ruling in the Marshall case, which more explicitly recognized native commercial fishing rights (*Record*, 30 Sept. 1999, A3).
3 Chief Kahgee passed away in early 2001. For consistency I use the present tense when presenting his interview comments, as I do with reference to several other deceased interviewees.
4 Judge Fairgrieve viewed 'traditional territory' as extending seven miles out around the peninsula. However, there is uncertainty as to whether this line completely encloses the bay at Owen Sound.
5 Regarding the Oka stand-off, see Fleras and Leonard Elliott (1992:92–9). In this incident native reserve members and their supporters barricaded roads in an effort to draw attention to their claim to a section of land that was slated for development by the village of Oka. The scenes of violence that followed have been, as Fleras and Leonard Elliott state, 'etched in our collective consciousness as Canadians' (1992:93).

3 Fishing in the Distant Past

1 Elaine Dewar's recent book, 'Bones: Discovering the First Americans' (2001), is presented in a literary/journalistic fashion, but it includes interesting insights into what we might and might not know about the first occupants of this continent. Dewar surveys current scientific work in this area, and assesses it quite convincingly.
2 The Palaeo-Indian period in Southern Ontario stretches from about 11,000 to 9500 BP. Regarding this time placement, and distinctions between early and late periods, see Ellis and Deller (1990:52–5; see also Funk 1978:16; Julig 1994:21–4).
3 Because of water fluctuations, Palaeo-Indian shoreline sites may currently be submerged along the peninsula's coast.
4 Ellis and Deller (1990:38) note an example of Palaeo-Indian peoples who lived where only small animals were available, but used the same tool kits employed by hunters who had access to big game.
5 Some stone tool types were dropped or were not as well made, while new tools and tool-making techniques and materials were introduced. Woodworking is more apparent, and greater regional variation is seen both in tool kits and in site types.
6 Due to quick decomposition, estimates of an increased presence of bone fishing tools, which could indicate more fishing, are problematic (Ellis et al. 1990:66).
7 Gorges are small splinters sharpened at both ends. Also referred to as 'bait holders,' they were likely used much like fish hooks (Rostlund 1952:113).
8 The earliest copper tools found in the Great Lakes region date to 5600 BP (Ellis et al. 1990:69).
9 While the peninsula is in closest proximity to the Saugeen tradition, it is also transitional to two other Middle Woodland traditions: the Laurel, centred on Manitoulin Island and farther north, and the Point Peninsula, centred east of the peninsula (Daechsel 1994).
10 Algonquian refers to a language group that at the time of contact was spread through the Great Lakes region, from the Atlantic to the Prairies. Iroquoian languages were spoken in the southeastern part of the Great Lakes region.
11 Researchers have speculated on possible Algonquian and Iroquoian connections going back to the Middle Woodland (e.g., Spence et al. 1990:168); however, to my knowledge, no links to the Middle Woodland Saugeen tradition have been suggested (Spence et al. 1990:168; see also Fox 1990b:171).
12 The linguistic term 'Iroquoian' includes several other groups besides those

located south of the lower Great Lakes who made up the Iroquois Confederacy, or League of the Iroquois (see Tooker 1978; Weaver 1978).
13 Additional information about Huron life-ways has been advanced through archaeological studies (e.g., Ramsden 1990).
14 The term 'Odawa' is preferred by some writers (e.g., Rogers 1978:760).
15 An extensive archaeological survey conducted by Fitzgerald (1979) revealed no new settlements west of the Petun centres, which supports Garrad's deduction (see also Fox 1990c:458).
16 See also Waisberg (1977:73).
17 Pukaskwa pits are depressions lined with stones. They are usually regarded as vision places or burial sites, but may have served a variety of other purposes including storage.
18 Other references to seventeenth-century fishing in the Mackinaw area are included in Rau (1884).
19 The French built several forts and trading posts in the Lake Huron region, and there is some suggestion that one or more posts were built on the peninsula; however, none have so far been conclusively located.
20 Historical documentation of this period is, unfortunately, limited since French traders, unlike earlier French missionaries and later British traders, seemed less inclined to keep detailed records of their activities.
21 For example, the men that Champlain encountered on the French River in 1615 are most often regarded as Ottawa, but are sometimes noted as Ojibwa (e.g., Rogers 1978:760; Schmalz 1991:14–15). Today's Ojibway (or Ojibwa), Chippewa, Mississauga, and Saulteaux have similar historical roots, and were closely tied to Ottawa, Potawatomi, and at times Huron peoples (Rogers 1978:760). In Southern Ontario these groups have historical links to Shawnee and Menominee as well (Rogers 1978:760). First mention of the people now thought of as Ojibway was in a 1640 French report, in which they were referred to as 'Saults' (Tanner 1974:351). 'Saulteaux' or 'Saulteur' are other French designations for the Algonquian peoples inhabiting the 'falls' or 'rapids' regions around the channels between Lakes Huron and Superior. Ojibway and Chippewa are generally regarded as synonymous, and are perhaps both derivatives of the term 'Ochipoe' (Skinner 1911, cited in Greenberg and Morrison 1982:91).
22 See Mason 1976:352–7; Ritzenthaler 1978:743; Rogers 1978:760–70; Greenberg and Morrison 1982:75; Greenberg and Spielbauer 1991:31–3.
23 Rogers refers to the time that I approximate as the British period, from 1760 to 1830, as the era of 'Land Cessions' (1978:763).
24 After the British assumed control, what is now Southern Ontario was known by several names as part of British North America. From 1791 to

Notes to pages 56–70   201

1841 it was part of Upper Canada, from 1841 to 1867 Canada West, and after 1867 Ontario.
25 Gourlay (1822:175–82) notes a large variety of fish species found in Upper Canada's rivers and lakes during the early 1800s.
26 Post factors noted their personal gill-net fishing success, as well as the wider fish trade (HBC B.109/a/2). Post employees recorded trips made to various locations around Lake Huron, including 'Saguingue.' The peninsula's Saugeen River was formerly referred to by that name, however, it is possible that these post accounts pertain to a location with the same name on Huron's western shore, as suggested by a 27 August 1829 entry that describes Saguingue as being 'on the other side of the Lake' (HBC B.109/a/2).

4 Change and Adaptation

1 In the late 1960s most of the Fishing Islands were returned by the federal government and are now native territory (Schmalz 1977:145–6).
2 Kincardine and Goderich are about forty and eighty kilometres, respectively, down the Lake Huron coast from Southampton.
3 Various estimates of the earliest uses of large seines and gill nets in Lake Huron are noted in Landon (1944:113), Barry (1978:106), and Spangler and Peters (1995:107).
4 Kane's 'salmon' is likely a 'lake trout,' which is a member of the salmonidae family. Various salmon, trout, and char are related within the salmonidae family, and the common names often overlap. Some 'trout' are closer in scientific classification to 'salmon' than to other 'trout,' and vice versa. In early and late historic-period literature, the terms 'salmon,' 'trout,' and 'salmon trout' are used in reference to Lake Huron's indigenous 'lake trout' or 'lake char' (*Salvelinus namaycush*). The generalized term 'salmon' is easily confused with the Ontario salmon, a variety of Atlantic salmon (*Salmo salar*) that was indigenous to the waters downstream from and including Lake Ontario (see MacCrimmon 1977:86–90). Various other species of salmon have been more recently stocked in the waters above Niagara Falls.
5 See also Brown (1932) for an interesting fictional depiction of the informal fish trade between natives and non-natives around the peninsula during this era.
6 Noting occasional acts of piracy, some have portrayed these fish-trade relations as highly competitive (e.g., Barry 1978:144; Lovisek 1991:87).
7 My sketch of the region's emerging commercial fishery is admittedly preliminary. Tough (1996), in his study of resource development in northern

Manitoba, depicts native involvement in emerging resource economies in greater detail, and with a sharper focus on disadvantages for native people related to power imbalances within emerging industries.

8 These confrontations occurred about the same time as the Dakota uprising in Minnesota, as noted by Tanner (1987:178).

9 Photographs of McGregor's descendants and other information about McGregor's career in this area are exhibited at the museum in Sheguiandah on Manitoulin Island.

10 There are slight differences between the chronology that Lytwyn presents, which he derived from public archive documents (1998, pers. comm.), and the one noted by Fox. Fox (1952:115) states that in 1848, after downturns in productivity, Dunlop's company was sold to two retired Hudson's Bay Company traders, John Spence and William Kennedy. Fox does not mention Cayley's tenure in his account of the Fishing Island companies, and Lytwyn does not mention Spence as Kennedy's partner. See also Weichel (1998:21–3).

11 Rowan states that after this deal was signed, the Americans put a duty on tin cases and 'drove a four-horse team through the spirit of the treaty' (1972:47).

5 Mixed Economies: Twentieth-Century Fisheries

1 Several of the peninsula's older non-native fishermen were interviewed in the 1970s by David Loftus, an Ontario Ministry of Natural Resources employee.

2 Verna Johnston also comments on the early and mid-century reserve fishing economy in a biography written by Roz Vanderburgh (1977:78–93, 166).

3 As well as indicating an indigenous lake trout species, the name 'lake trout' is sometimes used in reference to a stocked hybrid cross of original lake trout and speckled trout. The hybrid is also known as splake or back-cross.

6 'Conservation'

1 Henry David Thoreau is another writer (a 'transcendentalist') who articulated a preservationist vision. Grey Owl can also be seen as an ecocentrist or a preservationist, after he rejected the commonly held view that valued animals (the beaver in particular) only for the consumable products they might provide (see Dickson 1973).

2 Rarely is an environmental critique of modern society made without con-

trast to indigenous peoples' ecological relations (e.g., Wittbecker 1986:265–7; Johnson 1991:268–9; Jull 1991:453; Eckersley 1992:54; Suzuki and Knudtson 1992; Rasmussen 1993:177; McPherson and Rabb 1994:63). Native ecology is explicitly linked to ecocentric values by environmental philosophers such as Overholt and Callicott, who try to show the similarity between Ojibwa environmental relations and Leopold's land ethic (1982:154–5; see also Callicott 1989:207–15).

3 In Canada, the Berger Commission brought similar attention to traditional environmental knowledge. Traditional environmental knowledge, or TEK, is discussed in more detail in the next chapter.

4 Though some local areas likely suffered, widespread collapses are not clearly indicated until at least the turn of the century.

5 Though Olver et al. (1995) claim to be looking beyond utilitarian issues, they present principles that could as easily be based on instrumental as on intrinsic values (see p. 1587–90). Here and elsewhere they evoke the paradox of humans claiming to be able to represent the interests of other-than-humans.

6 Muir, as indicated earlier in this chapter, is regarded as the author of North America's first ecocentric perspective.

7 The genius of Leopold's land ethic may be in the paradoxical way that it allows one to understand humans as both separate from and connected to ecological domains. He made human impacts on the environment more vivid by first articulating a vision of the non-human-centred eco-community that could be affected.

8 The promotion of local management represents a challenge to Hardin's hypothesis (see McCay and Acheson 1987:2–6). Those who see already established local patterns as having important potential for making resource management more effective see Hardin's assumption that 'common property' is the same as 'open access' as problematic. Common property is often regulated, if only informally, within the protocols of local social relations, and is therefore not the same as open access.

9 Regarding historical accounts that have been cited in debates about native people's ecological impacts in the Great Lakes region, see Vescey (1980:9), Trigger (1981:27), McNab (1984:98–100), and Brightman (1987:123, 1993: 255–6). For ethnographic accounts of recent native conservation practices, see Feit (1973) and Tanner (1979). For critiques of Martin's hypothesis, see Krech (1981). See also Black (1981:112) and Trigger (1981:29–34). See Hames (1987:106) regarding the problem with claiming a determining link between ideas or beliefs and actions.

10 For discussion of ecological ethics in Palaeo-Indian times, see Krech (1999: 29–43). See also Martin (1978:169, 1992:33), Jones (1990), and Olsen (1990).

7 Local Perspectives on Conflict Issues

1 See note 4 in chapter 4 regarding definitions of 'salmon.'
2 Scientific and other forms of 'ecological knowledge' are discussed more directly in the following chapter.
3 The terms of this agreement have not yet been made public.
4 In her analysis of fishing-rights issues on the West Coast, Pinkerton notes that following the 1974 Boldt decision it took seven years before government representatives decided to abandon alternative legal strategies in favour of negotiating with tribal communities (1992:331).
5 Events that occurred during the last few years confirm these apprehensions. Several local fishers rejected participation in the band regulation system. Some were charged by the MNR for not reporting harvest amounts.

8 Traditional Knowledge

1 In this quote there is a possible contradiction between the dangers of polluting the gene pool (which assumes that introduced trout can breed) and the ineffectiveness of stocked trout (which apparently cannot breed). However, each critique is worth considering in itself.
2 Some folklorists, for example, see a 'traditional' song that has been recorded and promoted in the music industry, and thereby given a more permanent form within popular culture, as having been shifted out of the traditional domain, because it has lost its adaptive quality (Marrick Jarrett 1986, pers. comm.).
3 The specific method of transmitting knowledge through stories (e.g., being recited at ceremonies) is also likely to have an affect on their consistency (Trudy Nicks 2000, pers. comm.).

9 Toward Dialogue

1 See Carole Crumley's (1994) summary of historical ecology. For discussion of the three 'new ecologies' (the other two being ethnoecology and political ecology) that I build on in this book, see Biersack (1999) and Kottack (1999).
2 Several writers (e.g. Iverson 1987:141; Fogelson 1989:138; Sioui 1992:38; Trigger 1992:xi–xii) have noted that within native communities there is a great

deal of interest in the historical contexts of environmental issues. This presents good potential for collaborative research.
3 Most Canadian anthropologists have contributed to a fuller understanding of aboriginal history by highlighting cultural achievements and cultural continuity (e.g., Asch [1984]1988). Only occasionally (see, for example, Innis [1956]1988:32–3) are aboriginal contributions to the broader society given much attention.

References

Adlam, Robert G. 2002. Fish Talk. *Anthropologica* 44(1): 99–112.
Ankney, Dave. 1991. Conservation Laws Should Apply to All. *Angler and Hunter* (Nov./Dec.): 44, 49.
Armitage, Andrew. 1994. *The Bruce Peninsula Explorer*. Owen Sound, ON: Ginger Press.
Asch, Michael. [1984] 1988. Contemporary Native Life: Images and Realities, in *A Passion for Identity*, E. Mandel and D. Taras, eds. 389–98. Scarborough, ON: Nelson Canada.
BCHS (Bruce County Historical Society). 1967. *The Bruce County Historical Society Centennial Book* (n.p.)
Barry, James P. 1978. *Georgian Bay: The Sixth Great Lake*. Toronto: Clarke, Irwin.
Berkes, Fikret. 1987. Common Property Resource Management and Cree Indian Fisheries in Subarctic Canada, in *The Question of the Commons*, Bonnie J. McKay and James M. Acheson, eds., 66–91. Tucson: University of Arizona Press.
– 1990. Native Subsistence Fisheries: A Synthesis of Harvest Studies in Canada. *Arctic* 43: 35–42.
– 1999. *Sacred Ecology: Traditional Ecological Knowledge and Resource Management*. Philadelphia: Taylor and Francis.
Berkes, Fikret, and Dorothy Pocock. 1983. The Ontario Native Fishing Agreement in Perspective, a Study in User-Group Ecology. *Environments* 15(3): 17–26.
Biersack, Aletta. 1999. Introduction: From the 'New Ecology' to the New Ecologies. *American Anthropologist* 101(1): 5–18.
Billington, N., and P.D.N. Hebert, eds. 1991. International Symposium on 'The Ecological and Genetic Implications of Fish Introductions (FIN).' *Canadian Journal of Fisheries and Aquatic Sciences* 48 (Supplement 1).

Bishop, Charles A. 1981. Northeastern Concepts of Conservation and the Fur Trade: A Critique of Calvin Martin's Thesis, in *Indians, Animals and the Fur Trade: A Critique of 'Keepers of the Game,'* Shepard Krech III, ed., 39–58. Athens: University of Georgia Press.

Bishop, Charles A., and Toby Morantz, eds. 1986. Who Owns the Beaver? Northern Algonquian Land Tenure Reconsidered. *Anthropologica* 28 (1–2).

Black, Lydia. 1981. The Nature of Evil: Of Whales and Sea Otters, in *Indians, Animals and the Fur Trade: A Critique of 'Keepers of the Game,'* Shepard Krech III, ed., 109–54. Athens: University of Georgia Press.

Blair, Emma Helen, ed. [1911, vol. 1; 1912, vol. 2] 1969. *The Indian Tribes of the Upper Mississippi Valley and Region of the Great Lakes*. Repr. New York: Kraus Reprint Co.

Bocking, Stephen. 1997. Fishing the Inland Seas: Great Lakes Research, Fisheries Management, and Environmental Policy in Ontario. *Environmental History* 2(1): 52–73.

Boldt, Menno. 1993. *Surviving as Indians: The Challenge of Self-Government*. Toronto: University of Toronto Press.

Brightman, Robert. 1987. Conservation and Resource Depletion: The Case of the Boreal Forest Algonquians, in *The Question of the Commons*, Bonnie McCay and James M. Acheson, eds., 121–41. Tucson: University of Arizona Press.

– 1993. *Grateful Prey: Rock Cree Human-Animal Relationships*. Berkeley: University of California Press.

Brose, David S. 1978. Late Prehistory of the Upper Great Lakes Area, in *Northeast*, vol. 15, *Handbook of North American Indians*, Bruce G. Trigger, ed., 569–87. Washington, DC: Smithsonian Institution Press.

Brown, W.M. 1932. *The Queen's Bush: A Tale of the Early Days of Bruce County*. London: John Bale, Sons, and Danielsson. Owen Sound, ON: Bruce Peninsula Press.

Bruce Peninsula Press (Tobermory, ON). 1995. *Sunrise Ceremony Welcomes Spawning Fish*. Early May.

– 1995. *Greenpeace Visits Cape Croker*. Late September: 9.

Cadot, Rev. J.C. 1920. Bruce County and Work among the Indians. *Ontario Historical Society, Papers and Records* 18:21–4.

Callicott, J. Baird 1989. *In Defense of the Land Ethic: Essays in Environmental Philosophy*. Albany: State University of New York Press.

– 1993. Toward a Global Environmental Ethic, in *Worldviews and Ecology*, Mary Evelyn Tucker and John A. Grim, eds, 30–40. Lewisburg, PA: Bucknell University Press.

Chapman, L.J., and D.F. Putnum. 1966. *The Physiography of Southern Ontario*. Toronto: University of Toronto Press.

Churchill, Ward. 1988. Sam Gill's 'Mother Earth': Colonialism, Genocide and the Expropriation of Indigenous Spiritual Tradition in Contemporary Academia (Commentary and Debate). *American Indian Culture and Research Journal* 12(3): 49–67.

Cleland, Charles E. 1982. The Inland Shore Fishery of the Northern Great Lakes: Its Development and Importance in Prehistory. *American Antiquity* 47(4): 761–84.

– 1989. Comments on 'A Reconsideration of Aboriginal Fishing Strategies in the Northern Great Lakes Region' by Susan R. Martin. *American Antiquity* 54(3): 605–9.

– 1996. The Historical Development of the Great Lakes *Aboriginal Fishery*. Paper presented at Aboriginal Fishing Traditional Values and Resource Stewardship Conference, Bala, ON, 28 Sept.

Clifton, James A. 1975. *A Place of Refuge for All Time: Migration of the American Potawatomi into Upper Canada 1830 to 1850*. Canadian Ethnology Service, Mercury Series, Paper 26. Ottawa: National Museum of Man.

Coyne, James H. 1903. Galinee's Narrative and Map. *Ontario Historical Society, Papers and Records* 4.

– 1923. The Dollier-Galinee Expedition, 1660–70. *Ontario Historical Society, Papers and Records* 20:75–81.

Cruikshank, E.A. 1923. The Exploring Expedition of Dollier and Galinee in 1669–70. *Ontario Historical Society, Papers and Records* 20:5–8.

Cruikshank, Julie. 1990. Getting the Words Right: Perspectives on Naming and Place in Athapaskan Oral History. *Arctic Anthropology* 27(1): 52–65.

– 1995. Understanding Yukon History: Contributions from Oral Tradition, in *Native Peoples: The Canadian Experience*, B. Morrison and C.R. Wilson, eds., 286–315. Toronto: Oxford University Press.

Crumley, Carol L. 1994. Historical Ecology: A Multidimensional Ecological Orientation, in *Historical Ecology: Cultural Knowledge and Changing Landscapes*, Carol Crumley, ed., 1–16. Santa Fe, NM: School of American Research Press.

Crystal, M. Melvin. 1996. The Recognition and Affirmation of Treaty and Aboriginal Rights in Canada: The Constitution Act, 1982 and Regina v. Sparrow, in *The Recognition of Aboriginal Rights*, Samuel W. Corrigan and Joe Sawchuk, eds., 111–20. Brandon, MB: Bearpaw.

Daechsel, Hugh J. 1994. Review and Assessment of Known Archaeological Resources on the Bruce Peninsula Grey and Bruce Counties. Report on file with Parks Canada.

Davidson-Hunt, I.J., and Fikret Berkes. 2003. Learning as You Journey: Anishinaabe Perception of Social-ecological Environments and Adaptive Learning. *Conservation Ecology* 8(1): 5. hhtp://www.consecol.org/vol8/iss1/art5.

Delgamuukw v. British Columbia, [1997] 3 SCR 1110.

DeMille, Mary Susan. 1971. *Ethnohistory of Farming: Cape Croker 1820–1930.* Master's of Philosophy thesis, University of Toronto.

Densmore, Frances. 1970 [1929]. *Chippewa Customs.* Smithsonian Institution, American Bureau of Ethnology, Bulletin 86. Repr. NY: Johnson Reprinting Co.

Derman, Bill, and Anne Ferguson. 1995. Human Rights, Environment, and Development: The Dispossession of Fishing Communities on Lake Malawi. *Human Ecology* 23(2): 125–42.

DesJardin, Joseph R. 1993. *Environmental Ethics.* Belmont, CA: Wadsworth.

Dewar, Elaine. 2001. *Bones: Discovering the First Americans.* Toronto: Random House Canada.

Dickson, Lovat. 1973. *Wilderness Man: The Strange Story of Grey Owl.* Scarborough: New American Library of Canada.

Dodd, Christine F., Dana R. Poulton, Paul A. Lennox, David G. Smith, and Gary A. Warrick. 1990. The Middle Ontario Iroquoian Stage, in *The Archaeology of Southern Ontario to A.D. 1650*, Chris J. Ellis and Neal Ferris, eds., 321–60. Occasional Publication of the London Chapter, Ontario Archaeological Society, Publication Number 5.

Doherty, Robert. 1990. *Disputed Waters: Native Americans and the Great Lakes Fishery.* Lexington: University of Kentucky Press.

Duluth Declaration. 1995. *Duluth Declaration.* Saugeen First Nation.

Eckersley, Robyn. 1992. *Environmentalism and Political Theory: Toward an Ecocentric Approach.* Albany: State University of New York Press.

Elliott, Vincent. 1987. Fishing at Stokes Bay. *Bruce County Historical Society Yearbook.* 37–9.

Ellis, Chris J., Ian T. Kenyon, and Michael Spence. 1990. The Archaic, in *The Archaeology of Southern Ontario to A.D. 1650*, Chris J. Ellis and Neal Ferris, eds., 65–124. Occasional Publication of the London Chapter, Ontario Archaeological Society, Publication Number 5.

Ellis, Chris J., and D. Brian Deller. 1990. Paleo-Indians, in *The Archaeology of Southern Ontario to A.D. 1650*, Chris J. Ellis and Neal Ferris, eds., 37–64. Occasional Publication of the London Chapter, Ontario Archaeological Society, Publication Number 5.

Ellis, Chris J., and Neal Ferris, eds. 1990. *The Archaeology of Southern Ontario to A.D. 1650.* Occasional Publication of the London Chapter, Ontario Archaeological Society, Publication Number 5.

Ervin, Alexander M. 2000. *Applied Anthropology: Tools and Perspectives for Contemporary Practice*. Boston: Allyn and Bacon.

FON (Federation of Ontario Naturalists). 1993. *Putting Nature First: Conservation Principles to Guide the Settlement of Aboriginal Land Claims*. Don Mills, ON: FON (October).

Feder, Kenneth L., and Michael Alan Park. 1997. *Human Antiquity*, 3rd ed. Mountain View, CA: Mayfield.

Feest, Johanna E., and Christian F. Feest. 1978. Ottawa, in *Handbook of North American Indians, Northeast*, vol. 15, Bruce G. Trigger, ed., 772–86. Washington, DC: Smithsonian Institution Press.

Feit, Harvey A. 1973. The Ethno-Ecology of the Waswanipi Cree; or How Hunters Can Manage Their Resources, in *Cultural Ecology*, B. Cox, ed., 115–25. Toronto: McClelland and Stewart.

– 1991. The Construction of Algonquian Hunting Territories: Private Property as Moral Lesson, Policy Advocacy, and Ethnographic Error, in *Colonial Situations: Essays on the Contextualization of Ethnographic Knowledge*, vol. 7, *History of Anthropology*, George W. Stocking, Jr, ed., 109–34. Wisconsin: University of Wisconsin Press.

Fiedel, Stuart J. 1987. Algonquian Origins: A Problem in Archeological-Linguistic Correlation. *Archaeology of Eastern North America* 15:1–11.

– 1991. Correlating Archaeology and Linguistics: The Algonquian Case. *Man in the Northeast* 41:9–32.

Finlayson, W.D. 1977. *The Saugeen Culture: A Middle Woodland Manifestation in Southwestern Ontario*. Archaeological Survey of Canada, Mercury Series, Paper No. 61. Ottawa: National Museum of Man.

Fitting, James E. 1978. Prehistory: Introduction, in *Northeast*, vol. 15, *Handbook of North American Indians*, Bruce G. Trigger, ed., 14–15. Washington, DC: Smithsonian Institution Press.

Fitzgerald, William R. 1979. An Assessment of the Potential for Future Archaeological Research in the Area of Grey County Beneath the Niagara Escarpment. Report on file, Ontario Ministry of Culture and Communication, Toronto.

Flanagan, Tom. 2000. *First Nations? Second Thoughts*. Montreal & Kingston: McGill-Queen's University Press.

Fleras, Augie, and Jean Leonard Elliott. 1992. *The Nations Within: Aboriginal-State Relations in Canada, the United States, and New Zealand*. Toronto: Oxford University Press.

Fogelson, Raymond D. 1989. The Ethnohistory of Events and Nonevents. *Ethnohistory* 36(2): 133–47.

Forkey, Neil S. 1995. Maintaining a Great Lakes Fishery: The State, Science, and the Case of Ontario's Bay of Quinte, 1870–1920. *Ontario History* 87(1): 45–64.

Forsey, Helen. 1994. Gunning for Conservation. *Canadian Forum* (Jan./Feb.): 22–7.

Fox, William A. 1987. Dunk's Bay Archaeology. *Kewa*, Newsletter of the London Chapter, Ontario Archaeological Society 89(9): 2–8.

– 1988. Bruce Peninsula Archaeological Survey. Report on file with Ontario Ministry of Culture and Communication, Toronto.

– 1989. *The Hunter Site (BdHh-5). A Multi-Component Odawa Fishing Camp On Frenchman Point, Saugeen Reserve*. Report on file with Ontario Ministry of Culture and Communication, Toronto.

– 1990a. Ancient Onenditagui. *Cuesta, The Niagara Escarpment Magazine* (1990/91): 11–13.

– 1990b. The Middle Woodland to Late Woodland Transition, in *The Archaeology of Southern Ontario to A.D. 1650*, Chris J. Ellis and Neal Ferris, eds., 171–88. Occasional Publication of the London Chapter, Ontario Archaeological Society, Publication Number 5.

– 1990c. The Odawa, in *The Archaeology of Southern Ontario to A.D. 1650*, Chris J. Ellis and Neal Ferris, eds., 457–74. Occasional Publication of the London Chapter, Ontario Archaeological Society, Publication Number 5.

Fox, William Sherwood. 1952. *The Bruce Beckons: The Story of Lake Huron's Great Peninsula*. Toronto: University of Toronto Press.

Funk, Robert E. 1978. Post-Pleistocene Adaptation, in *Handbook of North American Indians, Northeast*, vol. 15, Bruce G. Trigger, ed., 16–27. Washington, DC: Smithsonian Institution Press.

Garrad, Charles. 1970. Did Champlain Visit the Bruce Peninsula? An Examination of an Ontario Myth. *Ontario History* 62(4): 235–9.

Garrad, Charles, and Conrad E. Heidenreich. 1978. Khionontateronon (Petun), in *Northeast*, vol. 15, *Handbook of North American Indians*, Bruce G. Trigger, ed., 394–7. Washington, DC: Smithsonian Institution Press.

Gateman, Laura M. 1982. *Echoes of Bruce County*. Southampton, ON.

Gatis, Sheila, ed. 1980. *Wiarton 1880–1980*. Wiarton, ON: Wiarton Echo.

Geertz, Clifford. 1973. *The Interpretation of Cultures*. New York: Basic Books.

Gill, Sam. 1990. Mother Earth: An American Myth, in *The Invented Indian: Cultural Fictions and Government Policies*, James A. Clifton, ed., 129–43. New Brunswick, NJ: Transaction.

Globe and Mail (Toronto). 1995. *Dispute Erupts over Chippewa Fishing*. September 11: A6.

Goddard, Ives. 1978. Central Algonquian Languages, in *Northeast*, vol. 15,

Handbook of North American Indians, Bruce G. Trigger, ed., 583–7. Washington, DC: Smithsonian Institution Press.

Gourlay, Rob G. 1822. *Statistical Account of Upper Canada: Compiled with a View to a Grand System of Emigration.* London: Limpkin and Marshall Stationers Court.

Graham, Elizabeth. 1975. *Medicine Man to Missionary: Missionaries as Agents of Change among the Indians of Southern Ontario,* 1784–1867. Toronto: Peter Martin Associates.

Great Lakes Fishery Commission. 1995a. *Fish Community Objectives for Lake Huron.* Special Publication 95–1.

– 1995b. *The State of Lake Huron in 1992.* Special Publication 95–2.

Greenberg, Adolph M., and James Morrison. 1982. Group Identity in the Boreal Forest: The Origin of the Northern Ojibwa. *Ethnohistory* 29(2): 75–102.

Greenberg, Adolph M., and Ronald H. Spielbauer. 1991. Prehistoric and Historic Linkages: Problems and Perspectives, in *New Dimensions in Ethnohistory,* Barry Gough and Laird Christie, eds., 25–41. Canadian Ethnology Service. Mercury Series, Paper 120. Ottawa: Canadian Museum of Civilization.

Griffin, David Ray. 1993. Whitehead's Deeply Ecological Worldview, *in Worldviews and Ecology,* Mary Evelyn Tucker and John A. Grim, eds., 190–206. Lewisburg, PA: Bucknell University Press.

Guillet, Edwin C. 1938. *Pioneer Life – Early Life in Upper Canada Series* (Book II). Toronto: Ontario Pub. Co.

HBC (*Hudson's Bay Company Archives*). HBC B.109/a/2. Ledgers from La Cloche, Lake Huron, John McBean C.F., to 31 May 1829.

Hallowell, A. Irving. [1960] 1976. Ojibway Ontology, Behaviour, and World View. in *Contributions to Anthropology,* Jennifer Brown, ed., 357–90. Chicago: University of Chicago Press.

– 1992. *The Ojibwa of Berens River, Manitoba.* Fort Worth, TX: Harcourt Brace Jovanovich.

Hames, Raymond. 1987. Game Conservation or Efficient Hunting, in *The Question of the Commons,* Bonnie J. McCay and James M. Acheson, eds., 92–107. Tucson: University of Arizona Press.

Hansen, Lise C. 1991. Treaty Fishing Rights and the Development of Fisheries Legislation in Ontario: A Primer. *Native Studies Review* 7(1): 1–22.

Heidenreich, Conrad E. 1978. Huron, in *Northeast,* vol. 15, *Handbook of North American Indians,* Bruce G. Trigger, ed., 368–88. Washington, DC: Smithsonian Institution Press.

Henry, Alexander. [1901] 1964. *Travels and Adventures; In Canada and the Indian*

Territories: Between the Years 1760 and 1776. James Bain, ed. New York: Burt Franklin.

Henry, Lorne J., and Gilbert Paterson. 1938. *Pioneer Days in Ontario.* Toronto: Ryerson Press.

Herzfeld, Michael. 2001. *Anthropology: Theoretical Practice in Culture and Society.* Malden, MA: Blackwell.

Hickerson, Harold. 1962. *The Southwestern Chippewa: An Ethnohistorical Study.* Memoir 92. American Anthropological Association, 64, no. 3, part 2.

Innis, Harold. [1956] 1988. (Conclusion from) The Fur Trade in Canada, in *A Passion for Identity,* E. Mandel and D. Taras, eds., 26–36. Scarborough, ON: Nelson Canada.

Inter Press Service. 1993. *Story Earth: Native Voices on the Environment.* San Francisco: Mercury.

Iverson, Peter. 1987. I May Connect Time, in *The American Indian and the Problem of History,* Calvin Martin, ed., 136–43. NY: Oxford University Press.

Jacobs, Wilbur R. 1980. Indians as Ecologists and Other Environmental Themes in American Frontier History, in *American Indian Environments,* Christopher Vecsey and Robert W. Venables, eds., 46–64. Syracuse, NY: Syracuse University Press.

Jameson, Anna Brownell. [1838] 1990. *Winter Studies and Summer Rambles.* Toronto: McClelland and Stewart.

Jasen, Patricia. 1995. *Wild Things: Nature, Culture, and Tourism in Ontario 1790–1914.* Toronto: University of Toronto Press.

Jenness, Diamond. 1935. *The Ojibwa Indians of Parry Sound, Their Social and Religious Life.* Bulletin No. 78, Anthropological Series, No. 17. Ottawa: National Museum of Canada.

Jennings, Jesse D. 1989. *Prehistory of North America.* Mountain View, CA: Mayfield.

Johnson, Lawrance E. 1991. *A Morally Deep World.* Cambridge: Cambridge University Press.

Johnson, Martha. 1992. *Lore: Capturing Traditional Environmental Knowledge.* Ottawa: Dene Cultural Institute and IDRC.

Johnston, Darlene. 1996. Saugeen's Fishing History. Unpublished.

Jones, Bruce A. 1990. PaleoIndians and Proboscideans: Ecological Determinants of Selectivity in the Southwestern United States, in *Hunters of the Recent Past,* L.B. Davis and B.O.K. Reeves, eds., 68–86. London: Unwin Hyman.

Julig, Patrick. 1985. The Sheguiandah Site Stratigraphy: A Perspective from the Lake Superior Basin. *Ottawa Archaeologist* 12(8): 2–13.

– 1994. *The Cummins Site Complex: And Paleoindian Occupations in the Northwest-*

ern Lake Superior Region. Ontario Archaeological Reports 2. Toronto: Ontario Heritage Foundation.

Jull, Peter. 1991. Lessons from Indigenous Peoples, in *Sweet Promises*, J.R. Miller, ed., 452–458. Toronto: University of Toronto Press.

Kaiser, Rudolf. 1987. Chief Seattle's Speech(es): American Origins and European Reception, in *Recovering the Word: Essays on Native American Literature*, Brian Swann and Arnold Krupat, eds., 497–536. Berkeley: University of California Press.

Kane, Paul. [1859] 1974. *Wanderings of an Artist*. Edmonton: Hurtig.

Karrow, P.F., and B.G. Warner. 1990. The Geological and Biological Environment for Human Occupation in Southern Ontario, in *The Archaeology of Southern Ontario to A.D. 1650*, Chris J. Ellis and Neal Ferris, eds., 5–36. Occasional Publication of the London Chapter, Ontario Archaeological Society, Publication Number 5.

Keeshig-Tobias, Polly. 1996. *The Illustrated History of the Chippewas of Nawash*. Wiarton, ON: Chippewas of Nawash, PointOne Graphics.

Kehoe, Alice. 1990. Primal Gaia: Primitivists and Plastic Medicine Men, in *The Invented Indian: Cultural Fictions and Government Policies*, James A. Clifton, ed., 193–210. New Brunswick, NJ: Transaction.

King, Cecil. 1994. J.-B. Assiginack: Arbiter of Two Worlds. *Ontario History* 86(1): 33–52.

Kinietz, Vernon W. [1940] 1972. *The Indians of the Western Great Lakes 1615–1760*. Ann Arbor: University of Michigan Press.

Koenig, Ed. 1996. Toward an Historical Ecology of the Saugeen Peninsula: Fish, Culture, and Changing Landscapes, in *Leading Edge '95 Conference Proceedings*, 39–41. Ministry of Environment and Energy et al.

Kohl, J.G. [1860] 1956. *Kitchi-Gami: Wanderings Round Lake Superior*. Minneapolis, MN: Ross and Haines.

Kottak, Conrad P. 1999. The New Ecological Anthropology. *American Anthropologist* 101(1): 23–35.

Krech, Shepard III, ed. 1981. *Indians, Animals and the Fur Trade: A Critique of 'Keepers of the Game.'* Athens: University of Georgia Press.

– 1999. *The Ecological Indian*. New York: Norton.

Lafitau, Father Joseph François, SJ. [1724] 1977. *Customs of the American Indians Compared with Customs of the First Times*, vol. 2, William N. Fenton and Elizabeth L. Moore, eds. Toronto: Champlain Society.

Lamorandiere, F. 1904. Wampum Strings. *Archaeological Report*. Ontario Department of Education.

Landon, Fred. 1944. *Lake Huron*. Indianapolis, IN: Bobbs-Merrill.

Larson, Douglas W. 1996. Cryptos, Critters, and Chronologies: A Year of Progress in Cliff Ecology, in *Leading Edge '95 Conference Proceedings*, 49. Ministry of Environment and Energy et al.

Leacock, Eleanor. 1995. The Montagnais-Naskapi of the Labrador Peninsula, in *Native Peoples: The Canadian Experience*, R. Bruce Morrison and C. Roderick Wilson, eds., 150–80. Toronto: Oxford University Press.

Leighton, Douglas. 1977. The Manitoulin Incident of 1863: An Indian-White Confrontation in the Province of Canada. *Ontario History* 69(2): 113–24.

Leopold, Aldo. 1933. *Game Management*. New York: Scribner's.

– [1949] 1989. *A Sand County Almanac*. New York: Oxford University Press.

Lister, Kenneth R. 1993. 'A Most Abundant Weir': Fish Trap-Weirs, Adaptive Strategies, and the Hudson Bay Lowland, in *Papers of the Twenty-Fourth Algonquian Conference*, William Cowan, ed., 262–79. Ottawa: Carlton University.

Lovisek, Joan A.M. 1991. *Ethnohistory of the Algonkian Speaking People of Georgian Bay – Precontact to 1850*. PhD diss., McMaster University.

– 2002. Transmission Difficulties: The Use and Abuse of Oral History in Aboriginal Claims, in *Papers of the Thirty-Third Algonquian Conference*, H.C. Wolfart, ed., 251–70. Winnipeg: University of Manitoba.

Lytwyn, Victor P. 1990. Ojibwa and Ottawa Fisheries around Manitoulin Island: Historical and Geographical Perspectives on Aboriginal and Treaty Fishing Rights. *Native Studies Review* 6(1): 1–30.

– 1992. The Usurpation of Aboriginal Fishing Rights: A Study of the Saugeen Nation's Fishing Islands Fishery in Lake Huron, in *Co-existence?* B.W. Hodgins, S. Heard, and J.S. Milloy, eds., 81–103. Peterborough, ON: Frost Centre for Canadian Heritage and Development Studies, Trent University.

MacCrimmon, Hugh R. 1977. *Animals, Man and Change: Alien and Extinct Wildlife of Ontario*. Toronto: McClelland and Stewart.

Mackey, Eva. 2002. *The House of Difference: Cultural Politics and National Identity in Canada*. Toronto: University of Toronto Press.

Magallanes, Catherine J. Iorns. 1999. International Human Rights and their Impact on Domestic Law on Indigenous Peoples' Rights in Australia, Canada, and New Zealand, in *Indigenous Peoples' Rights in Australia, Canada, and New Zealand*, Paul Havemann, ed., 235–76. Oxford: Oxford University Press.

Martin, Calvin. 1978. *Keepers of the Game*. Berkeley: University of California Press.

– 1981. The War between Indians and Animals, in *Indians, Animals, and the Fur Trade: A Critique of 'Keepers of the Game.'* Shepard Krech III, ed., 1–4, 190–6. Athens: University of Georgia Press.

– 1992. *In the Spirit of the Earth*. Baltimore: Johns Hopkins University Press.

Martin, Susan R. 1989. A Reconsideration of Aboriginal Fishing Strategies in the Northern Great Lakes Region. *American Antiquity* 54(3): 594–604.

Mason, Ronald J. 1976. Ethnicity and Archaeology in the Upper Great Lakes, in *Culture Change and Continuity*, Charles Cleland, ed., 349–62. New York: Academic Press.

McCay, Bonnie, and James M. Acheson. 1987. *The Question of the Commons*. Tucson: University of Arizona Press.

McEvoy, Arthur F. 1988. Toward an Interactive Theory of Nature and Culture: Ecology, Production, and Cognition in the California Fishing Industry, in *The Ends of the Earth: Perspectives on Modern Environmental History*, Donald Worster, ed., 211–29. Cambridge: Cambridge University Press.

McLeod, Norman. 1969. *The History of the County of Bruce, 1907–1968*. Owen Sound, ON: Richardson, Bond, and Wright.

McLeod, Rose M. 1979. *The Story of White Cloud, Hay, and Griffith Islands*. Owen Sound, ON.

McNab, Miriam. 1984. What Evidence Is There That Western Indians Were Conservationists? *Native Studies Review* 1(1): 96–107.

Merchant, Carolyn. 1992. *Radical Ecology*. New York: Routledge.

Miller, J.R. 1991. *Sweet Promises*. Toronto: University of Toronto Press.

Morgan, Rick. 1991. Algonquin Agreement Anything but Fair. *Angler and Hunter* (November/December): 45, 49.

Morrison, James. 1994. Upper Great Lakes Settlement: The Anishinabe-Jesuit Record. *Ontario History* 86(1): 53–72.

Murphy, Carl, and Neal Ferris. 1990. The Late Woodland Western Basin Tradition in Southwestern Ontario, in *The Archaeology of Southern Ontario to A.D. 1650*, Chris J. Ellis and Neal Ferris, eds., 189–278. Occasional Publication of the London Chapter, Ontario Archaeological Society, Publication Number 5.

NAC (National Archives of Canada). 1859. *Lease of Fishery in Upper Canada* (No.141 and 142). PAC, RG 10, Vol. 252, Pt. 2, No. 12601–12700.

Nader, Laura. 1996. *Naked Science*. New York: Routledge.

Newell, Dianne. 1993. *Tangled Webs of History: Indians and the Law in Canada's Pacific Coast Fisheries*. Toronto: University of Toronto Press.

Newell, Dianne, and Rosemary E. Ommer. 1999. *Fishing Places, Fishing People: Traditions and Issues in Canadian Small-Scale Fisheries*. Toronto: University of Toronto Press.

Norton, Bryan G. 1996. Integration or Reduction: Two Approaches to Environmental Values, in *Environmental Pragmatism*, Andrew Light and Eric Katz, eds., 105–38. London: Routledge.

Notzke, Claudia. 1994. *Aboriginal Peoples and Natural Resources in Canada*. Toronto: Captus Press.

OFAH (Ontario Federation of Anglers and Hunters). 1991. *Angler and Hunter*. (November/December).
– 1993. Self-Government and Comanagement in Ontario: OFAH Submission to the Royal Commission on Aboriginal Peoples. Peterborough, ON: OFAH.
– 1994a. *A Strategy for the Conservation of Ontario Fish and Wildlife Specific to Government/Aboriginal Agendas*. Peterborough, ON: OFAH (June).
– 1994b. *Problems Arising from Sparrow: Politics vs. Conservation*. Peterborough, ON: OFAH (September).
OMNR (Ontario Ministry of Natural Resources). 1991. *Anishnabek Framework Fishing Agreement*. Ontario Ministry of Natural Resources.
– 1992. *Interim Enforcement Policy*. Ontario Ministry of Natural Resources.
Olsen, Stanley J. 1990. Was Early Man in North America a Big Game Hunter?, in *Hunters of the Recent Past*, L.B. Davis and B.O.K. Reeves, eds., 103–10. London: Unwin Hayden.
Olver, C.H., B.J. Shuter, and C.K. Minns. 1995. Toward a Definition of Conservation Principles for Fisheries Management. *Canadian Journal of Fisheries and Aquatic Sciences* 52: 1584–94.
Orlove, Benjamin S. 1980. Ecological Anthropology. *Annual Reviews of Anthropology* 9: 235–73.
Overholt, Thomas W., and J. Baird Callicott. 1982. *Clothed-In-Fur and Other Tales: An Introduction to an Ojibwa World View*. Lanham, MD: University Press of America.
Pepper, David. 1993. *Eco-Socialism: From Deep Ecology to Social Justice*. London: Routledge.
Perez, Carlos A. 1997. Participatory Research: Implications for Applied Anthropology. *Practicing Anthropology* 19(3): 2–7.
Pinkerton, Evelyn W. 1992. Translating Legal Rights into Management Practice: Overcoming Barriers to the Exercise of Co-management. *Human Organization* 51(4): 330–41.
Preston, Richard J. 2002 [1975]. *Cree Narrative*. Montreal & Kingston: McGill-Queen's University Press.
Prevec, Rosemary. 1988. The Hunter Site BdHh-5 1988 Faunal Report. Report on file with Ontario Ministry of Culture and Communication, Toronto.
Radcliffe, William. 1974 [1921]. *Fishing from Earliest Times*. Chicago: Ares.
Ramsden, Peter G. 1990, The Hurons: Archaeology and Culture History, in *The Archaeology of Southern Ontario to A.D. 1650*, Chris J. Ellis and Neal Ferris, eds., 361–84. Occasional Publication of the London Chapter, Ontario Archaeological Society, Publication Number 5.
Rankin, Lisa K. 1998. Historical Context and the Forager/Farmer Frontier: Reinterpreting the Nodwell Site. PhD diss., McMaster University.
Rasmussen, Larry L. 1993. Cosmology and Ethics, in *Worldviews and Ecology*.

Mary Evelyn Tucker and John A. Grim, eds., 173–80. Lewisburg, PA: Bucknell University Press.

Rau, Charles. 1884. *Prehistoric Fishing in Europe and North America.* Washington, DC: Smithsonian Institution.

Record (Kitchener-Waterloo). 1995. Owen Sound: Police Watched Brawl Witnesses to Stabbing Say. September 5:A3.

— 1997. Saugeen Leader Resigns. April 5:F16.

— 1999. Federal Aid Sought as Tensions Mount in N.B. Fishery War. September 30:A3.

R. v. Jones, [1993] O.R(3d)14.

Reid, Jennifer. 1995. *Myth, Symbol, and Colonial Encounter: British and Mi'kmaq in Acadia, 1700–1867.* Ottawa: University of Ottawa Press.

Repplier, Agnes. 1929. *Pere Marquette.* Garden City, NY: Doubleday.

Richardson, Arthur Herbert. 1974. *Conservation by the People: The History of the Conservation Movement in Ontario to 1970.* Toronto: University of Toronto Press.

Ritzenthaler, Robert E. 1978. Southwestern Chippewa, in *Northeast,* vol. 15, *Handbook of North American Indians,* Bruce G. Trigger, ed., 743–59. Washington, DC: Smithsonian Institution Press.

Robertson, Norman. 1971 [1906]. *The History of the County of Bruce.* Toronto: William Briggs.

Robeson, Virginia R., ed. 1977. Upper Canada in the 1830s. Curriculum Series 22. Toronto: Ontario Institute for Studies in Education.

Rogers, Edward S. 1978. Southeastern Ojibwa, in *Northeast,* vol. 15, *Handbook of North American Indians,* Bruce G. Trigger, ed., 760–71. Washington, DC: Smithsonian Institution Press.

Rogers, Edward S., and Donald B. Smith, eds. 1994. *Aboriginal Ontario: Historical Perspectives on the First Nations.* Toronto: Dundurn Press.

Rostlund, Erhard. 1952. *Freshwater Fish and Fishing in Native North America.* Berkeley: University of California Press.

Rowan, John J. [1876] 1972. *The Emigrant and Sportsman in Canada: Some Experiences of an Old Country Settler; with Sketches of Canadian Life, Sporting Adventures and Observations of the Forest and Fauna.* Toronto: Coles Pub. Co.

Rubinstein, Robert A. 1994. Collective Violence and Common Security, in *Companion Encyclopedia of Anthropology.* Tim Ingold, ed., 983–1009. London: Routledge.

Satz, Ronald N. 1991. *Chippewa Treaty Rights: The Reserved Rights of Wisconsin's Chippewa Indians in Historical Perspective.* Transactions vol. 79, no. 1. Madison: Wisconsin Academy of Sciences, Arts, and Letters.

Scherck, Michael Gonder. 1905. *Pen Pictures of Early Pioneer Life in Upper Canada: By a 'Canuck' (of the Fifth Generation).* Toronto: William Briggs.

Schmalz, Peter S. 1977. *The History of the Saugeen Indians.* Ontario Historical Society, Research Publication No. 5.
– 1991. *The Ojibwa of Southern Ontario.* Toronto: University of Toronto Press.
Scott Colin. 1996. Science for the West, Myth for the Rest? The Case of James Bay Cree Knowledge Construction, in *Naked Science*, Laura Nader, ed., 69–86. New York: Routledge.
Shanahan, David. 1994. The Manitoulin Treaties, 1836 and 1862: The Indian Department and Indian Destiny. *Ontario History* 86(1): 13–32.
Sharma, Parnesh. 1998. *Aboriginal Fishing Rights: Laws, Courts, Politics.* Halifax: Fernwood Publishing.
Sillitoe, Paul. 2002. Globalizing Indigenous Knowledge, in *Participating in Development: Approaches to Indigenous Knowledge*, Paul Sillitoe, Alan Bicker, and Johan Pottier, eds., 108–37. London: Routledge.
Sioui, Georges E. 1992. *For an Amerindian Autohistory: An Essay on the Foundations of a Social Ethic.* Montreal & Kingston: McGill-Queen's University Press.
Smith, Donald B. 1987. *Sacred Feathers: The Reverend Peter Jones (Kahkewaquonaby) and the Mississauga Indians.* Toronto: University of Toronto Press.
Smith, W.L. 1923. *The Pioneers of Old Ontario.* Toronto: George N. Morang.
Sorrenson, M.P.K. 1999. The Settlement of New Zealand from 1835, in *Indigenous Peoples' Rights in Australia, Canada, and New Zealand*, Paul Havemann, ed., 162–80. Oxford: Oxford University Press.
Spangler, G.R., and J.H. Peters. 1995. Fisheries of Lake Huron: An Opportunity for Stewardship, in *The Lake Huron Ecosystem: Ecology, Fisheries and Management*, M. Munawas, T. Edsall, and J. Leach, eds., 103–23. Ecovision World Monograph Series. Amsterdam: SPD Academic Publishing.
Speck, Frank G. 1926. Land Ownership among Hunting Peoples in Primitive America and the World's Marginal Areas. Twenty-second International Congress of Americanists, 2: 323–32.
– 1935. *Naskapi: The Savage Hunters of the Labrador Peninsula.* Norman: University of Oklahoma Press.
Spence, Michael W., Robert H. Pihl, and Carl Murphy. 1990. Cultural Complexes of the Early and Middle Woodland Periods, in *The Archaeology of Southern Ontario to A.D. 1650*, Chris J. Ellis and Neal Ferris, eds., 125–70. Occasional Publication of the London Chapter, Ontario Archaeological Society, Number 5.
Spretnak, Charlene. 1993. Critical and Constructive Contributions of Ecofeminism, in *Worldviews and Ecology*, M.E. Tucker and J.A. Grim, eds., 181–9. Lewisburg, PA: Bucknell University Press.
Stewart, Frances L. 1974. *Faunal Remains from the Nodwell Site (BcHi-3) and from*

Four Other Sites in Bruce County, Ontario. Archaeological Survey of Canada, Paper No. 16.

Storck, Peter. 1994. Case Closed. *Rotunda* (Summer): 34–40.

Strachan, James. 1968 [1820]. *A Visit to the Province of Upper Canada in 1819*. Repr. New York: Johnson Reprint Corp.

Sun Times (Owen Sound, ON). 1995. Natives to Meet with Hodgson about Nets in Bay. August 15:16.

– 1995. Police Step up Controls: More Damage to Native Nets. August 28:1.

– 1995. Native Fishing Boat Sinks. August 28:1–2.

– 1995. Police Seek Witnesses: Two Stabbed in Downtown Brawl. September 5:1.

– 1995. Second Accident in Two Weeks: Boat Fire Suspicious OPP Say. September 5:3.

– 1995. Natives Mourn George, 1,000 Attend Funeral. September 12:11[a].

– 1995. Gustafson Lake Gun Fight Sours Peace Talks. September 12:11[b].

– 1995. 'It Stops Today': Saugeen First Nation Declares Itself Sovereign. October 3:1.

– 1995. CBC Links Racism to Fishing Incident. November 29:1.

– 1996. Sport Anglers Take Stock: Clubs May Close Hatcheries. May 15:1.

– 1996. Fish Plan Flawed: Biologist – MNR Catch Limit Based on Bad Science Nawash Study Says. July 7:3.

– 1997. Native Netters Free to Fish in Sanctuary. April 4:3.

Surtees, R.J. 1984. *Indian Land Surrenders in Ontario*. Ottawa: Department of Indian and Northern Affairs.

Suzuki, David, and Peter Knudtson. 1992. *Wisdom of the Elders: Sacred Native Stories of Nature*. New York: Bantam Books.

Tanner, Adrian. 1979. *Bringing Home Animals: Religious Ideology and Mode of Production of Mistassini Cree Hunters*. Institute of Social and Economic Research, Social and Economic Studies No. 23. St John's: Memorial University of Newfoundland.

Tanner, John. [1830] 1975. *A Narrative of the Captivity and Adventures of John Tanner*. Edwin James, ed. New York: Garland.

Tanner, Helen Hornbeck. 1974. *The Chippewa of Eastern Lower Michigan*. Chippewa Indians V, Garland Series: American Indian Ethnohistory (North Central and Northeastern Indians), David Agee Horr, ed., 347–77. New York: Garland.

– 1993. Book Review of *The Middle Ground: Indians, Empires, and Republics in the Great Lakes Region, 1650–1815*, by Richard White. *Ethnohistory* 40(1): 113–16.

Tanner, Helen Hornbeck, ed. 1987. *Atlas of Great Lakes Indian History*. Norman: University of Oklahoma Press.

Taylor, Paul. 1986. *Respect for Nature*. Princeton, NJ: Princeton University Press.
Thwaites, Reuben Gold, ed. [1905] 1970. *New Voyages to North-America, by Baron De Lahontan*, 2 vols. New York: Burt Franklin. (Reprint of a 1703 edition.)
Tonkinson, Robert. 1991. *The Mardu Aboriginies: Living the Dream in Australia's Desert*, 2nd ed. Toronto: Holt Rinehart and Winston.
Tooker, Elisabeth. 1978. The League of the Iroquois: Its History, Politics, and Ritual, in *Northeast*, vol. 15, *Handbook of North American Indians*, Bruce G. Trigger, ed., 418–41. Washington, DC: Smithsonian Institution Press.
Tough, Frank. 1992. Conservation and the Indian: Clifford Sifton's Commission of Conservation, 1910–1919. *Native Studies Review* 8(1): 61–74.
– 1996. *'As Their Natural Resources Fail': Native People and the Economic History of Northern Manitoba, 1870–1930*. Vancouver: University of British Columbia Press.
Trigger, Bruce G. 1976. *The Children of the Aataentsic: A History of the Huron People to 1660*. Montreal & Kingston: McGill-Queen's University Press.
– 1981. Ontario Native People and the Epidemic of 1634–1640, in *Indians, Animals, and the Fur Trade*, Shepard Krech III, ed., 19–38. Athens: University of Georgia Press.
– 1985. *Natives and Newcomers: Canada's 'Heroic Age' Reconsidered*. Montreal & Kingston: McGill-Queen's University Press.
– 1992. Foreword to *For an Amerindian Autohistory: An Essay on the Foundations of a Social Ethic*, by Georges E. Sioui, ix–xv. Montreal & Kingston: McGill-Queen's University Press.
Vanderburgh, R.M. 1977. *I Am Nokomis Too: The Biography of Verna Patronella Johnston*. Don Mills, ON: General.
Van West, John J., 1990. Ojibwa Fisheries, Commercial Fisheries Development and Fisheries Administration, 1873–1915: An Examination of Conflicting Interest and the Collapse of the Sturgeon Fisheries of the Lake of the Woods. *Native Studies Review* 6(1): 31–65.
Vecsey, Christopher. 1980. American Indian Environmental Religions, in *American Indian Environments*, Christopher Vecsey and Robert W. Venables, eds., 1–37. Syracuse, NY: Syracuse University Press.
Waisberg, Leo Gilbert. 1977. The Ottawa Traders of the Upper Great Lakes (1615–1700). Master's thesis, McMaster University.
Waldram, James. 1997. *The Way of the Pipe: Aboriginal Spirituality and Symbolic Healing in Canadian Prisons*. Peterborough, ON: Broadview.
Wallace, Anthony F.C. 1956. Revitalization Movements. *American Anthropologist* 58(2): 264–81.
Warren, William, W. [1885] 1984. *History of the Ojibway People*. St Paul: Minnesota Historical Society Press.

Warry, Wayne. 1990. Doing Unto Others: Applied Anthropology, Collaborative Research and Native Self-Determination. *Culture* 10(5): 61–73.
– 1998. *Unfinished Dreams: Community Healing and the Reality of Aboriginal Self-Government*. Toronto: University of Toronto Press.
Wathke, Brenna Michele. 1987. The Power of the Saugeen. *Bruce County Historical Society Yearbook*, 20–36.
Weaver, Sally. 1978. Six Nations of the Grand River, Ontario, in *Northeast*, vol. 15, *Handbook of North American Indians*, Bruce G. Trigger, ed., 525–36. Washington, DC: Smithsonian Institution Press.
Weichel, John. 1998. *Skeely Skipper: Southampton's Master Mariner Captain John Spence*. Bruce County Museum and Archives.
White, James, ed. [1913] 1969. *Handbook of Indians of Canada*. Repr. New York: Kraus Reprint Co.
White, Richard. 1991. *The Middle Ground: Indians, Empires, and Republics in the Great Lakes Region, 1650–1815*. Cambridge: Cambridge University Press.
Wiarton Echo (ON). 1995. Cape Fishermen Charged. September 13:14.
Wilson, Alexander. 1991. *The Culture of Nature*. Toronto: Between the Lines.
Wilson, Anthony. 1993. Van Der Peet and Gladstone: The Aboriginal Right to Fish. *First Nations Law* (Summer): 4, 5, 11.
Wittbecker, Alan E. 1986. Deep Anthropology: Ecology and Human Order. *Environmental Ethics* 8: 261–70.
Wolf, Eric R. 1992. *Europe and the People without History*. Berkeley: University of California Press.
Worster, Donald. 1977. *Nature's Economy*. San Francisco: Sierra Club Books.
Wright, James V. 1974. *The Nodwell Site*. Archaeological Survey of Canada, Paper No. 22. Ottawa: National Museum of Man, Mercury Series.
– 1981. The Glen Site: An Historic Cheveux Relevés Campsite on Flowerpot Island, Georgian Bay, Ontario. *Ontario Archaeology* 35: 45–59.
– 1994. Before European Contact, in *Aboriginal Ontario*. Edward S. Rogers and Donald B. Smith, eds., 21–38. Toronto: Dundurn Press.
Wright, Roland. 1994. The Public Right of Fishing, Government Fishing Policy, and Indian Fishing Rights in Upper Canada. *Ontario History* 86 (4, December): 337–62.
Wrong, George M., ed. [1939] 1968. *Sagard's Long Journey to the Country of the Hurons*. New York: Greenwood. [Originally published as Champlain Society Publication 25]
Wyonch, Cathy, ed. 1985. *Hewers of the Forest, Fishers of the Lakes: A History of St. Edmunds Township*. Owen Sound, ON: Township of St Edmunds.

Index

aboriginal, 198n.7
aboriginal rights, 62
adaptive management, 116
Akiwenzie, Chief Ralph, 22–4
Algonquian-speaking groups, 14, 43, 49–50, 53–4, 180
angling, recreational fishing, 77, 94–8, 104, 116, 125, 133–5. *See also* OFAH. *See also* tourism and recreational fishing
Anishinabe, 14–5
annual harvesting cycles, 41–2, 57, 62
anthropocentrism, 105–8, 116
aquaculture. *See* fish cages
archaeology, 38
Archaic fisheries, 40–1
Arriaga, Winona, 170–1

Berkes, Fikret, 44, 116, 120, 155
biases, anthropological, 8
Bond Head Treaty. *See* Manitoulin Island, treaty
Brightman, Robert, 119–20
British: era, 55–8; nation, 14
Bruce County, 9
Bruce Peninsula, 9
Bruce Peninsula National Park, 11

Bruntland Report, 110
Burnt Church, 4

Canada, 3–4, 110
Canadian, 185
Champlain, 51, 200n.21
changing resource use patterns, late historical period, 64–5
Chi-Cheemaun, 12
Chippewa(s), 14
Cleland, Charles, 44–7
commercial fishery, 23, 81–2, 85–9, 96–100, 103–4, 123, 180, 198n.2
community, 176
conservation, 19, 24, 105–21, 123, 126, 135, 143. *See also* sharing
conservationism, 106–8, 113, 118, 120
contact era, 48–52
Crawford, Steve, 127
Cruikshank, Julie, 38
cultural anthropology, 5
cultural identity, 36, 107, 143
cultural interaction, 60
current native fisheries, 30–6

Delgamuukw v. British Columbia, 38
Densmore, Frances, 69

deep ecology, 107
depletions. *See* fishery depletions
dialogue, 178–9,
discrimination, 93
Duluth Declaration, 24–5, 28, 33, 139–40
Dunlop, William, 72–3

early historical fisheries, 48–58
ecocentrism, 105–8, 110, 113–14, 116, 120–1, 143, 147
eco-feminism, 107
ecological anthropology, 5, 7
ecological Indian, 109, 116–21, 181, 184
economic shifts on reserves, middle twentieth century, 100–4
ecosystem, 112. *See also* ecocentrism
English. *See* British
environmentalism, 109–12, 181. *See also* conservation
environmentalist discourse, 105, 182
essentialism, 183
ethnoecology, 5, 7, 105, 181–3
ethnographic fieldwork, 5, 197n.8
ethnohistorical: research, 5; studies, 38
exotic fish, 127–32, 134–5

Fairgrieve Decision, 6, 19–25, 136, 193–4
farming, 64–5, 102–3
Fathom Five National Marine Park, 11
Federation of Ontario Naturalists (FON), 110–11
fieldwork, 15–8
Finlayson, W.D., 42
First Nation, 15, 197n.7
fish cages, 34

fish species, 49, 67–8, 70, 76, 82, 201n.25. *See also* lake trout. *See also* salmon
fishery, concept, 197n.1
fishery depletions: late historical, 75–7; twentieth century, 82, 96–101
fishery management: aboriginal, 141–51; government, 112–16
fishery rehabilitation, 100. *See also* fishery depletions
Fishing Act, 77–8, 112
fishing agreements, 25
fishing at Cape Croker, twentieth century, 82–93
fishing at Saugeen, twentieth century, 93–5
fishing beliefs and rituals, 50, 69, 158–9
fishing conflicts: current Saugeen-Bruce Peninsula fishing conflict issues and incidents, 24–30, 105, 122–51, 177–9, 183–6; early and middle twentieth century, 92–3; late historical, 71–5; various cases, 3–7, 197n.1
Fishing Islands, 27, 56, 62, 64–5, 71–4
fishing nets, 41–2, 46, 49, 77, 86, 92, 201n.3
fishing rights, 3
fishing tools and methods: archaeological, 40–2, 44–5, 49; historical and modern equipment and methods, 56, 67–70, 79–80, 83–7, 90, 97, 99–100. *See also* fishing nets
Flanagan, Tom, 39
food fishery. *See* subsistence fishery
Fox, William A., 52
French: ancestors, 14; era, 54–5; nation, 53

Garrad, Charles, 50
Georgian Bay, 13, 49
Gibbard, William, 71, 74–5, 78
glacial recession, 10
Great Lakes area, 10, 14
Great Lakes commercial fishery, 6, 66–70
Greenpeace, 111–12
group identity uncertainties, prehistoric and early historical, 180

Hardin Garret, 115
Heidenreich, Conrad, 50
Hickerson, Harold, 44
historical, 37–8
historical ecology, 5, 7, 178
historical period, 187
history, 36, 178–80
human, 107
hunting and trapping, at Saugeen, 93–4
Hunting Territories, 14
Huron, 49–50

identity politics, 110
Indian Peninsula, 66
indigenous fish species, 127–32, 134
information sources, prehistoric and historical, 188–9
inland shore fishery, 44–7
interviews, 6, 202n.1
interviewee list, codes and names 190–2
intrinsic value. *See* ecocentrism
Iroquoian-speaking groups, 43, 48, 180, 199n.12
Iroquois Wars period, 52–4

Johnston, Basil, 14–15
Johnston, Darlene, 15, 63

Johnston Ted, 126
Jones, Fred, 6–7, 158, 162–4, 167–8, 175
Jones, Howard, 21
jurisdictional issues, 24
justice. *See* legal system

Kahgee, Chief Richard, 24–5, 139–40, 142. See also Duluth Declaration
Keeshig, Donald, 169–71, 197n.4
Keeshig, George, 157–8, 162
Keeshig-Tobias, Lenore, 38
Kohl, J.G., 69

language, 144, 164
Lake Huron, 10, 13, 53, 67
lake trout, 6, 90, 96, 100–1, 202n.3. *See also* fishery depletions. *See also* salmon
lamprey, 96, 98–9
land cessions, 62–4
land claims, 29
land ethic. *See* Leopold, Aldo
late historical fisheries, 59–78
legal system, 140–1
Leopold, Aldo, 106–7, 114–15, 120. *See also* ecocentrism
licences (fish harvesting), 20–1, 24, 77
literature research, 15
logging. *See* lumbering
Lovisek, Joan, 46
lumbering, 66, 96
Lytwyn, Victor, 71, 113, 145–6, 189

MNR. *See* OMNR
MacKay, Eva, 109–10, 185
Mackinaw region, confluence of lakes Superior and Huron, 47, 53–4
management: as a non-native con-

cept, 141; resource, 16; wildlife, 106–7. *See also* fishery management

Manitoulin Island: fishing at, 70–1; geography, 10–12; inhabitants, Ottawa, 50, 52–3; treaty, 9, 63, 71, 73

maps: early, 48; eighteenth and nineteenth century, 56

marginalization, 184

Martin, Calvin, 119–20

Martin, Susan, 45

McEvoy, Arthur, 115–16

McGregor, Captain Alexander, 72, 202n.9

McLaren, David, 20–1, 125–6

media, coverage of fishing conflicts, 3–4

missionaries, 61

Mississauga, 54

mixed economies, 80–1

Muir, John, 106, 114. *See also* ecocentrism

Nadjiwon, Wilmer, 14

native, 197n.7

native involvement in commercial fishery, 69–70

native-rights conflicts in Canada, 28

natural resources, 3

nature, 107, 121

Nawash, 13–14, 61

Neutral, 50, 53

Newash, 13

Neyaashiingaming, 13

Niagara Escarpment, 11

Nicks, Trudy, 204n.3

Nipissing, 52–3

non-native fisherfolk on the peninsula, 79–80

OFAH (Ontario Federation of Anglers and Hunters), 26, 116–21, 123, 125–6, 137, 153, 182–4

OMNR (Ontario Ministry of Natural Resources), 16, 19, 24–5, 113–14, 123, 138, 152–3, 162, 185

off-reserve, 14

Ojibway (Ojibwa), 14, 55, 60, 63

Ojibway vocabulary, from Tanner [1830], 195–6

Oliphant Treaty, 13

Onenditiagui, 11

optimum yield, 116

oral histories, 38

Ottawa (Odawa), 50–2

overfishing. *See* fishery depletions

Owen Sound, 12–13, 27

Palaeo-Indian fisheries, 39–40

Petun (Tobacco, Khionontateronon), 50–1, 53

place names, 9

political ecology, 5, 7, 183

pollution, 96

populism, 185–6

Port Elgin fishery conference, 17, 127, 154–6, 167–8, 173

Potawatomi, 14, 61

prehistoric: date codes, 197n.2; fishing, 38–47; the term, 37; time frame, 187

preservationism. *See* ecocentrism

Preston, Richard, 44, 158

proto-language, 43–4

Proulx, Ernestine, 130

pukaskwa pits, 52

quotas, 19–20

quotes, 5–6

R. v. Jones and Nadjiwon. See Fairgrieve Decision
recreational fishing. *See* angling
regulating the fisheries: nineteenth century, 77–8; recent, 136–41. *See also* fishery management
Reid, Jennifer, 109
relocation, 61
reserve system, 65
reserves, 197n.5. *See also* land cessions
resources, 16, 144
revitalization, cultural: and tradition, 160–4; challenges, 164–8; movements, 164, 183–4
Rogers, Edward, 54, 60
Rostlund, Erhard, 46–7, 188

salmon, 127–32, 201n.4
Saugeen 29 reserve, 12–14
Saugeen Indians, 10
Saugeen Peninsula, 10
Saugeen River, 10, 12
Saugeen-Bruce Peninsula, ix, 4, 10
Schmalz, Peter, 90, 188–9
science and fishery management, 115, 152–5
self-government, 3
settlers, 11–12, 109
settlement of the peninsula, 65–6
social inequality, 122
Southampton, 12, 14
Southern Ontario, biological environments, 11
Sparrow, 1990 Supreme Court ruling, 19, 105, 138, 140, 197n.1
spear fishing, 95
Speck, Frank, 118
sport fishery, 122–35
sport fishing. *See* angling.

sharing, as a conservation ethic, 173–7
stocking practices, 100, 123, 126–32, 150–1. *See also* OFAH. *See also* Wilmot, Samuel
subsistence fishery, 23, 85–9, 95
summer fishing camps, Cape Croker, 92

Tanner, Helen Hornbeck, 50
Tanner, John, 56
totems, 196
tourism and recreational fishing, 81–2
tourist fishing at Cape Croker, 89–93
trading, 51, 53, 60, 62, 69–70, 201n.5. *See also* commercial fishing. *See also* subsistence fishing
tradition: and ethics, 169–73; concept of, 7. *See also* revitalization
traditional beliefs and practices, 164–6. *See also* fishing beliefs
traditional environmental knowledge, 152, 155–9
traditional knowledge, 152–77
traditional territory, 198n.4
traditionalism, 160–2, 167
treaties. *See* land cessions
treaty rights, 149
Trigger, Bruce, 119
twentieth century, timeframe, 187

UNESCO World Biosphere Reserve, 11
utilitarianism. *See* conservationism

veterans, 101–2

Warren, William, 15

Warry, Wayne, 16, 164, 184
Waukey, Ross, 171–3
Wilmot, Samuel, 77
wise use, classic conservationism. *See* conservationism

Wolf, Eric, 37
Woodland: fisheries, 42–4; time-frame, 187
World Wildlife Fund (WWF), 110–11
Wright, J.V., 52